'Full of unexpected twists and   the most
intriguing books I've read in recent times . . . the deep
storyline and unpredictable plot were outstanding . . .
you won't see that end coming . . . if you're looking for a
book that brings you to the edge of your seat, then go
for this, it won't disappoint'
Surjit Parekh

'Drugs, armed robbers, and cops working the grittiest
streets . . . Hardcase crime Northwest England style . . .
As good a bit of Lancashire Noir as you'll read all year'
Paul Finch

'The best police procedural thriller I have read this
year'
Gary Donnelly

'Price just gets better and better . . . A cracking read'
Nick Oldham

'Nobody fuses raw authenticity with a barnstorming
police thriller quite like Roger A. Price . . . Realism
bleeds from every thumping page, and in Inside
Threat, he layers it over a sparkling plot of deception,
betrayal, and sheer excitement . . . With a lead to truly
root for in DS Martin Draker, an air of constant
unpredictability, and a dynamite turn of phrase, Inside
Threat is, simply put, an outstanding thriller'
Rob Parker

ALSO BY ROGER A. PRICE

The Badge and the Pen Series
Nemesis
Vengeance
Hidden

Standalones
By Their Rules
A New Menace

DS Martin Draker
Inside Threat: Book 1

DARK EDGE PRESS

INSIDE
THREAT

ROGER A. PRICE

Published in 2022 by Dark Edge Press.

Y Bwthyn
Caerleon Road,
Newport,
Wales.

www.darkedgepress.co.uk

A CIP catalogue record for this book is available
from the British Library.

ISBN (eBook): B0B3D32K2F
ISBN (Paperback): 979-8-8349-1557-7

'Inside Threat began from an acorn of truth, which I have fictionalised and extended before lobbing it at my characters to sort out'
Roger A. Price

To
Kartin,
all the best

Noj '22

In loving memory of my father, John: Dad, this one is for you.

CONTENTS

PROLOGUE

Deso knew he wasn't the most academic, but he had street smarts better than most. He'd seen many of his mates buy drugs from new dealers only to get stung; either ripped off, usually by scousers, or nicked having bought from undercover cops. He'd never been caught out by either so was confident he'd suss out this new face from the off.

He met the guy under Blackpool's central pier, and although he'd never bought gear from him before, the bloke looked local, he was sure of that. More than familiar. Deso knew all was cool; street smarts; you can't buy it. You've either got it or you haven't. The sun was setting over the Irish Sea and bouncing its waning rays over the water and casting shadows everywhere. The light under the pier reduced even further and the guy stood with his back to the sea; he was just a silhouette. Street smarts, this guy had them too, so that meant he was no cop.

'What's this new cocaine like, man?' Deso asked.

'You'll be bouncing for hours, mate, trust me, it's better than anything you ever had.'

'I'm not sure, have you got any normal gear?'

'No, but I'll give you two wraps for a tenner;

introductory one-time deal,' the dealer said.

Street smarts, Deso thought, he didn't get to his early thirties without learning all the right stuff. This was a good deal.

'I'll even throw in a free pair of sunglasses; ease any over-dilation of your pupils.'

'Never been a problem before.'

'Your choice.'

'It's getting dark, no one is going to see me,' Deso said, as he handed his money over.

Once the guy had gone, Deso took himself to a quiet corner of the beach away from all the dog walkers and snorted a line of coke. The hit was almost immediate, and he felt higher than he had ever felt, well, apart from that first time; no one got that one back. But this was in a way, a new first, and he loved it. He was buzzing; full of energy, dancing and larking about, and man, did he feel horny. He'd give that bird from the squat a bell; she'd do anything to share his gear. It would be party time. He tried calling her, but her phone was off, he'd try again later.

But then the peak came and went; he was on his way back down. It had been one hell of a high but hadn't lasted as long as he'd hoped. That was the payoff, he mused. He found a rock to lean up against and decided to wait it out. Didn't want to do all his stuff too quickly, plus that could be dangerous. It was why so many dickheads went over when they shouldn't have. He'd chill it out and then go again. He'd ring the bird then, no point beforehand.

He dropped off and when he woke it was fully dark, it was only an hour later but felt like much longer. The moonlight was starting to stretch its glow from behind him. But his head was aching; it must be that which woke him. Perhaps he was dehydrated. It was a common fault of his. Then his eyes started to ache, and as his vison began to adjust to the gloom, he realised that he could see quite well given that it was night-time. Very well indeed. But everything seemed too bright, and the aching turned to pain. Spiteful, stabbing pain. It took Deso's breath away. This wasn't normal. He got to his feet and tried in vain to blink the agony away. But it just accelerated. It felt as if his eyes were on fire. God, what was happening?

Water, he needed water to cool his eyes, that's all, it must be a reaction to his dehydration. He headed to the sea, it seemed miles away with the tide out, but was not that far, not really, just seemed it.

He staggered forward as quickly as he could, but the pain was now white hot and he yelled out, no longer able to contain himself. By the time he reached the shore he felt like his entire face was alight, he'd never known pain like it. It was unbearable, and once he realised that he could no longer stand it, its effect magnified many times over.

Deso threw himself into the waves, desperate to get his head under the water of the ebbing tide. But there was no relief, it just seemed to get worse, maybe the salt aggravated it. He needed air and raised his head above the brine. But as he gasped for breath, the pain simply intensified once more. He didn't know what to do. The water was up to his waist now, and he was struggling to stand still, the retracting waters of the Irish Sea were pulling him, tugging at his sodden clothes, edging him ever further from the beach. He'd try again to put out the fire of pain, but with closed eyes to protect them from the salt, that might do it.

He plunged his head back beneath the surface, but the pain didn't lessen, but it didn't get worse either. Maybe that was a good sign; maybe it was passing its peak. He instinctively opened his eyes as he raised his head above the water, which was up to his mouth now. Then he was horrified to see that the water around his head had turned pink, illuminated by the moonlight bouncing off the waves. Then he lost his footing and felt as if some unseen force was sucking him down. He opened his mouth to scream, and in that instant all the pain disappeared.

It was replaced by a blessed blackness as he breathed in the cool water.

CHAPTER ONE

'I can hear someone coming,' Martin said.

'Me too,' Colin replied.

'I've no idea what to expect?'

'Nervous?'

'A little. It's been a while,' Martin said, as he turned to listen to the sound of footsteps which were growing louder and definitely heading their way. It gave him a second or two to take in their environment once again. They were behind a steel desk which had been screwed to the solid floor many years ago, judging by the rust. The two stand chairs they were using matched the empty one opposite: rusted steel frames with little cushioning on them. The walls in the small windowless room were white-painted brick, and the only illumination came from a single suspended strip light which reminded Martin of school classrooms.

'A bit OTT,' Colin said.

'I didn't know these places still existed,' Martin replied.

'There are loads still around; all redundant since the end of the Cold War.'

'Looks more pre-world war, but it's certainly cold.'

Martin realised that the footsteps had come to a halt

at the other side of the room's steel door which looked like it had been borrowed from a submarine.

The handle started to turn.

'As we discussed, I'm just here to make the numbers up; you're the expert,' Colin said, as the door started to open.

Martin knew that in such circumstances, there had to be two officers present; it safeguarded both sides. Though it was good of Colin to acknowledge it was Martin who had the relevant skills. Some senior officers thought they knew better simply because they had the highest rank. That said, Martin Draker was a detective sergeant who one day aspired to become a detective chief inspector, whereas Detective chief inspector Colin Carstairs was a frustrated detective sergeant in many ways; he always enjoyed the rare opportunity to join Martin in an operational matter. Though perversely, still from behind a desk.

The door fully opened and in walked a detective constable from Preston's Dedicated Source Unit – a specialist department whose sole purpose was to recruit and handle criminal informants – Covert Human Intelligence Sources, or CHIS, as the law termed them. Criminals had other names for them. The detective was dressed in casuals and said her name was Susan, which Martin knew may not be true. Though most CHIS handlers retained their real first names for ease, as did the CHISs, and simply adopted a false surname, so she might be called Susan, Martin mused.

Susan, nodded at both men, and then stood to one side to let her guest walk into the room. He was a man in his forties of Asian heritage dressed in traditional Muslim garb. He came to a stop next to Susan and nodded, too.

'This is Martin and Colin,' Susan said to her guest.

He gave another nod.

'And this is 0585, but you can call him Abdul,' Susan

said, before gesturing Abdul towards the vacant chair, which he took. 'I'll be back in an hour,' Susan finished, before turning and leaving, closing the submarine door behind her.

Martin knew that the following minutes were vital if they were to get anywhere; and none more so than the next few moments of silence, as each side of the steel table sussed the other out. The impasse started to feel intolerable, but Martin remained steadfastly quiet. A minute in and Abdul broke the silence.

'Abdul is not my real name.'

Martin guessed it probably was. 'Martin and Colin are ours,' he replied.

'I have much to lose, such as my life.'

Both Martin and Colin nodded.

'Are you aware of what I have told Susan?'

'We are among the chosen few,' Martin replied, wanting to emphasise to Abdul from the start that the intelligence was known only to a handful that actually needed to know.

'But I am not believed?'

'You are held in very high regard for the quality of significant work you have already done. It's just a failsafe, to make sure—'

'That what I tell you tallies with what I told my handlers?'

'Partly, but not entirely. And if what you have said is true – and we have no reason to believe that it is not – we will pursue him with everything at our disposal.'

'No cover-ups?'

'You have my word.'

'And there is no way my name can ever be associated with the information?'

'I'm sure Susan will have already explained how robust the structures are, and that within those closed systems, only three people know your true or full identity; The Authorising Officer, who gives you the lawful authority to do what you do, and your two handlers; all of whom you undoubtedly trust.'

Abdul nodded.

'We have been drafted in from the Northwest Regional Organised Crime Unit, and after today you will never see us again, it will only be your two handlers; this is an exceptional measure.'

'I have an exceptional story to tell.'

Martin had noted that Abdul was self-confident and articulate, intelligent and calm. But he had noticed a light film of perspiration start to shine on the man's forehead. And it was almost cold enough to see one's breath in here. He picked up a bottle of water from the floor and pushed it across the table to Abdul, who took it and drank a third of it in one go. It was a significant moment, not the drinking of the water, but the receiving of the bottle as a gift. A non-verbal agreement between them. The start of a mutual bond; irrespective of how short-lived it would be. An hour can be a long time without one.

Abdul visibly relaxed as he put the bottle down on the table and leaned back into his chair. 'Then let us begin,' he said.

'Thank you, and please, in your own good time,' Martin said.

Abdul raised and dropped his eyebrows, and then said, 'Detective Constable Jim Grantham is involved in a monthly importation of Heroin into the UK.'

Martin knew that it was time to stay silent, and just let Abdul tell his story. He knew what should be coming next. As shocked as he had been when first given the brief to double-check what Abdul had told his handlers, he'd been doubly shocked at the corrupt cop's identity because he and Colin sort of knew Jim Grantham. Not overly so, they had never met him, but they had worked in parallel on a case, he was apparently a decent guy. Jim to all intents and purposes appeared the archetypical hardworking, honest DC. If the intelligence Abdul was passing on was true, then he was anything but; you just couldn't tell nowadays; a thought which saddened Martin.

Abdul continued, detailing what he knew about Jim Grantham's heroin operation and how he had come about the information from one of Grantham's trusted lieutenants. Evidentially useless, as it was hearsay, but Abdul would never be called as a witness in any proceedings. He had received the information third-hand, but it didn't make it any less truthful.

Martin and Colin sat in respectful silence as Abdul spent the next twenty-five minutes outlining his tale. And as far as Martin could tell, it was exactly the same as the brief they had been given from his initial account to his handlers. He talked freely and without hesitation. Martin was sad to admit that he found Abdul totally believable. But he knew that an honest broker can still sell a dishonest tale. That would be his only query: who told Abdul, and why does he think it is true?

Abdul finished his account and immediately took the bottle of water and emptied it. Colin and Martin glanced at each other whilst Abdul was distracted with his drink, and Martin noted Colin raise his eyebrows as if to say 'sounds right'.

Then Martin questioned the provenance of his source, and Abdul fell silent for a moment.

The impasse was back, but this time Martin broke it. 'Well?'

'I've not told my handlers this bit yet,' he replied.

'Why not?'

'Because my brother told me in confidence, and to admit this bit means I could be identified.'

'But you are considering telling us now.'

'You don't know my true identity, so you don't know

who my brother is. As it stands.'

Martin knew this was true but could see another reason why Abdul may not have yet told his handlers this: if his brother had only told Abdul, and action is taken by the cops, then it could lead straight back to Abdul. It was a common fear with informants and Martin was used to dealing with it. He explained to Abdul that any action to be taken would be as a result of the police's own observations and enquiries. That they would ensure a thorough firewall between what Abdul had told them and the consequences.

'I know all this,' Abdul replied.

Martin could see him wrestling with something else. 'Is your brother involved, Abdul? Is that your problem?'

Abdul didn't answer straight away, but then nodded. Martin was about to launch into a further reassurance speech when Abdul spoke.

'My brother is a weak man who offends the teachings of the Prophet by his actions, and I am not concerned that he may also be arrested.'

'What is it then?'

'Grantham is working *for* my brother, and that is something I have not told my handlers yet. I have been wrestling with it, but I need my conscience to be clear. You won't like it.'

'You can trust us, Abdul.'

'Even though we have only just met, I do. I have the ability to judge people very quickly.'

Martin didn't answer.

Then Abdul let out a sigh, and continued, 'My brother is the one who actually goes to India every month and brings back the heroin. He travels there on official business, which is how he gets away with it. It's how I know that it's true.'

'Ah, I see.'

'That's not the worst of it.'

'Go on.'

'My brother's name is Mohammed Bashir.'

Martin watched Abdul rock back into his chair as if a great weight had left him.

Mohammed Bashir? The name was familiar. Was he a criminal? Then it hit him.

'I see recognition in your eyes; so now you will understand my nerves,' Abdul said.

'Mohammed Bashir, as in a senior member of the force's police staff?'

'Yes. He is head of IT. He works from your headquarters.'

CHAPTER TWO

Martin and Colin both shook Abdul's hand before he left, and Martin reassured Susan that her intelligence report was indeed accurate, but that Abdul had an addendum to it which he would tell her as she took him back to Preston.

Neither man spoke as Martin drove them to Lancashire Police's headquarters at Hutton on the outskirts of Preston. Martin was suddenly glad that Colin was the senior officer as it would be him who had to give the chief, Don Rogers, the good news. They were both badged officers from Lancashire but seconded to the Northwest Regional Organised Crime Unit (NWROCU) working from an office in Preston. They both had homes in Manchester as they had both started their careers there. The commute could be a pain, but Martin didn't really mind; he was divorced so had little to rush home to. It was more problematic for his boss, Colin, who did have a family to consider. He was also fifteen years older than Martin, in his late forties, and had warned Martin that once he leaves his thirties his patience for things, like commuting, would wane dramatically. It wouldn't surprise Martin if Colin moved home to somewhere nearer.

Even though Colin was two ranks superior to Martin they had a good relationship. He had heard banter liken them to Laurel and Hardy. Martin was slim and Colin was ex-slim. They also had a good relationship with Don Rogers, and he had used them before on sensitive issues. Coming from NWROCU sometimes brought a fresh perspective.

They were soon pulling up outside the headquarters' main building and ten minutes later were being ushered into the chief constable's plush office. Martin had lived in flats which weren't much bigger during his divorce. Rogers was soon from behind his huge mahogany desk and ushered both men to some leather easy chairs at the other end of the room. Salutations over, Rogers was keen to hear their report. Colin quickly ran through what was already known, confirming to the chief the intelligence with regard to Jim Grantham.

'And you believe the source?' Rogers asked.

'Hundred percent, sir,' Colin answered.

'Both of you?'

'Yes, sir,' Martin added.

'Good God, we are finding ourselves here far too often,' Rogers started.

Neither Martin nor Colin spoke. Both knew when to stay quiet and let the chief vent his frustrations. It might make the next bit easier.

'Is there something wrong with our recruitment procedures? Our monitoring systems?' the chief said to no-one in particular. 'We will need to revisit everything; we have to stop this.'

Martin and Colin exchanged a quick look at each other, but Rogers must have seen them.

'What is it?'

'Er, there's more, I'm afraid,' Colin said.

'Dear Lord, not another bent DC?'

'No, sir.'

'Well, what then? Spit it out, Colin.'

Colin did.

Martin had only ever heard the chief swear twice before, and on both occasions, it had only been a slipped word; he was a model of professionalism. Until today. When the tirade of expletives that followed came to an end, Rogers collapsed back into his Chesterfield armchair. Martin was impressed, the language he had just heard was fit to grace any CID office from the eighties or nineties; and included a couple of bastardised phrases which any Docker would have been proud of.

After clearly gathering his thoughts, Rogers leaned forward, 'And there can be no mistake that Bashir is involved?' he asked.

'According to the source, it was Bashir himself who told him,' Colin added.

'And why the hell would he do that?'

Colin turned to Martin to answer. He knew it would help prove the provenance to explain Bashir's relationship to the source, but that would identify the informant; and even chief constables didn't need to know that. The system which protected informants worked because it was so robust. Without it, they would never be able to attract high-level ones.

'The source is a long-standing friend of Bashir,' Martin said instead, 'they attend the same Mosque. The source knows he trusts him implicitly, but not why Bashir confided in him. Perhaps Bashir was sounding him out, trying to recruit him? But if he was, he failed; as the source made it plain to Bashir that he wanted no part in it.'

This seemed to placate Rogers, who after a few seconds added, 'So how do we progress with this?'

Colin gestured for Martin to continue, so he did. 'Well sir, we could either *orchestrate* Bashir's arrest for importation of heroin, or for the exportation of it. Both the chief and Colin were staring at him nonplussed. Martin continued.

***

An hour later, Martin and Colin were sitting in the headquarters' canteen enjoying a light lunch.

'I have to say, that was quite a plan,' Colin said.

'Thank you. I wasn't sure you or the chief would go for it.'

'Go for it, Rogers loved it. If it comes off, it's retribution times ten. Not that he's after vengeance; much.'

'And this way, if it goes tits-up with our arses in the air, nothing will be lost. We can continue investigating Bashir and Grantham without them being any the wiser,' Martin said.

'Are you sure you haven't been giving the chief some lessons in how to speak broad Anglo-Saxon?'

'I think he could teach me more after his earlier display.'

Colin laughed and then added, 'But what is said in the chief's office, stays in the chief's office.'

'Don't worry, I know.'

'Come on, eat up we've got a lot to do, and only fourteen days in which to do it.'

'At least you've stopped rubbing your chin.'

'Pardon?'

'You know, the way you rub it when you're stressed.'

'I don't, do I?'

'Yes, but it makes you look studious; to start with.'

'Next time I do it, tell me.'

Martin said that he would, but probably wouldn't, it was part of who he was.

An hour later, they were back in their office at Preston Central police station. It was next to a purpose-made murder/major incident room. Even when there wasn't a live murder investigation on the go, there was always plenty for the small but dedicated enquiry team to get on with. They didn't intrude in what they were doing, and the murder detectives didn't ask what they were up to either; a professional courtesy which ran both ways. Then Martin's mobile rang and jolted him from his thoughts, he checked the screen and smiled when he saw Cath's name light up.

'Hey stranger, are you planning to buy a nice girl a drink anytime soon?' she started.

'I'd love to, but might struggle getting back early tonight,' Martin answered.

'Does that mean you've got a job on?'

'Sort of, just helping out with something, but it could get late, I'm afraid.' He had only been dating Cath for a couple of months, but he really liked her. She had worked in the force's press office before moving into an analytical role within the Force Intelligence Unit, so she knew how the job could be sometimes. He also knew that before joining the police service she had worked as a journalist, so was always nosy, a great trait for an analyst.

'Now you've piqued my interest,' she said.

'Nothing I can share with you, sorry,' Martin said, as he noticed he also had Colin's attention. 'I'll give you a bell towards the weekend, maybe sort out a night then?'

'No worries, I'll let you get on, and to be honest, I've got a lead on my desk which is well overdue, I'll crack on with that and catch you later,' Cath said, before ending the call.

'Cath?' Colin asked. Though Martin knew it was a redundant question. He confirmed the obvious and then reassured him that he wouldn't be sharing any pillow talk with her, well not until the weekend at the earliest.

Colin just smiled and then added, 'She should have been a detective; she's wasted as an analyst.'

Martin was going to argue that what she did often drove the detectives' inquiries but decided against it. Colin was a bit old-school in his thinking, and besides, he'd no doubt meant his comment as a compliment.

CHAPTER THREE

Cath Moore was in her office at Lancashire Police HQ, and after some serious procrastination she knew she had to attack her 'Leads Tray' at some stage. She worked in a modern open-plan office and loved her new job. Not that she hadn't enjoyed working in the press office, or indeed working as a journalist before that at the *Manchester Evening Post*, but what she was doing now really affected people's lives. She drew up intelligence packages highlighting where the problems were to best inform the cops where they should concentrate their efforts. Of course, the overall strategic agenda was directed from on high, so she just dug around in the confines that she was given to work within. Street-level drug dealing was always on the list of priorities as were violent crimes. In fact, the list rarely changed much; anti-social behaviour was another staple.

In the past, the field work in intelligence gathering was always done by police officers, but as they didn't need their police powers, such as search and arrest; the force created the Field Intelligence Analyst role, which allowed non-badged staff to go out in the field to gather the information to add to the jigsaw that an Intelligence Package was. It was the field side of the job which had attracted her the most. In a lot of ways, it was like being an investigative reporter again. She had missed that when she'd left the paper, and she also missed her old newspaper editor, Judy. She promised herself to pop over and see her sometime soon. They had always had a great working relationship, and she had done her utmost to talk Cath out of taking the police press office job, but if she hadn't, she would never have had the opportunity to become a field analyst. The skills were all transferable and she felt like she had found her niche. She'd also met Martin, another bonus, or so she hoped it would be. Early days yet, but off to a good start. Apart from the job getting in the way, like tonight. She hadn't seen him in days and absence did make the heart grow stronger, or as Martin would put it, 'Abstinence makes the ardour harder'. She had tried to point out to Martin his misuse of the word abstinence as it normally related to food or drink, particularly drink, but Martin was having none of it. He said it worked in his adolescent rhyme and that was all that mattered.

She smiled at the memory, and then sighed as she reached for her Leads File and started to thumb through it. This dossier contained many titbits, from many different sources, some official, some not, and some just anonymous phone-ins. The latter were always the last to receive too much attention unless something jumped out. And today one did. It came from a woman claiming to be a healthcare professional of some description, no other details, but she was concerned with the state of some drug dependent patients who turned up at A&E. They were dealt with as cocaine abusers, but the caller had concerns. One being that they all suffered from vastly dilated pupils. So much so, that daylight was painful, and often they wore cheap sunglasses, irrespective of the weather, or whether it was day or night.

This resonated with Cath; she had been somewhere

recently doing some research into local drug markets, when lots of youths, who appeared down and out, were all wearing cheap sunglasses. She had written it off as some daft fad, but it gave the anonymous caller's information a basis of fact. And that was all she needed sometimes to pique her interest. She had learned long ago never to ignore it. And it sounded drug-related, but where the hell had she seen them?

She spent the next hour ringing around all the A&E departments in the Northwest, to try and illicit other similar observations from doctors or nurses, but not surprisingly, she didn't get very far. Then she tried speaking to an old school friend of hers who was a ward manager at a local clinic. She commented that she had seen lots of cocaine overdose patients, but hadn't recalled anything out of the ordinary, they either survived, or they didn't. And if they didn't, it was usually the heart that faltered.

'Who cares, it's just another addict wasting the NHS's resources?' Cath didn't say out loud. But she could understand why some would think like that. 'Thanks, Jill, we'll have to have a proper catch-up over a coffee sometime,' she'd ended the call with. And then felt immediately guilty at using the same hackneyed line she'd used the last time she'd asked Jill a favour.

But the caller had voiced other concerns, one being that of the several cases she had seen of the sunglass-wearing patients, all but one had died. And she said that was far higher than the norm. She'd raised her concerns with her bosses, but no one was interested.

Cath's first thought was that it may just have been a bad batch of cocaine. She knew that the average purity was below fifty percent, so perhaps the dealers had used a toxic adulterant and once that batch was spent, the problem would be over. She then spent an hour going through all recent press releases from either the police, or any of the locally based drug intervention teams. She found no new health warnings talking about a bad batch of drugs. She checked the 'date received' stamp on the lead, and it was only a few days old; maybe the problem had still to mature?

Lastly, she put a call into a local Drug and Alcohol Action Team, and drew a further blank, so decided it was stimulation time and headed to the coffee machine. Her supervisor, Sergeant Eleanor Crosby was already there.

'Working on your next intel package, I hope?' Eleanor asked.

'Just following a drug related lead – could involve a bad batch of drugs, not sure yet.'

'Excellent, keep at it, especially if there is a public health angle to it,' Eleanor replied.

Cath said that she would and gave Eleanor a quick update. She then asked Cath to join her in her office. She wanted to hear more.

'Bad batch?' you say.

'Could be, but who knows if it's a one-off? Could be part of a larger supply which is about to wreak havoc and death on our streets.'

'That's a cheery thought. Tell me about the sunglasses again?' Eleanor asked.

So Cath did.

'You mean like the cheap kiss-me-quick crap you might see on a Blackpool seafront stall?'

'Eleanor, I could kiss you quick, you're a star,' Cath said.

'Blackpool, is that where you saw them?'

'It wasn't actually, although they may have originated from there, but you've jogged my memory. It was in Preston City centre, I passed them en route to Blackpool for a meeting about a week ago.'

'I guess you are shooting off to Preston, now?'

'I guess I am,' Cath replied.

'Can Martin or Colin in Preston help?' Eleanor asked. 'They may have some local knowledge,' she added quickly.

Cath felt herself blush at Eleanor's choice of cops to approach; news travels faster when it's gossip. 'Possibly, but I'll have to wait, they are both on a hush-hush job.'

'Hush-hush job? Would love to know more about that,' Eleanor said.

'Me too, but Martin's keeping quiet.'

'Okay, keep me posted.'

Cath said that she would and then put her mug back on her desk and retrieved her car keys. It was time to head into town.

CHAPTER FOUR

Fourteen days after meeting Abdul, Martin and Colin were in India, housed close to Delhi's Indira Ghandi International airport, the capital's main civil aerodrome and the busiest in the country, or so it seemed. It was like any other major multi-terminal airport, modern, spacious, and busy; very busy. Apparently, Mohammed Bashir was a regular visitor, sometimes on police business trying to garner interest in the Indians to buy Lancashire's IT software, using cultural channels – which had been far more regular than Don Rogers had realised – and sometimes he flew in and out over a weekend when he was not working. He apparently flashed his Lancashire Police identity badge as if it was a warrant card. He didn't claim to be an actual serving police officer but allowed the illusion, nonetheless. This, coupled with the frequency of his visits, meant he was always given the VIP treatment and waved through immigration and never searched. The Indian police had quickly established all this and revealed that imperial hangovers still existed, even though India had long been an independent country. And such special treatment was often extended more so when the visiting British official was of Indian heritage.

No doubt Bashir relied on this; Martin had commented when first made aware. However, what troubled the Indians was that according to their enquires, Bashir travelled light, often with only a briefcase, though he was never made to wait in line for it to be scanned, he was always flagged through. It was a high-risk strategy on Bashir's part. He couldn't know in advance that he would always get the VIP treatment, though it had looked like he had up until now.

One hypothesis was that he had either bought a customs official off, or at the very least was very friendly with one. But how could he guarantee he would always face the same individual? According to the Indians it was always easy to assume corruption, but they had done extensive background checks on the staff and had yet to come up with any evidence of collusion from their side.

Martin and Colin had been advised that they could trust the Indians at Senior State level, and that a lot of their investigative techniques were mirrored from the UK. Even their laws were often close copies of what came out of Westminster. The local and more rural forces were perhaps a different thing altogether.

Initially, Martin had outlined two possible ways forward in the chief's office two weeks ago: one; to allow Bashir to return to the UK on his next jaunt and then search him, or, two; let the Indians do so on his departure.

The benefit of letting the Indians do it were several-fold, but firstly, it would take the job well away from Martin and Colin. It would look like the Indians were either acting on their own intelligence, or it was simply a random search. Either way, it was far removed from the UK and therefore far removed from Abdul. The source had to be protected at all costs. Those were the rules, and this often provided some of the hardest challenges; get a result while it appeared to have come from a different direction.

The second main benefit in allowing the Indians to do it, was that he would languish in a rat-infested jail for between two to five years before his case even came to trial, where after, on conviction, he would receive a very heavy sentence in the most impoverished of environments. This was the bit that Rogers particularly liked about the plan.

Martin ended his musings as Sub-Inspector Aadi Das entered the room. Normally for police to obtain permission to enter and work in a foreign country – even a friendly one – it would take many months. But being a very friendly country, the Indians had granted an extrajudicial permission for Martin and Colin to enter India, but under a strict caveat that they were spectators only, with no official capacity. Perhaps, the ex-colonial ties were working for them too.

Since arriving in Delhi the previous day, they had been restricted to staying in an airport hotel and this small room, which was airside on police premises within Terminal 1.

'Gentlemen, so sorry to have left you here for so long without company or refreshments,' Aadi said.

'Not at all, you have much to do, we are just looking forward to watching events unfold,' Colin said.

Aadi nodded and then walked across the small room to a table above which was an array of TV monitors. He picked up a remote control and brought them all to life. They showed several views within the check-in side of departures inside the terminal, including passport control and immigration.

Martin had grown fond of Aadi very quickly but was well aware of the advice he and Colin had been given from the Foreign Office prior to flying to Delhi. 'The Indians are very helpful, and can seem obsequious even, but don't believe all the platitudes; some of it is just a cultural politeness they don't expect you to test. In other words, don't take advantage. They could soon become very offended if they think a Brit is trying to pull the colonial right to be treated better than anyone else'.

Colin had suggested it may be one of the reasons that they had been offered so much help so quickly; they probably hated Bashir's arrogance and couldn't wait to cut him off at the knees.

'Our top surveillance team is currently following Bashir on his way to the airport in case he is met by any criminals en route,' Aadi said.

'Excellent,' Martin replied. 'Is he alone?'

'In a taxi on his own, apart from an attaché case, which is his only luggage,' Aadi said.

'I hope he has the drugs in there,' Colin added.

'So do I, chief inspector, we have gone to a lot of trouble and expense on this investigation.'

'For which we and Her Majesty's government are eternally grateful,' Colin said.

Aadi nodded and then added, 'His taxi is pulling up near the terminal now, so we should soon find out. I have to go; I will see you later.'

Aadi didn't wait for a reply, and swiftly left.

Martin and Colin sat transfixed watching the screens. The departures seemed busy as one might expect, but not overly so, which should make it easier for them to follow the action. The first screen was showing the entrance to the terminal, so Martin concentrated on that one. They didn't have to wait long.

Three or four minutes later, Bashir walked into the terminal building. Martin recognised him straight away, as did Colin. He was in his forties, of average height and build, wearing grey flannels and a dark blue double-breasted jacket. He had a black attaché case in his right hand. 'Looks like he has just parked his yacht up,' Martin noted.

Colin smiled but stayed focused on the TV monitors.

After several minutes, Martin saw Bashir emerge on the last screen, which covered the immigration and customs area. Martin noted a 'fellow passenger' start to hang back a few metres behind Bashir, and he guessed that he was part of the surveillance foot-team. The reason why he was hanging back became obvious; Bashir was stalling.

Martin leaned nearer the screen, as did Colin. Bashir seemed to be looking around. Was he looking for someone, or had he spotted the surveillance? 'I hope he's not blown the team?' Martin said.

'You're the expert in these matters, Martin, what do you think?' Colin asked.

'I hope not. He will no doubt be on his highest alert at the moment, but he's a police civilian for God's sake, not some anti-surveillance savvy organised gangster.'

Then it appeared that Bashir's attention was more drawn towards the customs officers manning the desks.

'You see that?' Colin said.

'Dead right, he's looking for someone on the desks.'

'Probably, the same guy who ushers him through every time.'

'And it appears he can't see him.'

'I hope Aadi's men are clocking all this.'

'I hope they are in close,' Martin said.

'Why?'

'If his contact is not there and he bolts, they need to stop him before he can ditch his briefcase. He needs to be holding it when they pounce.'

Martin could feel the tension rising and half expected Colin to start a chin-rub, but he didn't. Maybe that was a good sign. He watched the TV even closer. Bashir was stood ramrod straight, frozen to the spot, still looking at the desks, and then all around. He looked far from comfortable. The case, Martin noticed was a cheap moulded plastic one. It would have a couple of document dividers on the inside of the lid, but little else. If there were drugs in there, they should be pretty obvious.

'I don't like the look of this,' Colin said.

Martin didn't answer but agreed. He watched on. Bashir hadn't moved, and the area was becoming busier. People kept walking past and obstructing their view. Each time that happened, Martin's heart almost stopped until Bashir became visible again.

Then Bashir pulled his mobile phone out. This was starting to go to rat-shit. But Bashir didn't use the phone, in that he didn't appear to make or receive a call. He just looked at it.

'Text,' Colin shouted, as Martin thought the same.

He then saw Bashir use his thumb on the phone's screen. 'And he's just sent a reply,' Martin added. His face was nearly touching the TV as he leaned in even closer to see if he could get a look at what it said.

Then a minute later a nondescript-looking youth appeared next to Bashir. Neither man looked at the other. The youth was carrying a cheap moulded plastic attaché case. He put it down, and Bashir put his down and immediately picked up the new case and walked off. The youth collected Bashir's case and hurried away in the opposite direction and out of view into the crowd.

'Did you see that?' Colin said.

'I did; but we now have a dilemma.'

The door burst open and in rushed Aadi looking stressed and flustered, and Martin knew why. Which case had the drugs?

If Bashir's contact at customs was not where he should have been then perhaps the youth was his safety net, and he'd switched cases to send the drugs back to Delhi.

Or maybe the youth was always the mule, the one carrying the drugs until Bashir was ready to go through customs. Perhaps, his contact *was* where he should have been, it was just that the youth carrying the drugs was late to the party? Bashir's original case may even contain the cash payment.

The three men quickly voiced the scenarios between themselves.

'Where is the youth now?' Martin asked.

'We've lost him in the crowd,' Aadi said, before he cupped his right ear. 'Oh, hang on, wait.' He was clearly concentrating hard on what his radio earpiece was telling him. Then he added, 'He's reappeared outside, walking away from the airport – minus the case.'

'Shit,' Martin said.

'What about Bashir?' Colin asked.

'He's gone through customs, still with *a* case.'

'Is he airside now?' Martin asked.

'Yes, he is walking in the general direction of his flight's gate.'

'If you pull him now, it will obviously not be a routine search,' Colin added.

'And if he has *the* empty case, the job's blown. He'll not try again, unless he's an idiot, which he's not,' Martin said.

'But if he still has the drugs in his case?' Aadi said.

'Your call sub-inspector; but I know what I'd do,' Martin added.

CHAPTER FIVE

Martin voiced his opinion but neither Colin nor Aadi responded. Aadi had his hand cupped to his ear once more and Colin shrugged his shoulders. It was a toss of a coin situation. Surveillance operations often came down to going with a hunch as they often didn't go according to plan. Criminals were either very organised or habitually disorganised, and either could wreck the most detailed of planning. That said, this job – on paper at least – had seemed straightforward. Martin should have known better.

Aadi nodded at Martin and spat what sounded like a command into his coat lapel before he turned to face them both. 'I agree. We have one foot unit following the youth and I have ordered a drugs and cash dog to search the route he took in egress with support from two customs officers looking for a discarded case.'

'I hope you don't think I was trying to—' Martin started to say.

'Tell my grandmother how to suck an egg? No, I realise we are all officers, and you were thinking it out loud,' Aadi said.

Martin was relieved that he hadn't offended him, and said, 'Your knowledge of our ridiculous metaphors is impressive.'

Aadi smiled.

'How long before Bashir is due to board?' Colin asked.

Aadi looked at his watch, and then answered, 'Twenty minutes, maybe a little less.'

The next few minutes passed quickly as the three of them agonised over the two scenarios. Aadi spoke several times into his lapel in what Martin guessed was Hindi. Then Aadi turned to face them, his expression stern. 'The search for a discarded case, both physical and with the dog has proved fruitless, so I have instructed that the youth be stopped.'

Showtime.

The following minutes slowed to a crawl as Martin and Colin stared at Aadi expectantly. After what seemed like an eternity, Aadi raised his hand to his ear in earnest. Then he spoke. 'The youth has been very open; he says he was paid by a stranger to deliver the case to Bashir. He did not know what was in it and assumed that he is just a businessman who is very busy.'

'Sounds like your officer is happy with him?' Colin said.

'Indeed, he has told him that he was surprised to be asked to take the second case away. His brief had been only to deliver one, but he felt it would be disrespectful to decline.'

'What did he do with the second case?' Martin asked.

'As he was instructed by Bashir, he delivered it to a waiting taxi driver who took it and drove off without comment. The youth was surprised why the man could not have done this simple task himself, and just assumed that he was a very important person.'

The pay-off, Martin thought.

'So we are none the wiser?' Colin said.

'I'm afraid not,' Aadi replied.

'Strange to have a taxi driver waiting to take away an

empty case?' Martin said. 'It must have had either drugs or cash in it.'

'My thoughts too, Sergeant,' Aadi said. 'You would think that he would just tell the youth to keep it, or bin it, or do whatever he liked with it, if it had been empty?'

'Agreed,' Martin and Colin said in unison.

Martin watched as Aadi cupped his right ear once more and waited intently to hang on his every word when they came.

'Bad news,' Aadi eventually said. And then explained that the dog handler had meandered past the gate for Bashir's flight and his dog had walked past a seated Bashir and his new case and had failed to give the handler any indications.

Shit, Martin thought, but then said, 'They are usually pretty good.'

'They are, but nothing is one hundred percent,' Aadi said.

'So we are still none the wiser, but the clandestine nature of the first case's removal suggests that Bashir has either been spooked, for whatever reason, and sent the drugs back, or received them and paid for them?' Martin said.

Both Colin and Aadi nodded.

'How the hell can we tell which it is?' Colin said.

'I am under orders to make sure,' Aadi said. 'Bashir will have to be searched before he can board the plane. Let's hope it is the latter scenario, and we are worrying for nothing. I will return shortly.' And then he turned and left.

Double shit, Martin thought, before he discussed the ramifications with Colin.

'We're in their hands,' Colin said.

'I know, but it will obviously spook him more than he has been already if it's the rat-shit scenario. It may even put a stop to any more runs,' Martin answered.

'For a while perhaps, but don't forget how greedy these types of bastards are. They may change things, but I doubt they'll stop, we will just have to rely on the source.'

'If we can encourage him to report further, he looked like the world had lifted from him when he told us his tale. It may take a lot to get him to re-engage with Bashir,' Martin said.

'And he's still his brother.'

'True,' Martin said, 'but he clearly hates him.'

Both men sat in silence in quiet contemplation. From the euphoria of seeing Bashir arrive at the airport with the briefcase, to the crushing feeling of impending defeat, Martin felt depressed. The extreme highs and lows of police work must be akin to a drug addict's rollercoaster ride.

Eventually, Aadi reappeared, and Martin knew that it was not good news as soon as he entered the room.

'I have bad news and bad news,' Aadi started.

'Better give us the bad news first,' Martin said.

'The search was negative. Nothing in Bashir's case, bar a few souvenirs.'

'How did he take it?' Colin asked.

'The handler tried to hide the reason for approach in that he claimed his dog had shown a vague interest in Bashir for a second time, having walked past him minutes earlier.'

'Did he accept that?' Colin asked.

'He seemed to, or put it another way, he didn't show that he was offended.'

'What were the souvenirs?' Martin asked.

'Just trinkets,' Aadi said, 'put it this way; it was not five kilogrammes of heroin.'

Martin could only shake his head in frustration.

'In fact, the dog had a sniff at the air from inside the case while it was being searched, and again showed no real reaction,' Aadi added.

Martin realised that they were now in the damage limitation stage; if Bashir accepted the dog handler's reason for searching him, he would just be glad that he was clean. But even if he did, he would no doubt change his whole method of operating; he wouldn't risk this again. And if he was spooked by his customs contact not being present, he might even think that he had sold him out to the cops. Either way, it could hopefully still keep the UK side of things in play.

'So what's the other bad news?' Colin asked.

'An officer has checked the CCTV and the youth is clearly seen being approached as he left the terminal building by a taxi driver, who took the case. But unfortunately, his features are not clear, and the taxi licence plate cannot be seen.'

'At least you know that the youth is telling the truth,' Colin added.

Although Martin was not entirely convinced of his innocence, he had to accept that it would be impossible to prove otherwise. They both apologised and thanked Aadi in equal measure, and Colin voiced that he hoped the lack of a result would not cause him trouble with his bosses due to the costs involved.

'Thank you for your concern, but the swapping of the cases will be my get out of jail card,' Aadi said, before grinning. Martin was starting to think that the Indians did love a metaphor or two.

Martin and Colin were already booked on a later flight, so all they had to do now was return to the hotel to check out before coming back to the airport. Aadi offered them a lift, but they declined, they had used up too much of his time as it was, and in any event, Martin fancied a walk and some fresh air. Aadi said his goodbyes and then led them out of the room and back to the departure lounge. As soon as they left the building Martin regretted turning down Aadi's offer of a lift. The heat was stifling and instant, and even though they could see their hotel, they jumped into the first waiting taxi.

'What the hell do we do now?' Martin asked.

'I'll have to chew that one over for a while, what do you reckon?'

'Not sure, if I'm honest.'

'One thing at a time. I've got to ring Rogers next and give him the good news.'

CHAPTER SIX

Bashir knew that he was not a brave man; he accepted that he could be standoffish, arrogant even. But he had learned a vital lesson today; familiarity does indeed lead to slackness. He had done this route many times and never with any problem. In fact, today had appeared no different. But he had nearly died of fright when that dog walked past sniffing him at the departure gate. But that was nothing to the fear he felt when the damn thing returned and the cop claimed his stupid mutt had shown some interest in him, and he would have to be searched. He had to try very hard not to show his fear. Nor did he wish to confirm any suspicions by being overly complaintive. He'd passed the test, but his legs had nearly given way several times. He'd started to shake after the cop and his mutt had walked away, probably the adrenalin rush; he was just grateful it hadn't kicked in minutes earlier; the cop may have misread it.

But he was in two minds; in some ways he had passed a test, so why should things have to change. He mused that it all depended on whether the stop and search had been random or not. He was no expert in these matters, but it had looked random. He'd have to wait until he got back to Preston and check with his expert partner, she would know. He'd take his lead from her. He'd have to. He just hated the thought of having to change all their systems if they didn't have too. One thing was for sure, if he'd had the five keys of white in his case like the time before last, and all the previous runs, he would have been down the steps with no light of day ever to look forward to. It was that thought which had unnerved him during the search; what might have been.

Bashir took his seat, economy class, so as not to draw attention, and rested the cheap case on his lap. Then his phone vibrated to announce an incoming text, which he duly read. The money had been safely delivered by the taxi driver. Excellent, at least the supplier would be satisfied. Bashir then unclasped and opened the case on his lap. Three or four cheap-looking tacky trinkets lay inside. Nothing else. Apart from the egg timer. He held it up; it was made from hand-crafted mahogany and was of much better quality than the other souvenirs. Heavier too, substantially so.

He then fired off a one-line text to his home contact before turning his phone off. A steward had just announced that all phones or devices should be switched off or put in flight mode.

He picked the egg timer up and upended it to watch the grains within it swap ends with celerity. He rubbed it and smiled. Then a stewardess approached and told him that his case would have to be stored in an overhead locker for take-off. Bashir smiled at her before replacing the egg-timer and closing the lid. He then handed the case to her and watched which locker she put it into. He then leaned back into his seat and started to relax. He'd soon be airborne and out of this shithole of a country.

Once they were off the runway, Bashir relaxed even further, and started to muse about how much money he had made so far. How he had significantly passed the upper limit he had set himself, but it had just become so easy to do and so hard to give up. His initial plan was to leave the police and do one once he had reached his limit. He could set up anywhere and be comfortable, not greedy, and not in a way that would attract attention. As it was, he hadn't touched any of it yet, on purpose. But with these new developments it was worth the risk to continue, he could increase his worth tenfold or more, and then he and his wife could live in luxury for the rest of their days. Somewhere far away where no suspicions would be raised. But for now, he knew that he needed to keep his feet on the ground, and as soon as they were back on terra firma that's what he intended to do. Starting with a hard conversation with his other partners. It was time to adjust the percentages a little; after all, it was he who was taking all the risks, it was his heritage and appearance that they didn't have.

Then the stewardess approached, breaking his reverie. 'Can I get you any drinks, sir?' she asked.

'No thanks, I don't drink, I'm a Muslim,' he replied, trying to keep a straight face. Bashir then returned to his thoughts.

One issue was how to eventually get all the cash into the banking system without raising a red flag. He was well aware of the SARs in the UK. The Suspicious Activity Reports which all UK financial institutions were bound in law to report to the police. A sudden deposit of several hundred thousand pounds would no doubt jump to the top of the SARs to-do list on some fraud cop's desk.

He'd initially intended laundering the dosh somehow, in dribs and drabs from many different directions, but hadn't reckoned on the profits reaching such heights when he'd started this game. Which, if everything went to plan, would become so much more. He did have half an idea, but that would have to wait a while before he could explore it further. Time to get his head down, he was due back in work tomorrow, the thought deeply depressed him. Especially as he was due in a top tier management meeting chaired by that buffoon of a chief constable, Don Rogers.

***

'How did the chief take the news?' Martin asked Colin as soon as he entered his hotel room.

'His swearing is definitely getting better. Are you sure you've not been giving him private tuition?' Colin asked.

'As opposed to what? Public tuition?'

Ignoring the comment, Colin continued, 'On the plus side, they have managed to identify a serving female inspector at Blackpool who is in an inordinate amount of telephone contact with Bashir.'

'What's her name?' Martin asked.

'He wouldn't say over the phone.'

'That must have placated him somewhat?' Martin asked.

'Not really, he was ranting about "the bent bastard being a fucking inspector".'

'Do we know that she is actually bent?'

'Not really.'

Colin picked up his holdall, and Martin reclaimed his from inside the room's front door.

'Come on, we've got a plane to catch,' Colin said.

CHAPTER SEVEN

Martin said his goodbyes to Colin once they were in the arrivals lounge. Colin was headed to a pickup point where his wife was waiting, and Martin intended on catching a train into Manchester from the airport. Colin had offered him a lift, but it was out of his way, plus the train would be quicker. He'd agreed to get into their Preston office early so they could prepare for their inevitable meeting with Rogers, who would require an in-depth debrief from them both.

He texted Cath as he wandered to the train station level of the airport and was relieved that she was at home. He couldn't wait to see her. He'd no doubt face a barrage of questions from her, but he knew he would have to keep quiet on this job, at least for now. He considered whether he should stop by his to freshen up and change his clothes, but decided against it, he didn't want to delay seeing her. As he made the decision to go straight to her place, he smelled his right underarm; not sure whether any body odour would transcend his clothing, not sure why he had felt the instinctive need to find out. A woman walking past gave him a wide berth.

An hour later he was knocking on Cath's front door. She answered and seemed pleased to see him. Once settled inside with a glass of Merlot, he asked her what she had been up to.

'You first, globetrotter, sounds far more interesting,' she answered.

'You know, I can't; well not yet anyway.'

'When then?' she asked.

'It maybe a while, I'm afraid.'

'Well, that's no fun,' she moaned.

'I promise I'll tell you when I can.' Then wishing to move the conversation on, Martin asked again what she'd been up to.

'Well, I followed a lead in Preston, re drugs,' she answered.

Martin sat up to listen.

'Got your attention now?'

'Go on,' he said.

'I've been looking for a group of young people which I'm sure I've seen hanging around near the train station in my recent past.'

'What for?' Martin asked.

'To see if they are still wearing cheap sunglasses.'

Martin picked up the opened bottle of Chilean Merlot from the coffee table and asked how many of them she had drunk? Cath laughed and then explained about an anonymous lead she had received from an alleged health professional re cocaine addicts and bad gear.

'Did you find any?' Martin asked.

'No, but I did speak to a homeless guy near the station who knew what I was talking about. Said that he had been offered some but was suspicious as it was half the normal price. Plus, he'd heard that it was "very bad shit".'

Martin was always amazed at how Cath got people to open up to her and tell her all sorts. Perhaps not being an actual cop helped. Maybe he should try 'being an analyst' when faced with someone he would expect to be difficult, see how he got on. But he knew it was more than that;

Cath had this charm about her, a way of putting strangers at ease. 'You should have been a detective,' he said.

'So you've said many times, but I couldn't take the pay cut,' she answered.

Martin grinned and asked if she thought it was just a bad batch of gear knocking about. She said that she wasn't sure. He asked her what her next step would be.

'Blackpool. According to the homeless guy, the dealer knocking it out is also giving away cheap sunglasses, and he comes on the train from Blackpool where it is more prevalent.'

'You need to be careful over there,' Martin said, with genuine worry.

'I'm a big girl, and you're a big girl's blouse, Martin. I'll be fine.'

'When are you going over there?'

'Not sure yet. When are you back in work?'

'Colin wants me in Preston for seven tomorrow morning.'

He watched Cath look at her watch and he instinctively did the same. 8.30 p.m. already.

'In that case, hurry up and finish your wine,' she said.

'Why, are we going out?'

'Nope, but all this mention of girl's blouses reminds me that I want your help taking mine off,' she answered, as she stood up and started to wander towards her bedroom.

Martin doubted that he had ever emptied a glass of wine so fast.

***

There was only one thing worse than dreaming about having a wee, and then waking up with a bladder the size of a space-hopper, and that was dreaming about a car or house alarm going off before awaking to find a mobile ringing in the dead of night. As an operational detective, the latter was never as easily dealt with as the former.

As he focused on the screen, he could see that it was four a. m. Cath stirred next to him and put her bedside table lamp on as Martin sat up and started to orientate himself. Having noted the time, he saw the identity of his caller was 'Colin – DCI'. He pressed the green icon to answer.

'You took your time,' Colin said.

'I was dead to the world,' Martin said.

'Drinking or shagging?'

'Jet lag and one glass of wine.'

'Only one glass?' Colin asked.

'Yes.'

'Well, you've definitely been up to the other then,' Colin said.

Martin wasn't used to Colin being quite so playful, especially at this time of the day, and especially as it had to mean that a job was on. Then Colin explained, and Martin ended the call saying that he'd see him in an hour; give or take.

'Murder most horrible?' Cath asked, who was now also sat up. But with the quilt pulled up to cover her modesty.

'You'd have thought so, but no. A robbery team are due to strike in a few hours, and they want me and Colin on it,' Martin answered. He now realised why Colin was in such a good mood. A further rare occasion for him to get out operationally. First Abdul, then Delhi, and now this; at this rate he'd start to miss his desk and strategy meetings. 'Sorry about the disturbance, but I've got to have a quick shower and then go.'

'No worries, just gen me up later – if you can of course.'

'Your charm won't work on me,' he replied.

'Just did, you'd be amazed what you say in your sleep.'

Martin grinned as he headed to Cath's bathroom.

When he came out there was a mug of tea and a slice of toast waiting for him, bless her. Then she handed him her car keys in exchange for his. Shit, he'd forgotten he'd come straight from the airport. 'What about you?' he asked.

'I'll taxi round to yours later and grab your motor.'

'Thanks, you're a star,' he said.

'I am, and it'll cost you, but for now, just scram so I can get back to sleep.'

CHAPTER EIGHT

It was ten past five when Martin rushed into Preston Central police station. The one advantage of travelling up the M61 from Manchester at this time of day was that he could rag the motor, and although there were still quite a few heavies about, the fast lane was mostly clear. Unlike in a couple of hours from now.

Colin was already at his desk. A steaming polystyrene cup of nuclear hot sludge was waiting for him. He picked it up and then thought better of it. 'Cheers, but we must really invest in our own kettle.'

'There's gratitude,' Colin said.

'What time is the briefing?' Martin asked.

'It's in ten minutes, at half past.'

'Is it an armed op?'

'Yep.'

'Why us, Boss?'

'The force Serious and Organised Crime Unit are running it, but they invited us along for a reason.'

Martin was perplexed, but let Colin explain. Apparently, a nasty team of villains are planning to attack a cash-in-transit van in Preston. A four-handed team which SOCU had been running surveillance on for months as they did any number of recce runs.

'And today's the day the teddy bears have their picnic?' Martin asked.

'According to their intelligence, yeah.'

'Sounds like a job our firm could have run? What's our role?' Martin asked.

'It certainly sounds a tasty job. But the reason we are in tow is that the gang's leader is none other than Dan the Man,' Colin said.

'What?' Martin said with incredulity.

Colin just nodded. Martin and Colin had circulated Daniel (Dan the Man) Manning eighteen months ago as wanted for the murder of his ex-girlfriend. Manning was a brute of a career criminal with many previous convictions for robbery and varying degrees of assault; usually GBH. Martin knew that they had a strong case against Manning but the last intel they had on him suggested that he had fled to the Costas. 'I thought he was on his toes in Spain?' Martin asked.

'I know, which is why enquires keep drawing a fat zero over there,' Colin replied.

'How long did you say the SOCU have been watching this team?' Martin asked, as he felt his temper rising.

'Several months,' Colin said, and then added, 'but before you get too excited, the SIO claims that they only identified the "Dan" target yesterday. Otherwise, they would have moved in and nicked him for our offence.'

'Very convenient. You believe their SIO?' Martin asked.

'We'll never know.'

Martin had come up against this issue in the past, proactive teams wanted to catch their targets committing robbery, or with the drugs or whatever, and get the whole gang that way, rather than spoil the party by nicking the main man for an outstanding matter. To be fair, he understood the frustration that such a quandary created, with the argument being that to jump on one head prematurely in that way could lead to the rest of the team escaping justice. A moral dilemma: and if the offence the target was already wanted for was a lesser one, say in this case, burglary, then an SIO could arguably justify a decision *not to arrest* but catch the bad guys for the more serious offences. The alternative argument, however, was that the police could be seen to be allowing an offence to take place which they could have prevented by arresting the target for the lesser offence. And when the original offence was one of murder; there was no way Manning should not have been arrested. The only excuse would be that they didn't realise who he was.

He shared his concerns with Colin.

'As long as we get our murderer into custody, then I'm happy. It'll be for the SOCU SIO to convince a trial judge that they had no idea who Dan the Man was?' Colin said.

'Clue's sort of in the nickname,' Martin said.

Colin then looked at his watch, and Martin looked at his. It was 5.29 a.m.

'Come on, we'll miss the briefing,' Colin said.

Five minutes later, Martin and Colin were stood at the rear of a large group of officers who were a mixture of detectives, surveillance officers, and firearms officers in plain clothes.

The briefing was being conducted by a DI named Gary Falstaff, who neither Colin nor Martin knew. And it sounded as if things were already going tits-up. Intelligence and/or observations had put three of the gang at their home addresses at bedtime the previous evening. The only one not 'housed' was Daniel Manning. Marvellous. He had been lost the previous evening and had not   as yet – returned to his last known address.

'How do we know the job's still on?' one detective asked.

'They may have sacked it?' another added.

'According to intelligence only received in the last few hours, the job is most definitely on. The cash-in-transit van will be attacked as it approaches the counting house in Preston,' Gary said.

'Do we know which van, Boss, or could it be any?' a DC asked.

'It is a specific van, but *we* don't know which one. But we do know exactly where they plan to do it. So surveillance on the targets will hopefully, bring them onto the plot, while you lot are lying in wait. We'll have both ends covered that way,' Gary said.

'What about Manning, Gary?' Martin shouted from the back.

'We'll have to wait for him to come to us, which he will,' Gary answered.

Then Martin heard a murmur of mutterings from some parts of the room, and Martin guessed why. But so too must have Gary as he immediately intervened.

'And just so the suspicious bastards among you are clear; Manning is not the snout who we have suddenly lost a grip on, he is actually wanted for murder, which we only discovered yesterday, so it is imperative that we find him, whether the job goes down or not.'

The room fell silent again.

'This is why Detective Chief Inspector Colin Carstairs and Detective Sergeant Martin Draker from the NWROCU are with us today,' Gary added, and pointed to Martin and Colin at the back of the room. Everyone turned round and looked at them.

Gary then checked his watch, and said, 'Okay, let's synchronise our watches at 5.45 a. m., and I want everyone on plot for 6.30 a. m.'

As everyone started to shuffle out of the room Gary made a straight line for Martin and Colin. As he arrived, he handed Martin a copy of the operational order and thanked them both for turning out at this ungodly hour. Martin started to thumb through the op order as Colin spoke.

'Where exactly do you want us, Gary, we don't want to get in the way of the surveillance or armed support?'

'I'll be in a command car with a loggist, and not be part of the surveillance as such, it'll free me up to have a better overview; you can join me in there if you wish?'

Both Martin and Colin nodded, and Gary said he'd see them in the garage in ten minutes, and then rushed off.

'Should be fun,' Colin said, as they hurried back to their office to grab their stuff.

'I just hope our man shows,' Martin replied.

Ten minutes later, Martin and Colin were in the garage and met by Gary and his loggist, a DC named Shelia. Gary jumped in the driver's seat of a large Volvo estate car and Shelia got into the front passenger seat. Martin and Colin jumped in the back. Gary turned on the car's surveillance radio loudspeaker and did a radio check with one of the team to ensure that the car's equipment was working properly, which it was.

Twenty minutes later, they drew up onto a large industrial estate in Ribbleton, which is a large area on the eastern side of the city. A mix of residential estates and industrial parks on its outer fringes. Some were newly built, where a clear expansion programme was under way, and some were much older. The one they drove onto was one of the newer ones. Gary pulled over onto a disused car park. Judging by the weeds growing across it, Martin reckoned that it had few visitors. They usually built the infrastructure first, and buildings second in these places.

'How far from the counting house are we?' Colin asked.

'It's over on the other side of the estate, a way off, and the identified attack zone is across the main road, too. We are well out of the way here, yet it'll take just two minutes to get out when needed,' Gary answered.

Martin knew that the villains could have spotters all

over, so where they parked was important. The surveillance teams were the only ones allowed close to the zone, and Martin knew from his surveillance training they would be well-hidden through a variety of innovative guises and techniques. He also knew that they could be in for a long wait.

After a couple of hours, Gary took a call and Martin could see him stiffen in his chair as he listened. Martin was on his phone to Cath at the time but hurried off when he saw this. Gary said little until he ended his call. He then pressed the radio transmit button on the steering wheel and spoke. 'Victor One to all teams, intelligence update from the Whiskey Team; Target Two is mobile in the vehicle mentioned on your op order; all units please acknowledge.'

Then each unit in turn acknowledged the update before Gary turned in his chair to face Colin. He explained that Target Two, using the known bandit vehicle had left his house, but had checked all over and under the car before driving off. The Whiskey surveillance team was following him. It might not mean anything yet, but his cautiousness was a good sign, he'd not done it before when they'd followed him. Martin knew that some criminals went to that effort every time they drove, but according to Gary, not this lot.

The next thirty minutes confirmed Gary's suspicion that the target vehicle being driven by Target Two, had collected Targets Three and Four from their respective home addresses. But it was what happened at the last address which had got Gary excited. Target Four had left his house carrying what looked like a nylon plumber's bag with long implements within it. According to the foot team, the long objects were about two feet in length and there were more than two of them. But that was all they could say.

'Pretty good observation work by your Whiskey team,'

Martin said.

'Cheers,' Gary replied. 'But it's not enough for us to strike. I know we are all thinking sawn-offs, but what if the bag just contains plumber's piping and tools? This is a top team, and they could just be testing. Seeing if they are being followed.'

'They deployed a lot of anti-surveillance moves, previously?' Martin asked.

'Some, every time we have run out on them when together, but this is the first time we have seen the plumber's bag, so I'll keep an open mind for now,' Gary replied.

Martin agreed, not that it was his shout, or that he had any say or input in Gary's decision-making. Nor did Colin, for that matter, even though he was of senior rank.

Over the next thirty or forty minutes, Gary received regular updates from the Whiskey team. The targets were taking them on a mystery tour, including doubling back, going around roundabouts several times and even suddenly stopping for no good reason, when they would all jump out of their vehicle and just stare at passing traffic. All pretty standard stuff for an experienced surveillance team to have to deal with. They just hung back and watched from a distance while the targets played silly beggars. The last update Gary received was more encouraging. It appeared that the targets had eventually settled down and had stopped pissing about. Hopefully, they were now reassured that no one was following them, so the Whiskey Team could settle down and carry on following them.

But there was still no sign of their fourth member, the elusive Dan the Man.

'Perhaps it is game-on day, but Manning doesn't want to get his hands dirty?' Martin mused aloud.

'Could be. I mean anything is possible. I know that would not be what you two want to see, but if past observations are anything to go by, Manning has been with them each and every time they have done a recce run to Preston,' Gary replied.

Martin could only hope.

'Where are the targets currently heading?' Colin asked.

'Still in Manchester, towards Old Trafford cricket ground, last I heard.' Gary replied.

CHAPTER NINE

Cath hadn't sleep well after Martin had gone, conscious that she needed to be up earlier than normal in order to get his car. She was toying with the idea of heading over to Blackpool today but would have preferred to use her own car rather than Martin's Mondeo.

By eight-thirty she was in Martin's motor. She'd rang Eleanor, who was always in the office around 8 a. m., and as there was nothing critical waiting for her at HQ, she decided to go straight to Blackpool; she may as well use Martin's petrol as he was using hers. She may get the chance to share a coffee with him on her way back, if he wasn't too busy, and they could swap their cars back over. She was dying to know exactly what he was up to today; a robbery team sounded interesting. He might not be able to tell her about his trip to India at the moment, but maybe today's job would be different.

She rang Martin, and he said he'd meet her later if he could.

She ended the call and set off to Blackpool. It was about fifty miles from Manchester and at this time of day would take two hours. As she drove, she mused about what the homeless guy in Preston had told her, how the drug had made his 'friend' double over, how the daylight hurt him to a point of being nearly unbearable. She'd asked if his friend had gone to hospital, and he'd said no, but thereafter he had started to become less communicative.

She'd wondered if he had been, but the guy didn't want to say as it could identify him. She used her phone hands-free and rang the Royal Preston Hospital. She'd rung them initially from the office the other day when she'd rang them all but hadn't been convinced by any of the answers she'd received. At least she could be a bit more specific now. Thirty minutes later, she was still none the wiser. She didn't really blame the busy hospital staff, getting an annoying call from a police analyst was not what they lived for. She might pop in later, might get a bit further, but she'd leave it until later in the day, she didn't want to piss off the same person she'd just spoken to. Plus, a different person might give a different answer.

The next forty-five minutes passed fairly quickly, but she kept the radio on. She did check out Martin's CD collection, which was all bluesy stuff, she liked it normally, but she could only find the dirges type, so gave up. She was more an upbeat Blues Brothers sort of girl, rather than the Mississippi Delta stuff.

As she approached the end of the M55 motorway she couldn't help but feel a warm nostalgic sensation on seeing Blackpool Tower. It reminded her of her childhood, when it had been a game in the car to be the first to see the tower. And how her sister, Linda, always seemed to see it first. Cath was too easily distracted. She shook the memory from her mind as she concentrated on the Satnav; she'd set it for Talbot Road in the centre where she knew there was a large bus terminus. The station, she knew, had two things addicts liked. A needle bin and toilets. It also had car parks nearby.

Cath parked Martin's car and went on foot. There were no obvious drug addicts anywhere around the bus station or toilets. She then hoofed it towards the nearest chemist as many nowadays had needle exchange facilities, or even allowed registered addicts to receive methadone – a heroin substitute prescribed by doctors. Then she realised her mistake. Heroin users may use needles if their habit is particularly bad, but cocaine was smoked usually, just as heroin could be, but it was not typically injected. She was looking in the wrong place.

But she had a thought and carried on to the chemist and asked to speak to the pharmacist. A robust woman with a ruddy complexion came to the counter. Cath introduced herself and showed her Accredited Lancashire Police Staff card. She noted the woman's demeanour stiffen on seeing it. 'I'm just wondering if you could point me in the right direction if I wanted to chat with a street cocaine user.'

'I'm sorry I can't help you,' the woman said, and started to turn away.

'Please, it's not what you think. Let me explain?'

'We have enough bad press in this town,' the woman said.

'I'm trying to help,' Cath said.

'They need help, not arrest.'

'Couldn't agree with you more; it's the dealers I'm really interested in.'

The woman looked at her, so Cath launched into her pitch and mentioned the possibility of a bad batch of cocaine and the potential threat to life.

The woman stepped forward. 'And what makes you think that?' she asked.

Cath explained everything, including the sunglasses thing. This seemed to strike a chord with her. Cath saw it in her eyes.

'I've noticed a lot of youths who look like users walking around with sunglasses on, even in the rain,' the woman said.

'Where would I find them?'

'Central Promenade is a good place to start, and as it's an overcast day, you should see them if they are about.'

Cath thanked the woman and promised her that she really was here to help.

Twenty minutes and one tram ride later, Cath was at Central Pier in the middle of Blackpool's six-mile-long promenade. Again, the tram ride had taken her back to her youth, she felt sad when she considered her reason for being here today, compared with the fond memories she had of Blackpool as a child.

She hung around the entrance to Central Pier with all its noise and flashing lights emanating from within. The hustle and bustle of people walking to and fro past it, and in and out. But no sign of sunglass-wearing youths. She found a stairwell and walked down to the beach which was empty bar the odd dog walker. She turned to look around and then saw what she was after under the pier itself. Sat on the sand directly under the network of structural supports was a young couple; both wearing sunglasses.

She approached slowly, not wanting to startle them, and as she neared them, she could see that they looked to be in their early twenties, both dressed in baggy jogging bottoms with a baggy hooded top. Both looked unkempt. She wasn't sure which sex they were until only a few metres away; both had short dark hair, and the sunglasses didn't help. As she neared, they both turned to look at her. One was a little smaller than the other, and slimmer too. By the shape of her mouth Cath reckoned she was female.

She spoke first, confirming her gender as she did, 'What do you want?'

'Just to chat, for a minute, if that's alright?'

'You a cop?' the taller of the two – who was definitely male – asked.

Cath thought if she said she was an analyst working for the police it would amount to the same thing, so decided to use her old profession instead.

'No, just a newspaper reporter, but don't freak out, I do want to help.'

'Look lady, we are up to our tits in do-gooders, no offence,' the female said.

Cath quickly explained why she was there.

'That's why we are under here,' the man said. 'It's darker, and the pain's only just starting to go.'

'Why bother with it if it hurts your eyes so much?' Cath asked.

'It's like nothing you've ever done; I mean before you start to come down, that's when the pain hits your eyes. Just got to ride it out,' the female said.

'Is it a bad batch?' Cath asked.

'We're not that daft,' the man said. 'It's new shit. It's synthetic Charlie, made in a lab not a jungle. They will be able to make as much as is needed.'

'Once they get it right, once they stop this eye grief, then it'll be great,' the female said.

'You do know people have died from it?' Cath added.

'If they have, then they are dickheads, probably overdid it, greedy bastards,' the female said.

Cath knew she wouldn't talk these two around; drug addicts had an answer for everything, it was part of being an addict. It was why they needed the help they didn't want; they couldn't help themselves. She knew many people in society didn't care, thought that they brought it all upon themselves, which she had to admit was true to some degree. But in her experience addicts were often vulnerable and weak from a variety of reasons and circumstances: and shouldn't any civilised society be judged by how they treat those who are most in need?

She felt sorry for these two. She sighed, and then asked, 'What's this synthetic cocaine called?'

'Sky White,' the female said, and added, 'we'll need to get some more soon. Can you lend us a twenty?'

Cath shook her head slowly. The female shrugged, and then told her partner that her eyes felt bearable now. He said his did too, and then they both tentatively removed their sunglasses, a few millimetres at a time. Stopping several times in the process, as if they were testing their eyes against the natural light, until they'd both removed them. They looked at each other.

'You okay?' the man asked.

'Yeah, you?' the female replied.

He nodded, and then they both turned to look at Cath.

Cath let out an audible gasp. Both of them still had pupils which appeared massively dilated. The eyes seemed to be bulging out from their sockets and what area was left beyond the pupil was red and fiery; it was like looking into the face of zombies.

They both put their glasses back on.

'That good?' the female said.

'Sorry, it was just a shock,' Cath said.

'Well, we don't want to draw attention. Should be okay properly in half an hour,' the female said.

Cath doubted that very much.

'We gotta go,' the man said.

'One last question?' Cath said.

'Go on,' the female said.

'Where can I find a dealer of Sky White?'

Both looked at each other in obvious contemplation, before the man spoke, 'Look, we know we should get off this shit.'

Cath was impressed, if they could admit that to themselves, then there was a chance for them both.

'But we just aren't ready yet,' he said, and turned to the female, 'are we babe?'

She just shook her head, but Cath was unconvinced by it. The man stood up and started to walk away before pausing to look back. The female stood up and started after him. The man then turned and continued to trudge through the soft sand.

As the female passed Cath, she whispered, 'Railway station, but come after we've scored; tonight, ask for Minty.'

Cath put her hand on the woman's shoulder, pausing her for a moment. She quickly placed her calling card into the woman's hand. One of her blank ones without all the police stuff on it. Just her name and a phone number. It paid to have both kinds to give out.

She glanced at it, and said, 'What's this?'

'I have contacts,' Cath said, and quickly added, 'if and when you are ready to come off this shit, call me. Maybe I can help get you both into a treatment programme.'

The woman smiled and closed her fingers around the card.

The man had stopped and was looking back. He shouted, 'What you saying?'

'Just thanking us for chatting,' the female replied, and then hurried after him.

CHAPTER TEN

By ten o'clock everyone in the command car was starting to feel hungry, and everyone had sandwiches with them except Martin. Colin took pity on him and shared his salmon paste treats.

'Unlike you to come unprepared?' Colin said, and grinned.

'I was busy, okay? Satisfied?'

'I'm glad; it might calm you down a bit, now you seem to be in a proper relationship with Cath.'

'Just after salacious gossip, more like.'

Colin laughed.

Then Gary's phone rang again, and Martin noticed that he did that stiffening posture thing followed by lots of listening and little talking. Intelligence update incoming.

He ended the call and pressed the radio transmit button. 'Victor One to all teams, intelligence update; the Target vehicle containing Targets Two, Three and Four has now joined the M61 northbound headed our way. All teams acknowledge.'

All the units acknowledged receipt of the information in sequential order.

'Sounds like game on?' Colin asked.

'Unless they are just doing another recce,' Gary

replied.

'God, I hope not. I mean how many times can you watch a T-junction with vans full of cash coming and going? The intel good?' Colin asked.

Gary didn't answer straight away but looked at them both in the back of the car pensively. Martin knew that Colin – who was not that experienced in intelligence gathering protocols – was walking into dodgy ground. Intelligence could come from a variety of methods: observations, telephony data, bugs, undercover officers, snouts or even telephone line taps, and the operational team acting on it should never know the details. It was supposed to provide a firewall between those who gathered the intel, and those who acted on it. Create transparency and reduce the chance for corrupt practices. Colin had been a reactive detective in the main before he'd joined NWROCU, but he'd soon pick up the protocols.

Gary eventually answered, with, 'Let's just say it's Bx2x5.' Colin looked at Martin, who knew that B meant that the source of the info was known to be reliable, 2 meant that the info was believed to be true – perhaps Gary had been able to corroborate it, or part of it – and 5 was a handling code. It meant that the one receiving the information could not share it with anyone without prior approval from the originator of it. In other words, it's good, but Gary couldn't explain why it was good. 'It's all good, and we don't need to know why,' Martin said.

Colin took the hint, and sat back in his chair, before saying, 'Sorry Gary, I didn't mean to pry.'

Gary just nodded before he turned back to the front. Martin picked up his copy of the operational order and Colin quickly did the same. It would do no harm refreshing their memories of the order's proposed method of operation. It detailed where everyone should be at the business end and how the armed strike was planned to be executed. Though, Martin had enough experience to know that things like this rarely went according to plan and improvisation caused by the fluidity of events often dictated things. The intention was to arrest the bad guys as soon as the SIO decided they had gathered enough evidence – on top of what they had amassed previously – to bring about a successful prosecution for conspiracy to rob, rather than actual robbery itself. Therefore, to be in a position to effect the arrest *before* the bad guys attacked the van. And even though there was a contingency plan in the operational order to cover that, things could happen too fast sometimes.

'Looks like a good plan,' Martin offered.

'Thanks, Martin,' Gary said. 'I just hope that we don't need to revert to plan B.'

'I've been on a few plan Zs in my time,' Martin said, trying to lighten the tension that was starting to build in the car.

'You and me both,' Gary said.

'I remember one job in Manchester, when the strike plan was to front and back the robbers in their vehicle. One AFO – authorised firearms officer – was to throw a hammer at the windscreen to break it, closely followed by another AFO lobbing a stun grenade into the vehicle via the broken screen. Then in the ensuing mayhem in the vehicle, other AFO's would attack and put the armed challenge on all the occupants, containing them,' Martin said.

'What happened?' Gary asked.

'The dick with the hammer missed, it glanced off the roof, but the grenade was already on its way,' Martin said.

'And it didn't break the windscreen by itself?' Gary asked.

'No, it bounced off and landed in someone's garden

before going off.'

Martin noticed the loggist Shelia starting to grin.

'But the really bad news was that the robbers managed to drive away in the confusion and the cheeky bastards did an armed blag on a different post office and opened fire on a randomly passing police van.'

Shelia stopped grinning.

'Fortunately, no one was hurt, and we later locked them all up,' Martin said.

'Thanks for that, Martin, but you are really not helping,' Gary said.

'Sorry,' Martin said, 'just trying to lighten the mood.' He felt a sharp dig in the ribs from Colin's elbow and took the hint.

Thirty minutes, and the rest of Colin's salmon paste sandwiches later, the Whiskey team leader came over the Victor Team's radio channel asking for permission to join the party, which was duly given. They were now all on the same channel, and the target vehicle had just left the M6 motorway at junction 31A and was minutes away from their location.

Everyone in the command car was on full alert and hanging on to every word which came over the net from the Whiskey Team's car, which was eyeballing the area.

The target vehicle still had Targets Two, Three and Four on board, with no sign of Target One – Manning. The vehicle was on Ribbleton Lane heading east from Preston City straight towards them. Martin knew from the order, that the entrance to the side of the estate where the strike zone is, was Wallace Avenue.

'Whiskey Seven with the eyeball, target vehicle is slowing, all teams prepare for a halt. No indications. Brake lights showing. It's a left, left, left onto Wallace Avenue. Whiskey Two, can you go with it?'

'Whiskey Two, yes, yes,' the car radio speaker announced.

All four sat in silence as the radio commentary reported that the target vehicle was travelling very slowly along Wallace Avenue towards the junction with Park Road, which would be on its right as it approached. The counting house was further down the street.

Then suddenly, one of the outer teams asked for urgent permission to speak. The eyeball car granted it. Interrupting a lead surveillance vehicle's commentary was rare, Martin knew, and was only ever done when critical. Or all hell would break loose at the conclusion of the day. Martin had been at surveillance debriefings where fights had broken out when someone had interrupted an eyeball for no good reason and the target was lost because no one could hear the eyeball screaming over his radio. Only one voice can be heard at one time on a surveillance channel.

The interrupting unit was Victor Four; and he had good reason. A cash-in-transit van was heading down Park Road towards its T-junction with Wallace Avenue. It was about one minute away from the junction, Victor Four reckoned.

'Fuck me, it's happening,' Shelia said.

'Don't put that in the log,' Martin said, and received a second dig in the ribs. He didn't mean to be overly flippant; it was just his coping strategy in stressful situations.

Control of the airways was quickly handed back to the eyeball, who reported that the target vehicle had passed the junction and had turned around. The driver was now heading back the way they had come.

Collison course.

Martin wondered how the robbers could be so accurate; they must have a spotter somewhere down Park Road. Gary grabbed a quick permission to speak from Whiskey Seven. 'Victor One to all firearms teams, prepare to strike on my command, or if you see an aggressive action towards the cash van first.'

The eyeball car had now deployed a foot unit to take up the commentary and she had found a position that gave her a view of both roads and the junction itself.

'Whiskey Seven Foot with the eyeball. Target vehicle has stopped ten metres short of the junction. Engine running. I have a view of the approaching cash van; ETA twenty seconds.' The car radio speaker announced.

Gary jumped on the net and no longer asked for permission to speak. There was no time. He interrupted when Whiskey Seven drew breath.

'All AFOs, Condition Amber,' Gary said.

Martin knew that meant 'prepare to strike'. The next level was Condition Red, which meant they had enough evidence to arrest for conspiracy to rob. Condition Red: strike, strike, strike, would mean party time.

But two things still bothered Martin. One: where was Manning? It was his team after all. And two: the van was heading away from the counting house, not towards it. Martin didn't know the ins and outs of how the cash-in-transit vans worked.

He listened in.

'No change with the target vehicle and the cash van is fifteen seconds away,' Whiskey Seven Foot said, over the car's radio speaker.

'All teams, Condition Red,' Gary shouted.

'No change with target vehicle, and cash van is ten seconds away.'

'All teams Condition Red; strike, strike, strike.'

But the moment Martin saw Gary's finger release the transmit button on the car's steering wheel, the speaker burst back into life.

'Abort, abort, abort,' Whiskey Seven Foot said.

What the hell just happened?

'Target vehicle is mobile, past the junction before the cash van arrived, and is heading towards the main road.

Victor One, are you getting this? Is anyone getting this?'

Martin thought his heart would stop. One of the surveillance teams on Ribbleton Lane – the main thoroughfare – announced that it was in a position to continue following the target vehicle. All the AFOs acknowledged the command to 'abort', which strictly should have come from Gary. Then Gary's phone rang.

'It's Whiskey Seven Foot,' Gary announced to the car, before answering the call. It came through the vehicle's Bluetooth this time.

'What the fuck just happened?' Gary asked.

'I don't know, Boss, but they moved off just before the cash van reached the junction. The bandits have turned right onto Ribbleton Lane back towards Preston, and the cash van, a minute later, went in the opposite direction. I don't know if it was the wrong van, another dummy run, or if they were spooked. I had to make a split-second decision. Did I get it right?' Whiskey Seven Foot asked.

Gary said that she had done the right thing, if they'd had struck on the bandits as they were driving away, nowhere near the van, then they'd have struggled to prove to a court that the bandits were about to rob the van. And if it was another dummy run, then the plumber's bag probably contained plumber's tools, this time.

Martin realised that the decision to abort had been taken out of Gary's hands, and as such there was no point in criticising the foot unit. It was done. They should just keep following while they tried to work out what had happened. Martin also thought that they had more than enough to arrest the bandits, especially if the intel was deemed to be so accurate and there were guns in that plumber's bag. But he didn't say so, there was no point. And the good guys lived to strike again.

'Could it have been another dummy run?' Colin asked.

Gary was now driving out from their end of the estate,

and at great speed, but replied, 'I really don't know what the hell to think.'

'Could have been the wrong van, could have been spooked by something which is absolutely nothing to do with us,' Martin said.

'Could be waiting for Manning, still,' Colin added.

CHAPTER ELEVEN

If the last thirty minutes had been confusing – and heart stopping, almost – then the next thirty were no better. The surveillance team had to be at the top of their game as the target vehicle went this way, and then that. But it had stayed generally within a half-mile radius of the industrial estate where the counting house was located.

Were they waiting for Manning, of which there was no sign, doing another recce, or waiting for the correct van? All in the command car joined in the brainstorming, even the loggist. In fact, Shelia had been spot-on, Martin thought, when she had reckoned that they could disregard the 'spooked' theory, because they were still here.

Gary had parked up at one stage and left the vehicle to have a hushed conversation on his phone out of earshot.

'He's probably chasing the intelligence gatherers for an update,' Martin said.

Gary got back in the vehicle, 'Any change?' he asked.

'No, they are still sat in their vehicle parked in Asda's car park.'

'Any updates?' Martin asked.

'Unfortunately, not. How long have they been at Asda now?' Gary asked.

'About twenty minutes,' Shelia replied.

Then an awful thought hit Martin. He leaned forward, and asked Gary, 'How sure are we that the junction is the strike location?'

'It's what the intel told us, and we are intelligence led,' Gary said.

We should also be intelligently led, Martin didn't say, but instead said, 'But things change as we all know.'

'Granted, even the most organised villains can be disorganised,' Gary said.

'And reactive,' Martin said.

Now Colin leaned forward, 'What do you mean?' he asked.

'What if the van, the right van, has for argument's sake broken down? We don't know why that van in particular, perhaps they have a man on the inside who can give them its exact movements and timings,' Martin said.

'Or exact contents?' Colin added.

'We've been looking at that, but as you know it's hard to look properly until we nick the team and can approach the firm overtly,' Gary said.

'No criticism, all granted, mate. But these guys – if they have come to do the job today – will be all pumped up, yeah?'

'Yeah,' Gary replied.

'And if the original plan is off, then perhaps all this toing and froing has been their frustrations kicking in. Trying to find a suitable target to rob whilst they are here and up for it.'

Gary nodded slowly.

'And where have they been sat for the last twenty minutes?' Martin added.

'Asda. Shit! Where cash vans service the ATMs,' Gary replied.

'I'm not saying I'm right, but it's a hypothesis perhaps worth considering?'

Gary quickly put a couple of teams on the outer roads so they could warn of any approaching cash vans. Then he ordered the armed units to get as close to the target vehicle as possible.

Ten minutes later the targets moved to a quiet spot in the car park. This made the surveillance a little more difficult, but the strike plan a hell of a lot safer for the public. The targets would now have a good view of both the entrance to the car park, and the row of ATMs. This had to be it.

The next question was, do they await the arrival of a cash van, or pre-empt it? Shelia had made enquires with Asda's head of security, and he rang back to say that a cash van was due to refill the ATMs within the next half an hour. Gary said that ATMs could hold anything from between ten and a hundred grand at a time. There were four here, and who knew how many ATMs one cash van could service. The amounts could be vast.

Then one of the outer foot units reported sighting a cash delivery van inbound towards Asda. Decision time. For the first time, Gary asked Martin and Colin what they thought. Martin could only empathise with the guy, what with the abort from earlier on; he must really be feeling the pressure now. DIs weren't paid enough.

Colin answered, 'In the light of all the information you have, I'd say go for them as soon as that van enters the car park. And regardless of the outcome, I'll back you up if the "should have" squad kick in. Most of who may have very senior rank but will have never been sat where you are now.'

Martin could see Gary's shoulders loosen slightly, and he added to Colin's words, 'And for what it is worth, I agree.'

'And so do I, Boss,' Shelia added, with a grin.

The plan was to use three plain cars, each carrying three AFOs. The target vehicle was currently backed into a space which had a grassy mound behind it. There were no vehicles parked within ten spaces at either side of it. Two AFO cars would take a side each, and the third would block the front of the targets' vehicle. The AFOs would be out and would throw in an armed challenge before the bad guys knew what hit them.

Gary went to Condition Red.

The van entered the car park and headed towards the row of ATMs.

Gary called Condition Red: strike, strike, strike.

Then it went quiet for what seemed like an eternity. Eventually, the radio sparked back into life with the lead firearms officer calling Gary. 'Victor One, all three targets detained without incident. No shots fired.'

A cheer went up in the command car. Then the radio continued. 'But the suspects are unarmed, I repeat, unarmed. The plumber's bag contains plumber's tools.'

'Shit, shit, shit,' Gary shouted, as the euphoria in the car turned sour.

'But there's something else, sir, and you're going to need to see this,' the lead AFO said.

'We are two minutes away, but what is it?' Gary asked, as he fired up the car's engine.

'They are all laughing at us,' the lead AFO said.

CHAPTER TWELVE

Colin broke the silence in the command car by telling Gary that he and Martin would jump out and get a cab back to the office. Gary had enough to do without babysitting them further. They'd catch up with him later. As they wandered to the main road, Martin accessed the Uber App on his phone and arranged transport, which would be five minutes, give or take.

'Laughing at them?' Colin asked.

'It was all one big piss-take,' Martin replied.

'They still might have enough, given the many recce runs they have done. Notwithstanding, anything else that might come from any house searches,' Colin said.

'I doubt they'll get anything from their homes, and I'm pretty sure that they'll get fuck-all from any interviews with them. This team have been at this game a long time,' Martin said.

'It was still the right call, and we should still back Gary up if he needs it,' Colin said.

'Absolutely,' Martin said. But neither voiced the unspoken thought in Martin's head as to what had actually gone on. The bad guys knew that they were being followed and had been playing with the cops. Their plan had not been without its risks, they could have got themselves shot. Then the shit really would have hit the wind turbine.

'But why do it? Why not just abort their whole plan? Why go to all this trouble to wind us up?' Colin asked.

'Either to send a message to the cops, which I have to admit would be exceptionally arrogant—' Martin started to say.

'And totally counterproductive,' Colin interrupted.

'—or as a distraction? I mean, where the hell is Manning?' Martin added.

'A jolly thought,' Colin said.

Martin was sure that Colin's chin would have been benefiting from an involuntary rub, had they not been walking.

A minute or two later they reached the main road, and their Uber was waiting for them.

Fifteen minutes after that they were sat back at their desks when Colin's phone rang. Martin watched as he took the call and could tell by his expression that it wasn't Camelot calling. He finished his call as he stood up. 'Grab the car keys, Martin; we've got a job on.'

They both rushed to the garage and Colin gave Martin the location; Preston Docks, which Martin knew was now a busy commercial retail area with motor parks, a cinema, restaurants, pubs and business parks. It also had a supermarket and petrol station. Once mobile, Martin asked Colin what was happening.

'Apparently, there was an armed robbery about an hour ago—' Colin started.

'Please don't say on a cash-in-transit van?' Martin interrupted.

'I'm afraid so.'

'Distraction indeed.'

'Should keep your thoughts to yourself,' Colin said.

Martin could only begin to imagine what Gary would be feeling when he heard the news. But then asked, 'So where do we come in?'

'The robbery was on a van delivering cash to the ATMs at a supermarket,' Colin said.

'Anyone hurt?' Martin asked.

'Fortunately not, but shots were discharged so the security guys are in a bad way shock-wise.'

'Who's got the robbery?' Martin asked.

'Local CID,' Colin replied, and then carried on. 'They used a stolen getaway car, nicked from Manchester last night. And as you might expect, it was dumped within minutes, where they will have left the area in a clean car which no one will have seen.'

Normal practice, Martin thought, still unsure, where they came into it. But he just let Colin carry on.

'And the initial getaway car has been found burned out on the other side of the docks,' Colin added.

Again, standard practice, Martin thought. But he was now waiting for the 'but'.

'The brigade has extinguished the fire, but there will be little left, forensically. It's just a tin shell now. Apparently, it was fiercely ablaze when they got there. Plenty of accelerants had been used,' Colin said.

'But?' Martin asked.

'They did leave one thing behind,' Colin replied.

'A body?'

'I'm afraid so. And the local CID have asked for all the help they can get. Plus, this has Manning written all over it. No doubt Gary will want to get involved too.'

'Knocked some poor sod down?' Martin asked.

'Not sure yet, but it's odd, if that's the explanation.'

'How come?'

''Cause what's left of it is in the car's boot.'

Martin just shook his head. Poor bastard. His first guess would be the car's owner. He knew how hard it was to nick cars nowadays without their electronic keys. And if the keys came with the owner, then, well?

Probably a carjacking job. But did they really need to kill the owner. He just hoped that they had done so before they set the motor alight.

**

Bashir couldn't wait to get rid of the contents of his attaché case. It was bad enough having to keep it in his house overnight after arriving home from India. Even worse, that he was due back in work that next morning. He'd left it in the boot of his car and drove the short distance from Penwortham – on the outskirts of Preston, where he lived – into the compound at Hutton which was the headquarters of the Lancashire Constabulary. He managed to park in the small car park at the front of the main building, which was supposed to be reserved for visitors, but a space is a space, and it always irked him that as a senior member of the police staff he didn't have his own designated parking spot.

He knew he'd be busy admin-wise for the first half of the day, and he had a management meeting after lunch which he had to attend. He groaned at the thought, as it would be chaired by the chief constable, Don Rogers; he couldn't stand the man. A boorish narcissist. But with any luck, he could get away a little early, when he would head over to Blackpool. The sooner he could hand his case over to his expert partner, the sooner he could relax properly. He hesitated as he approached the entrance foyer to the main building and put a quick call into his comrade-in-crime.

'It's me, I'll get away from here as soon as I can this afternoon, and give you a shout when I'm nearby,' Bashir started.

'I'm going to be a bit busy, myself, another fucking drug death has come in,' the female recipient said.

'Nothing to do with us, is it?' Bashir asked.

'No, just some tosser of a cokehead, but it shags your whole day up,' she said.

'I'll only need five minutes to hand it over.'

'Yeah, yeah, I know. Bell me when you see the Tower,' she said, and ended the call.

The woman was all heart, Bashir thought as he put his phone away; she took after him.

CHAPTER THIRTEEN

Martin could smell the scene before he saw it. A mixture of acrid smoke residue lingering in the air with a noticeable hint of petrol fumes, paraffin, or similar. They were on the westerly side of the dock area, beyond the basin and marina, in among a network of small industrial cul-de-sacs. The smell was growing stronger, and Martin could see blue lights bouncing off the buildings' walls as they turned into the dead end where the scene of the crime was. It was a short road of forty or fifty metres with a number of minor units on the left-hand side, each with a small parking space in front. All looked deserted, long since used. On their right, was a high brick wall which looked like the rear of a far larger industrial unit that had its front on a neighbouring road. Martin couldn't see any CCTV cameras.

Fifteen metres in there was a blue and white ticker tape across the road. Martin parked next to the fire engine on their left. A uniformed constable stood in front of the tape with a clipboard. At least someone had begun a scene log straight away.

Martin and Colin got out and headed to the boot of their vehicle to don the appropriate white paper over-suits and plastic over-shoes. He took a second or two to take in the first images of what lay beyond the tape.

The remains of a BMW, with its four doors still open, faced the brick walled dead end at a slight angle. It had been stopped in a hurry. The boot and bonnet were open, which the fire brigade would have done. Nothing flammable was left. Just a singed and heat-twisted shell, still smouldering. Then Martin noticed another element to the aroma, and it made him gag; the unmistakable stench of burnt flesh.

Two firemen were sat in the lead tender, with a firewoman stood at its front. She had a white helmet on with a couple of black rings around it. She was obviously the senior fire officer. She made straight towards them, and they introduced themselves.

'Our team will stay and damp down a bit longer if that's okay. The engine block has become very hot and is liable to re-ignite if we don't,' she said.

'That's fine,' Colin said. 'Do what you have to do, but no more than is absolutely necessary, please.'

She nodded, and said, 'The bit you want to see is at the other end. I'll show you. And there is something else.'

Martin and Colin followed her, pausing to give the officer with the scene log their details.

'Can we take a roundabout route?' Martin asked, as all three of them ducked under the tape. 'You never know,' he added.

The fire officer took the hint and led them round the edge of the building and then around the other side until they were all stood facing back towards the road. Martin couldn't imagine forensics would find much, but at least they were approaching the vehicle from a sterile side. They edged slowly towards the rear of the vehicle and Martin noted that Colin had now pulled his paper mask over his face. Martin pulled his up too.

In the boot was a sight that would stay with them all for a long time, Martin was sure of that. What had once been a human being was now blackened charred remains. It looked like a hog roast gone wrong. One that had been overdone by a couple of days. The head was still intact but looked more like a featureless ball. It also looked too small. The torso was similar, and the legs were far too short. Martin looked closer, whilst trying to stifle his gag reflex. There were no feet at the ends as the legs ended halfway down the shins. His first thought was that they had been amputated; it's what it looked like, but why?

As if reading his thoughts, Colin spoke, 'I've been to house fire fatalities where the bodies have appeared similar.'

Martin looked at him. It was a relief, if only for a few moments.

Colin continued, 'Temperatures have to reach above 3,000 centigrade for bone to melt, and when it does, the extremities such as hands and feet are obviously the first to go.'

Martin turned to the fire chief, and asked, 'Would this fire have reached that temperature?'

'Without a doubt, maybe even more at its height,' she said, confidently.

Martin then realised he hadn't seen the hands, or the arms for that matter, and looked back into the boot. He could see that the arms appeared to be behind the body, it was lying on them. He turned his head to one side to try and confirm this.

'I didn't want to disturb the body,' the fire officer said, 'but I reckon the arms have been secured behind the back ante-mortem.'

'What was the other thing you wanted to show us?' Colin asked.

'This,' she replied, and then bent down to pick up a blackened A4 size box. It had been laid to one side of the car.

Martin noted that she was wearing thick gloves, and that the object was still smoking. Both he and Colin stepped closer to have a better look.

'Don't get too close, it's still hot,' she warned.

Martin looked at the curious object intensely, as did Colin. It was about twelve inches long, six inches wide, and about an inch thick.

'It had been propped up behind the body, at the end of the boot, at the back of where the rear seats would have been,' she said.

'So it couldn't be overlooked?' Colin asked.

'Exactly. We noticed it as a jet of water from one of the hoses dislodged it. The firefighter who saw it is of the opinion that it had been wedged into the framework of the rear seats.'

'So we didn't miss it?' Martin asked.

The fire chief nodded.

'Any idea what it is?' Colin asked.

'That I do know,' the fire chief replied. 'It's a fireproof document case.'

Martin and Colin exchanged a look of incredulity.

'How much heat can they withstand?' Colin asked.

'Industry standard is 1,000°C, some can do 2,000°C,' she replied.

'But wasn't it much hotter in here?' Martin asked.

'On the body, yes, because of the accelerants used on it. But not so hot everywhere else. Plus, this is what's left. It had initially been put inside a larger fireproof box, which fell apart. That probably took the brunt of the heat. And we were on scene pretty quickly,' she finished.

'Well, whatever is in there, someone has gone to a lot of trouble to ensure we find it,' Martin said.

'Bizarre,' Colin added.

'And who the hell was that?' Martin said, pointing at the cadaver in the boot.

'And why?' Colin added.

'Over to you two with those quandaries, I'm afraid,' the fire chief replied. 'I'll be off now, gents.' She turned and started to retrace her steps from the scene.

Martin and Colin jointly thanked her, and once she was out of earshot, Colin asked, 'You thinking what I'm thinking?'

'Yes, I think I am.'

CHAPTER FOURTEEN

Cath made her way back to where she had parked her car and couldn't help but feel sad for the couple she had just left. She didn't even know their first names. Living on the fringes of society, treading water, and never moving forward. She wasn't sure if she could provide the help she had offered, but she did have contacts, and Martin would have more. He of all people should be able to help. She grabbed a sandwich and a drink from a deli and ate lunch in her car. When she'd finished, she gave Martin a call. She wanted to ask if he did have access to fast-track drug treatment programmes, just in case. And whether he fancied meeting up in Preston for a coffee where she could get her car back. She had a few hours to kill before her appointment at Blackpool's north railway station.

Martin said he couldn't chat as he was up to his nuts in it, or 'Colin's chest' as he also put it. 'Busy?' she asked.

'Yes,' he replied.

'The robbery job come off then?' she pushed.

'Not as planned and we've now got a fresh murder on the go. Look, gotta go, bell you later,' he said, before ending the call without waiting for a reply. He must be very busy. But a 'fresh murder' he'd said. An expression she'd heard before, though she wasn't quite sure what was so fresh about a dead body. Police parlance always made her smile. She drove leisurely back to Preston and went to the Royal Preston Hospital's main A&E reception. It was gone 2 p.m. when she arrived, so hopefully the woman she'd spoken to earlier would have finished her shift. She had, but her replacement was no more helpful. If she wanted data, she would have to contact the relevant administration department by letter or email. But she did glean that cocaine induced drug deaths were twice the number that they had been over the same period last year.

She then drove to Preston railway station in the hope that she might find the homeless guy again, but she couldn't see him, so drove off down Fishergate Hill away from the city centre. She pulled up at a red traffic light and as she glanced around waiting for the lights to change, she saw him. He had his sleeping bag over his shoulder and was mooching slowly down the hill. She didn't actually recognise him from behind, but she recognised the dirty, white-coloured Highland Terrier trotting beside him. She wound down her front passenger window, and as soon as the lights changed to green, she caught up with him and pulled over. 'Hey, how's it going?' she shouted.

The guy stopped and looked at her, and after a couple of seconds she could see recognition in his eyes. 'So, so. You haven't got any change, have you?'

Cath pulled a twenty pound note from her purse but hesitated to hand it to him. She knew she shouldn't be doing this. He reached in through the open window. 'You on drugs?' she asked.

'Nah, I'm clean now,' he replied.

She wasn't too sure he was telling her the truth, since he'd previously told his tale about his 'friend' who'd taken Sky White. He grabbed hold of the loose end of the twenty, but Cath held it firm. He stopped pulling, but they both had tension on the note.

'What?' he asked.

'Do you know a Sky White dealer from Blackpool called, Minty?' she asked.

'Never heard of him,' the man said, before pulling the note free.

In truth, she'd let go of her end. She added, 'Another twenty, if you tell me the truth.'

He hesitated, it was all the tell-tale sign she needed, so she said, 'Thirty and that's my final offer; we're not playing Wheeler Dealers, by the way.'

The man smiled. 'Okay, he's a dealer, but he hasn't got any wheels, well none that I know of. He uses trains everywhere. Reckons it's safer. No filth, or what little filth they have on the railways are all dim; according to Minty. Can I have my thirty now?'

Cath took the money from her purse and handed it to the man. This time *he* hesitated as he grabbed hold of it.

'You seem like a nice lady, and I know you're not proper plod – no offence – so listen to me when I say be careful.'

'In what way?' she asked, as the man took the notes and stuffed them into a grubby back pocket of his jeans.

'He's a nasty bastard, or he certainly can be. Most are shit-scared of him,' the man said, before he turned and continued his way down the hill.

Typical of her luck, she thought. She'd love to ask Martin to join her, but she knew how busy he would be; day one of a murder. But she was a big girl, she'd be okay. But first, she'd try a personal visit to Blackpool's Victoria Hospital and see if she could get any further there than she had at Preston Royal. She waited for a break in the traffic before continuing down Fishergate Hill, she looked out for the homeless guy but there was no sign of him.

Traffic was steady, but light-ish as Cath drove down the A586 between Preston and Blackpool. The Satnav directed her to Blackpool Victoria Hospital situated on the eastern side of the town. She passed brown signs showing directions to Stanley Park and Blackpool Zoo, which broke another memory bubble from her childhood. She used to love seeing the big cats but was scared of the snakes; her sister was the exact opposite. It was mid-afternoon by the time Cath walked into the hospital and she hoped it would be a quieter time of day; if hospitals had such quieter times, these days.

She was in luck; and then she wasn't. It was relatively quiet, but the receptionist came out with the same defensive narrative, she'd have to write to their admin department blah, blah, blah. And she'd have to leave as they were busy. Maybe Cath was losing her touch. She thanked the woman anyway and turned to leave when the rubber-edged double doors between the outside automatic door, and the inside suddenly burst open. A trolley was being rushed through feet first, pushed by one paramedic whilst another walked quickly alongside it, keeping pace. On the stretcher, Cath could see a scruffy-looking man in his thirties. He was on his back with an oxygen mask over his face while the paramedic at his side somehow managed to continue chest compressions.

Cath just watched in awe as the trolley was met by two nurses who ushered it into an open cubicle. Her first thought was that the poor occupant of the stretcher was a road accident victim, but she wasn't sure why she should assume that. She noted that the receptionist had disappeared, so took her opportunity to get as close as she could to the action. The nurses were joined by a doctor, but they were all so preoccupied no one closed the cubicle privacy curtain. She watched as they all worked on getting him to breathe.

'What have we got?' the doctor asked the paramedics, who were both now stood to one side as a nurse had taken over the chest compressions, and the other nurse wired the patient up to various monitors.

'Drug overdose, believed to be cocaine,' the one who had been doing the chest compressions replied.

'Okay,' the doctor said, and then asked the nurse by the monitors to pass him an adrenalin injection.

She nodded, and as she passed it to him, added, 'Still no heartbeat.'

The doctor administered the hypodermic and prepared the patient for use of a defibrillator. He told the nurse working the chest to stand clear. She did. He put the handheld pads onto the now bare chest of the patient and Cath watched as the charge it released made the patient's torso convulse up and then down. 'Charging', she heard someone shout. 'No response,' shouted someone else.

'According to witnesses, he had inhaled vapers from burnt cocaine, apparently a new type,' the paramedic added.

This made Cath take even more notice as she looked on, already transfixed. A second charge was given, again with no result, and after a few minutes of hurried activity, she saw the doctor take a small step backwards and shake his head. It was the slightest of movement from side to side, almost as if done involuntarily. She also noted the expression on the doctor's face. Sad, yet resigned. He glanced at his watch.

'I'm going to call it. Are we all in agreement?' he asked.

Both nurses and the two paramedics nodded.

'Time of death—'

'What the hell do you think you are doing?' a voice bellowed from behind Cath.

Cath turned to see the receptionist glaring at her.

'Who is that?' the doctor asked. 'Are you a relative?' he added.

'She's not and she's just leaving, sorry about this,' the

receptionist said, as she roughly took hold of Cath's arm and started to pull her away. Cath didn't resist, she just smiled a weak apology at the woman and allowed her to march her off.

She risked a final glance over her shoulder as she left. The doctor and paramedics had moved out of the cubicle, followed by one of the nurses. The remaining nurse was starting to pull a sheet over the deceased addict's head. That's when Cath got her first, and last, proper glimpse at the corpse's face. She shuddered as she recognised the eyes; red and swollen with hugely dilated pupils. She then recognised something else which made her shake with horror. It was the man with no name from under Central Pier. A pitying sadness engulfed her as she snapped at her escort. 'Okay, I'm going; for now. I know what I just saw.'

The receptionist pushed Cath through the rubber-edged doors to the outside doors which slid back automatically, and said, 'What you saw were over-worked health heroes trying to save someone's life.'

Cath stopped in the open doorway. 'I know that, truly, I am on your side. But there is a bad batch of cocaine about, and you will find many more of these victims coming through these doors if people like me don't highlight the dangers.'

The woman let go of Cath's arm and eyed her for three or four long seconds.

'I'm not here to make the hospital, or Blackpool look bad, I promise,' Cath said. 'It's much bigger than that.'

'Okay,' the woman said, and walked outside. Cath followed and the automatic doors slid shut behind them.

'Off the record?' the woman asked.

'Off the record,' Cath affirmed.

'We are getting twice or even treble what we would expect to see.'

'How long has this been happening?' Cath asked.

'Only the last couple of weeks or so. Everyone hoped it was just a temporary spike, but I'm not so sure.'

'And do they all have those ungodly eyes?' Cath asked.

'All of them,' the woman answered, before she turned and headed back into the hospital.

Cath reached her car and climbed in. She sat in quiet reflection for a moment, and then wept, which she hadn't expected to. It just hit her. As a reporter in the past, she had seen many sad things, and although she had grown a thicker skin when dealing with them, she had never become desensitised. She had instead just learned how to swallow it. But something about having seen that young man lose his fight to survive had broken through her protective outer shell. The fact that she'd met him only a few hours ago was obviously part of it. But it was more than that; something about the way he had put his arm round the woman as they had trudged off the beach. It showed a shared caring that they had. They were addicts, but not by choice. They wanted to get clean, just didn't know quite how to, so they looked out for each other against the outside world. It showed a touching vulnerability that shone between them as they had walked away, arm in arm.

And now there was a grieving other half to this duo, out there somewhere, all alone and hurting even more than she could have probably ever imagined.

Cath took a moment to gather herself as she dabbed away the tears. Her resolve started to return, partly fuelled by anger. Now she was determined to get to the bottom of this. She started the car engine. Next stop, Blackpool North railway station.

CHAPTER FIFTEEN

Colin and Martin had been pretty busy as soon as they had reached the nick. The incident room was frenetic. Martin was preoccupied; he went through the motions but was secretly seething inside. That bastard Manning had set them up. It left a lot of unanswered questions; least not that Manning knew the cops were looking at his robbery team. And more worryingly, that he'd known they were following them today. Giving him a great distraction to do the real robbery. But why he had felt the need to murder someone into the bargain, Martin didn't know. And to leave the body in such a manner, too? And what the hell was that fireproof document box all about? Martin couldn't help but feel that Manning was toying with them; but why?

Colin beckoned across the incident room for Martin to join him in their office. He nodded, and then finished his conversation with the HOLMES Manager who was setting up the computer terminals for the inquiry. HOLMES was a closed software system where everything that was done on a major investigation such as a murder, was kept, cross-referenced and used to help highlight lines of enquiry. It also stored all the gathered evidence such as witness statements, and listed all the exhibits as they came in. It had been brought in after The Yorkshire Ripper enquiry of the late seventies, and had pretty much stood the test of time, notwithstanding numerous upgrades.

Martin closed the door behind him as he entered their shared office. 'Any news from Gary?' he asked as he took the seat at his desk.

'No, it's still early days, but he doesn't expect to find anything incriminating during the house searches, and as of yet, they have all gone "no comment" during interview,' Colin replied.

'As expected,' Martin noted, and then added, 'what about their gathered evidence from earlier surveillance?'

'Mostly circumstantial. Yes, they may have all visited the area many times, but as they didn't actually get around to attacking a van, or had any weapons with them today, it's not looking good.'

Martin knew that circumstantial surveillance evidence could be gold when proving the preparation that had gone into a crime, but when there was no actual crime to link it to, it could be worthless. 'I take it that they had no masks or other paraphernalia with them?' he asked.

'No, unfortunately. No "robbers' kits". The best hope was the plumber's bag, which we now know was a dummy.'

'Bet none of them are plumbers,' Martin said.

Colin didn't respond.

'And I take it we have no sign of Manning?' Martin asked.

'None. And as requested, Gary had all the surveillance logs searched to try and attach Manning to a current address, but he was always picked up on the main road, nowhere near any residential properties, in Trafford. And his last known address is an old one.'

'What a pisser.'

'Indeed. He had crashed at one address they knew

about, but that was some time ago and has now been disregarded, too. So, assuming he didn't travel too far to his pick-up point, his real residential location should be close to those. Give us a place to start looking at least,' Colin said.

'I just can't see what Manning is up to? I mean why point the spotlight on himself this way?' Martin asked.

'I agree, it probably is Manning, but we should keep an open mind until we know more,' Colin replied.

Martin agreed with his boss, but his gut was screaming that Manning was their man. He just couldn't work out what the man was doing. There was clearly more to this than the obvious. 'How are we getting on with the document case?' Martin asked.

'It's at the lab now with an exhibits officer and they are taking samples from its exterior before they try to open it.'

It was Martin's turn to nod.

'Anyway, that's not why I called you in here. I've just had the chief on the blower, and as you might expect, he's as happy as a turkey on the run-up to Christmas. He's expecting both of us in his office ASAP.'

Twenty minutes later, Martin pulled their car up at the visitor's parking spaces outside the Lancashire Constabulary headquarters' main entrance. They walked over, entered, and after booking in, made their way up the staircase. As they started to climb it, Martin instinctively looked up as he placed his foot on the first step. Someone was coming down on his side. He smiled, as did the descending individual, who duly moved to one side. It was Bashir; Martin had to concentrate on not showing a reaction of any kind. Colin was behind him so he couldn't tell whether he'd noticed or not. Halfway up the first flight of stairs, Martin risked a glance over his shoulder beyond Colin, and watched the back of Bashir's head cross the reception area to the exit.

As they rounded the first landing onto the second flight of stairs, Martin turned to face Colin and said, 'Did you see the bastard?'

'What bastard?' Colin replied.

'Bashir.'

'Where?'

'Walked right past you.'

'Oh, that was him? Glad I didn't notice. Not sure how I would have reacted.'

'We need to chase the handlers up, get them to find out from Abdul what happened,' Martin finished as they arrived on the floor of the chief's plush office.

His staff officer showed them in. Don Rogers was waiting for them at the Chesterfields. Martin kept quiet while Colin briefed the chief on all that had taken place in Delhi. Up until now, he'd only had the essentials.

'Conclusions?' Rogers asked, as Colin paused for breath.

'Not too sure. Something must have gone wrong, but as far as we can tell the money was handed over, and we've no reason to feel that he was spooked,' Colin finished.

'Sergeant?' Rogers asked Martin. He knew that the question would rankle with Colin slightly, but it was Rogers's way. They had become accustomed to his cross-referencing and corroboration-seeking tactics, which wasn't such a bad fault. 'He certainly didn't look spooked five minutes ago.'

Colin explained that they had just passed him on the stairs, even if Colin had missed it.

'I can't bring myself to look at the man,' Rogers said, and added, 'I was supposed to chair a meeting a little earlier where he would have been present, had to get my dep to cover it.'

'What about the original source of the intelligence?' Martin asked.

'Another anomaly. As soon as I heard from Colin while you two were still over there, I tasked the intel super to chase that up. But so far, the handlers have been unable to get hold of the source,' Rogers replied.

Martin groaned inwardly, he hoped they'd not all been played; that there was no connection between Bashir's case being empty, and the source suddenly having gone AWOL.

'You two verified the source,' Rogers said.

Martin wasn't happy where this was leading, so interjected. 'As far as we can know, sir, the money was handed over. Had the suitcase been empty, then the taxi driver wouldn't have collected it from the hired stooge, surely? So, if the cash was paid, it must have still been game on?' Martin said.

'But then it wasn't,' Rogers said. 'Look gents, I'm not blaming anyone, I know how unpredictable these things can be. I'm just kicking the ball around.'

'Well sir, my gut still tells me that Abdul was on the level. There must be another reason for Bashir's suitcase having been empty,' Martin said.

'Martin's the expert in these matters, but I was totally convinced of his authenticity too,' Colin added.

'That's why I wanted to see you both in person, to look you in the eyes as you both told me so. In the light of anything to the contrary, I'm happy with your submission, gents. Now tell me about the murder?'

'Just one last point on the source?' Martin said.

Both Rogers and Colin turned to face him. He continued, 'When we debriefed him, it didn't come easily from him, as lies often flow. It was a great weight and he seemed troubled with it. I wouldn't blame him if that was his last act of public service. It would explain his refusal to answer his handlers' calls.'

Colin nodded. Then so did Rogers, before he added, 'Fair point, Sergeant. Now on to the murder.'

Colin quickly briefed the chief including their working hypothesis that Daniel Manning was behind the robbery, the decoy robbery and the murder. The chief nodded as Colin spoke. When he had finished, the chief asked Martin if he had anything to add, so he asked him about the uniformed inspector that had apparently had a lot of telephone traffic with Bashir.

'Debbie Yates; a uniformed PACE inspector at Blackpool Central. Used to be a DS and after gaining promotion to inspector, she has tried several times to become a detective inspector but failed, and according to her divisional commander, has sulked about it ever since. Confirming in her view, why Yates is not suitable to be a DI,' Rogers said.

'What was the issue with her?' Colin asked.

'She was promoted uniformed inspector in order to widen her managerial learning, and had she accepted this willingly, she would no doubt be a DI by now. But instead of getting to grips with her job, she threw her toys out of the pram. So her divisional commander formed the opinion that she had training needs, and gave her an action plan to follow.'

'I gather that didn't go well?' Colin asked.

'The plan followed her toys; bad attitude all round.'

'Any ideas for why the regular contact with Bashir?' Martin asked.

'No, but the head of professional standards tells me that they remained in contact over the weekend while Bashir was in India, which of course proves nothing, but is very interesting, is it not?'

The chief was right, it proved nothing, Martin thought, but was highly suspicious, nonetheless.

'I know you two are busy, and as of this morning, very busy, but I want to keep a very tight lid on who is involved, or in the know, with this job,' the chief started.

Martin guessed what was coming next, and he was

right. Rogers wanted them to stay on it. Notwithstanding, that they had a murder to help investigate and a murderer to find; for this one and for the earlier offence in Manchester. Colin tried to argue, but Rogers was having none of it. He told Colin to free up Martin who he wanted to follow any leads that came from the telephone data, and to try and find the source as a matter of urgency. Just in case he could add anything.

They all shook hands, and Martin and Colin left the chief in his office. Once they were outside the building, Colin spoke first. 'It's not too much more for you to do, to be honest; I just have to push back sometimes so he thinks we are doing him a bigger favour than perhaps we are.'

'I agree, and I'm happy to do some digging around on this Debbie Yates,' Martin said.

'Be careful not to leave any footprints.'

Martin didn't respond.

Colin took the hint, and said, 'Sorry I didn't mean . . .'

'None taken, but firstly, I'd like to try and find Abdul,' Martin said.

'Agreed.'

'I do hope he hasn't rubber-dicked us.'

'You'll never make inspector with phrases like that.'

Martin just laughed, and then tried ringing Cath as they walked to their car. He got her voicemail. He didn't leave a message; she was obviously busy. He'd call again later.

CHAPTER SIXTEEN

Bashir couldn't wait for the meeting to end; nevertheless, he was grateful that the oaf of a chief constable hadn't chaired it, which he thought was unusual as the autocrat usually ran everything he could. His stand-in was the deputy chief constable who Bashir didn't mind. Small mercies. But if it all went to plan, he wouldn't have to put up with this lot much longer. He'd be far away and sunning it bigtime on some island. He might even be able to afford his own island, who knows? But for now, he couldn't wait to get over to Blackpool and hand the attaché case to his expert partner. He never fully relaxed, until the handovers were done.

He walked the few metres from the front of the police headquarters to the visitors' car park and glanced over his shoulder while he popped the boot lid, just to check that no one was looking and that the case was still there. Which of course it was. He jumped in and set off towards Preston, from where he would pick up the A586 from the docks which would take him to Blackpool. Bashir hated Blackpool and everything it stood for, with its rock concerts, arcades, stag and hen weekends. Tawdry British seaside avarice. Except the drug addicts. He should hate them, but where would he be without them.

God bless them. Though he couldn't help despising them, nonetheless.

The traffic into Preston wasn't too bad, which was rare, and as soon as he left the docks behind, it thinned out even further. The sooner he could get in and out, the better. He hadn't seen his brother in a while, so after dinner he would nip in and visit; even if they did end up having some sort of moral argument, about this or that. Truth be known, he quite enjoyed the banter and debate.

He ended his thoughts and rang a number via his car's Bluetooth, which was answered on the second ring. 'It's me,' he started; 'you still tied up at work?'

'I'll be free in an hour or so. What time are you coming?' the female recipient asked.

'Just leaving Preston.'

'Look, get yourself over here and grab some food and I'll bell you when I'm free,' she said.

Bashir agreed and ended the call. He cursed the delay for a number of reasons, not just the obvious, or the fact that it put his own evening plans on hold. Just the thought of spending time and eating in sin city wasn't his idea of fun. But what could he do if some daft addict had gone over, presumably through greed? There was little he or his expert could do about it. Marketwise, he wasn't concerned; one dies, and another one pops up, especially in Blackpool. He slowed down and tried to relax into the drive.

***

Cath found the railway station quite easily; it was only round the corner from Talbot Road bus station. But she was surprised at how small it seemed as she drove into the car park. Though as she thought about it, the main West Coast line between London and Glasgow ran through Preston. The line to Blackpool from Preston was a track to nowhere. And Blackpool *was* the end of the line. It only had to accommodate passengers who wanted to come to or leave the town. Hopefully, it would make her search for Minty the dealer, a bit easier.

She eyed a parking space at the end of the car park by two perimeter walls and remembering what Martin had once told her, she parked face-in with a rear view of the comings and goings of the station. Martin had explained that parked this way, you were harder to see through a rear window and that the seats themselves provided cover. Whereas the other way round, you stuck out like a Preston North End football fan would do in this town.

She adjusted the interior and the door mirrors and settled down in her seat. Sometimes Cath thought that she would have made a good detective. She was often told so, and she knew that she was a good investigative analyst. But she'd stick to her day job as she soon became bored at looking at nothing. And it was tiring too. Not least with the added difficulty of looking via her car mirrors. And she couldn't relax for a second in case she missed something. She remembered Martin also telling her about a robbery team he had been working on, and that the only way into the unknown robbers was by monitoring a stolen car they had garaged to use as a getaway vehicle. The trouble was that the team had planned so far ahead, that they kept committing armed robberies around the country, but never used the knock-off car Martin and his team were watching. They used others that they had stored previously. Eventually they came and used the stolen car and Martin's team followed the bad guys and caught them red-handed on the Southwest coast. When Cath asked how long they had to lie in wait, she had been gobsmacked when he'd replied, 'Three months.' But on the plus side, it helped him pass his Inspector's exams, as he'd used the time sat in a car studying while waiting for the tracker on the target vehicle to give them the good news. He just had to stop failing the promotion boards next.

Cath had been sat for thirty minutes and was getting fidgety, so she decided to go and have a look on the platforms. It apparently had six according to Google so shouldn't be too busy. Then as she started to walk towards the entrance to the station, she saw what she was hoping to see; an addict approaching. She didn't know what Minty looked like, but she could spot an addict. Great timing. She slowed her approach and followed the hooded youth at what she thought was a discrete distance. He entered the complex and shuffled his way onto the main concourse.

Cath followed him through the large glass atrium into the station which inside looked modern and spacious – it was a bit like the TARDIS – and it was quite busy. She kept seeing the hoodie as he weaved in and out of people, but she kept losing him too. Every time she did, she felt her heartrate quicken. It was hard work this surveillance malarkey. Where was Martin when she needed him? She remembered having put her phone on silent when she'd arrived outside and quickly checked it. There was a missed call from the man himself, but no voicemail, so it hadn't been urgent. She'd call him back later.

She closed the distance between hoodie and herself and felt that she was starting to get the hang of this business. Until she saw her hoodie come to an abrupt stop for no obvious reason. If she'd still been looking at her phone, she'd have probably run into the back of him. As it was, she veered off and plonked herself down on a steel bench in front of a wall near some toilets, about twenty feet away. She then saw the reason for his sudden halt. Another hoodie was walking straight towards him. Another addict? Or Mr Minty himself? She wasn't sure, but she didn't have to wait long for a possible answer. The hoodie she'd followed in suddenly produced a hand with a bank note of some denomination in it. It looked purple; a twenty? But the second hoodie kept his hands in his pockets and just shook his head. Then she saw her hoodie lean forward and appear to say something in confidence to new hoodie. New hoodie stood back and reached into his back pocket. This was it, she thought.

But new hoodie didn't produce a bag of drugs, he pulled out a brown bank note and handed it to her hoodie, who quick as a flash, took it, turned, and ran back the way he had come. Cath watched him as he ran and was trying to assimilate what on earth was going on. She soon wished she hadn't, because in so doing she had taken her eye off new hoodie. Realising her mistake, she looked back to where she had last seen him. He was on a direct trajectory towards her, but now only feet away. He was looking straight at her and didn't look happy.

CHAPTER SEVENTEEN

Martin dropped Colin off at Preston Central nick, who said he'd check with the DS he'd asked to follow up on the Missing From Homes, existing or new. Somebody was going to miss the deceased at some stage. Martin said he'd try to find Abdul and then come back to the office. Colin unclipped his seatbelt as Martin asked, 'What about a press appeal? I know it's early days, but we can hold back on the circumstances for now, just ask anyone to get in touch who has been unable to get hold of a loved one today that they might have expected to?'

'Might be a bit soon yet,' Colin said. 'Let's see what comes in over the next twenty-four hours. Then do an appeal. We can ask your Cath for help to get the appeal onto TV, using her press office connections.'

Martin nodded his agreement and smiled to himself as Colin got out of the car. It was the first time he had heard Colin refer to Cath as 'your Cath'. He liked the sound of it. The thought made him check his phone, but she hadn't sent him any messages. He'd try again in a while.

Firstly, he rang the number he had for Abdul's lead handler, Susan. The call was answered on the first ring. 'Susan?' he asked. There was a pause of a second or two before she replied. Switching into source handler mode

Martin guessed, so added, 'It's DS Martin Draker here, not a snout, but you can call me Susan.'

She laughed, 'In that case, Sarge, you can call me Wendy.'

Martin laughed too and told her to call him Martin as Susan was his Sunday name, and then enquired about Abdul.

'His phone appears to be off, and we are reluctant to call in at his home address. His wife was never happy with him working for us in the first place.'

'Thoughts?' Martin asked.

'We think he's had enough, and we can't blame him. We have one outstanding payment to give him for the last intel he gave us, so he'll have to make contact at some stage if he wants it. That will give us a chance to gain a final debrief from him, if indeed he's done being a secret agent.'

'How much is he due?'

'As you know yourself, it's all generated automatically by the CHIS software, and never much; it's only £500.'

Martin knew that the payments were never enough to keep the handlers happy as they had to manage the raised expectations of the sources, and that could be difficult. The computer payment system had been brought in by the Home Office to prevent corruption, allow for transparency and scrutiny, and to standardise the amounts, at least the handlers could blame the system. 'Computer says "no".'

'It would have been a lot more had the suitcase actually contained drugs,' Wendy added.

Martin agreed but said, 'Still, £500 is worth having, so hopefully he'll be in touch once he's skint.'

'I'll bell you as and when,' Wendy said.

Martin thanked her but pushed her on his need to speak to him and suggested he could knock on the front door of his home address on a pretext, as a normal detective, as opposed to a sneaky-beaky one, like Wendy. 'It will get around the wife issue you have,' he added.

Wendy agreed and gave Martin the address, he promised to ring her afterwards. She confirmed that Abdul was actually his real first name. Martin thanked her and they said their goodbyes.

He put the address into the Satnav and was pleased to see that it was the Avenham district of Preston, which was only a few miles away.

Abdul lived in a modest terraced house on a small side street within Avenham. Most of the houses in the cul-de-sac had Asian cultural adornments in the ground floor front windows, but Martin did notice one house in the middle of the pavement-fronted row, with an England flag in front of the glass, with the letters EDL scrawled across it in black marker pen. No doubt community relations on this road came to a dead-end like the street did.

Martin turned round and purposely pulled over two or three houses past Abdul's. He got out and walked to the front door and knocked. An Asian woman in her thirties dressed in traditional Indian garb answered. Martin quickly produced his warrant card and stated that he was from the local CID at Preston, that he was just making routine house-to-house enquires and asked if they had had any problems with the neighbour with the flag in his window. Martin was thinking on his feet, and particularly despised how some far-right factions misused the flag of St. George for their own twisted political means. It had almost become synonymous with its misuse instead of what it should and did stand for. The Nazi Swastika sprang to mind. That had started out as a symbol of life and good luck, used by many cultures over thousands of years, until the fascists came along.

The woman said that she didn't want to say and was clearly uncomfortable with the question. He asked if her husband was at home. She said not, and that he was working away, then she was joined by an Asian man who was a generation older, and Martin noticed that she immediately showed a non-verbal deference to him and slid into the background as he filled the doorway. Martin went through the introduction and question again. The man identified himself as the woman's father-in-law who was visiting while his son was away, and then spent five minutes listing all the anti-social behaviours that the flag-abuser got up to. Martin was genuinely shocked and made a mental promise to make sure that the uniform inspector for this area was made fully aware of what was going on – if he or she wasn't already. The man just shouted abuse at all his neighbours whenever he saw them, and if anyone dared park a car outside his house, he would go on a rant rampage, even though he had no car of his own. It sounded as if he just kept himself inside the criminal law, but his actions nonetheless were very anti-social. Just what Anti-Social Behaviour Orders were invented to prevent. He didn't know all the ins and outs of getting an order, but he knew that hearsay was admissible, and if it came from a DS, it should carry some weight. Martin took notes as the man vented his frustrations, and almost forgot the real reason why he was there. When the man finished, Martin asked about his son. Maybe, he would have something to add?

'My son is a very busy man and is away working at the moment. We expect him back in a day or two.'

'Perhaps, you can give me his phone number and I can call him?' Martin asked.

The man hesitated, so Martin added, 'He lives here, so surely he can add to what you have said.'

'I speak for his family in his absence, but I take your point, Detective,' the man said, and then gave Martin his telephone number, and added, 'but please say that you have spoken to me first. And be warned that he may not answer. As I say, he is a busy man, and his phone is not always turned on.'

Martin nodded his reply and then thanked the man for his candid counsel. He turned to leave and as he did so the elderly man said, 'He must not know where the information has come from,' as he nodded in the direction of the flag-abuser's house.

'Absolutely,' Martin replied.

'And you will act on what I have told you?' he asked.

'Absolutely,' Martin answered again. And he would.

Martin waited until he was back in his office, before he tried the telephone number the old man had given him for Abdul. It went straight to voicemail. Martin left a message identifying himself but added that he wasn't ringing regards to the last matter they had spoken about. He mentioned the troublesome neighbour and the fact that his father had given him the number. Martin hoped that would tempt him to call back pronto. He could always engineer the conversation around the original reason for his visit once he had him on the line. Next, he rang Wendy and briefed her and passed the number to her. She said that it wasn't a number they had for him, so she wouldn't ring it just yet, she'd give Martin's approach time to work. Martin then asked whether Abdul had ever raised any concerns about the abusive neighbour.

'On many occasions, and we also passed the information on, albeit indirectly, to the local geographic inspector, but according to Abdul, nothing ever seemed to change. As his covert handlers, there was little else we could do, unless he could give us any information of any crimes the man may have committed, but he was never able to do so,' Wendy replied.

Martin was pretty sure that putting a dog turd through a letterbox probably wasn't legal, but he understood that these things could be hard to prove. He wouldn't prejudge until he'd spoken to the local inspector, but did add, 'If Abdul's become disengaged with you, maybe the problems in the street, and the apparent lack of a police response, are something to do with it.'

Wendy didn't respond. The question was largely rhetorical, he knew. She thanked him for ringing her and then ended the call.

Martin turned to face Colin, who had been listening and who then asked, 'How did you get on?'

'Not too good from our point of view, but interesting nonetheless,' Martin replied, and then explained.

Then he asked how Colin had got on with the Missing From Home enquires.

'Drawn blanks so far.'

CHAPTER EIGHTEEN

Bashir had finished his meal at a local Indian restaurant some time ago, and although it was still relatively early, he was keen to leave before the first of the evening's drunks arrived. He wasn't sure what time that would be, but in Blackpool he guessed it could be anytime. He didn't know how the staff put up with some of their clientele. He knew he couldn't do it.

He was about to ring his expert again, when a text from her arrived. At last, she was available and told him to meet her in the usual place. He paid his bill, left a tip and exited the premises as quickly as he could. He drove the few miles to where their regular meeting spot was, parked in the empty yard out back, got his case out of the boot and made straight for the fire door. It was ajar so he guessed she was already there, though he hadn't noticed her car. Thinking about that, she'd probably parked round the corner and walked the last bit. He should have probably done the same, but he was too lazy. He had a quick glimpse around and behind him, and then entered through the door. It was dusk now and he couldn't see beyond the perimeter wall. It would be dark in half an hour, which was even better.

He walked up the steel staircase and entered the

room, it was an old office with three or four dust-covered desks crammed into one side of the space, leaving a couple of chairs in the middle. The whole area was only about ten metres square, if that. Sat on one of the chairs was his expert and partner, uniformed inspector, Debbie Yates.

'Sounds like you've had a busy afternoon?' Bashir asked.

'Busy day, thanks to that daft addict going over,' Yates replied.

Bashir knew that Yates was always busy and was amazed at how she managed to keep her tubby figure with all the rushing around she did, she obviously found time to eat. Though to be fair to her, this town was filled wall-to-wall with takeaways, and he shuddered to think what the calorie count of the average Blackpool fast-food meal was. The curry he'd just eaten was starting to repeat on him.

He'd known Yates for a few years now; he'd initially met her at an IT Conference in the town and had got on well with her. She didn't drink and neither did he, so as the other delegates spent the evenings of the weeklong event getting pissed, they had chatted on their own. He had never looked at her romantically, and he was sure she had not done so of him, but they did have a shared resentment. She was a very disgruntled ex-detective sergeant who thought she was being overlooked as a detective inspector because she wasn't an arse-licker. She'd also moaned that female DIs had to be lookers too; and she wasn't. Bashir wasn't sure that her latter moan was still true in this day and age, but he hadn't argued with her.

He, on the other hand, always felt that as a senior civilian officer he was never shown the respect that his peers in uniform were given. He was certainly paid far less. It suited the oaf, Rogers, to proudly claim that they had Bashir, an Asian employee at the similar position and status to a superintendent; box ticked. But for some reason, only gave him half the responsibility – and therefore power – that supers might have, and half the wage. He'd applied three times to have his job description re-written and re-banded to a higher level, but even though it had received widespread support from HR, Rogers had always refused. Bastard.

So when his current financial opportunity came along, he jumped at it. He just needed someone who knew about drugs and the markets, as he knew jack-shit. He'd kept in touch with Yates after the conference and had been more than a little trepidatious when he'd first tentatively approached her, but he'd need not have worried; she jumped at the chance.

'It wasn't some of our stuff, was it?' he asked, as he took a seat facing Yates.

'Who cares; they'll write it off as a coke or crack overdose as they always do. Probably cardiac failure. The pathologist will go straight to the heart, find the cause and then stop there. It's only with homicides that we use Home Office pathologists who go a lot further. *They* usually start by scraping fingernails.'

Bashir thought that all suspicious deaths had to be investigated by a DI, but he didn't want to openly ask Yates in case it set her off on another rant, so instead said, 'Are the local CID interested?'

'Suspicious, yes. Even if it's not homicide. If it's unexplained, then a DI is supposed to investigate it on behalf of the coroner, just to be on the safe side.'

'So how did you get roped in?' he pushed.

'I volunteered to that stupid bitch of a divisional commander that I was happy to have a first look at all drug deaths to free up the CID, and then call in the DI if something was amiss.'

'That's good for us,' Bashir said.

'That's what I thought; it also keeps me away from the daily shite I normally have to do. Plus, I used my ex-DS credentials to swing the deal, and as the divisional commander has never been a detective, she went for it. In fact, the dozy cow couldn't detect a turd in a hot-dog bun.'

Bashir placed the briefcase on his knee, and said, 'Anyway, here we are.' He then flipped the catches and opened the case to reveal its only contents, which was now just the ornate egg-timer. He picked it out and passed it to her. She held it up and inverted it and watched the off-white grains follow gravity's path into the lower glass tube.

'It's amazing how much gear these few grains make, ideal for importation. No big heavy kilo bags for you to carry any more,' she said.

'That's as maybe, but it wasn't you who got pulled up by the Indian cops. I nearly passed out. I'm not sure it's safe to do the next run the same way.'

'Are you mad; it's now the safest way.'

'How do you reckon that?'

'Think about it, the gear is so small that it fits in an egg-timer, and it looks innocuous. It won't show up as suspicions in any x-ray. And the ultimate test was the drugs dog. If that hound, with its specially trained nose a hundred-thousand times more sensitive than the thing in the middle of your face can't detect it, then happy days.'

Bashir had to admit, she had a point. But wondered if Sky White was too new for the dogs; they may not have been trained to recognise it yet. He voiced as such.

'Don't forget that it's synthetic cocaine, so chemically it has many similarities to the jungle juice the cokeheads are used to, so the dog should still know it. But it's very small in quantity, sealed in a glass tube and will have some differences. This is the best test we could have hoped for.'

She may be right, though it wasn't her who'd had to undergo it. He was also worried about why he'd been stop-checked, and described it to her in every detail, then shut his case and sat back and waited for her expert view.

'They didn't go straight to you?' she asked.

'No, like I said, the handler walked up and down a few times, and even after he supposedly randomly stopped me, he searched someone else down the line afterwards.'

'Well, that's all good. When he asked you to open the case, did he say it was a random stop and search – and he just happened to have a dog with him – or did he say the dog had indicated some interest in you or the case?

It was a very good question which Bashir had not previously considered too deeply. Which came first, the search or the dog? He thought about it and replied, 'I'm sure he said that the dog had shown an interest in my case.'

'But when you opened the case, the dog didn't show any further interest?'

'How the hell do I known how a damn police dog shows an interest. It wasn't wagging its tail if that's what you mean.'

'Think?'

'I can't remember,' Bashir said. 'Look, there was nothing "obvious" inside the case. Just the trinkets and the egg-timer; so the concealment worked. They were obviously expecting to see bags full of drugs and as there were none, happy days, as you would say.'

'You idiot.'

'What?'

'That's not the same case you used for the heroin jobs, is it?'

'Shit,' Bashir said.

'Problem solved, there would still be microscopic traces of heroin in the case. That's what the dog smelled. Bin it, you idiot. And use a new one every time, just to be on the safe side.'

Bashir felt reassured, but also embarrassed.

Moving the conversation on, he asked, 'How does the stuff work, anyway?'

'That's the beauty of this stuff, the guy who is knocking it out puts a couple of grains into a pan of hot water and boils it up. Once cool, he pours five mills into a syringe with a cap on and tells the user to boil a bit on a spoon and inhale the fumes or pour a mil or two into a vaper. That method could take off big time. More discrete, no one looks twice at a vaper.'

Bashir was impressed, and he could see why the main man was so excited. This stuff could be made anywhere, eventually, so no importations would be needed if it took off.

'You never told me where half the money goes when I carve it up?' Yates asked.

'I don't really know,' he replied.

'If you ever start turning up wearing a Rolex, I may have to ask you again.'

Bashir wasn't sure whether Yates was joking or not but could understand her concerns. 'Trust is everything,' he said.

'So don't break it.'

'Look, the guy who set this all up, knows all about the lab over there. If things go as well as we hope, then he wants to replicate the lab over here, then the risks are massively reduced. Well, for us. But he's waiting to see how it takes off first.'

Yates nodded, but he could sense the unasked question.

'They need to get the mixture right first. This eye thing isn't good,' Bashir said.

Yates nodded more vigorously. Then said, 'They do. If too many daft bastards keep overdosing on it, that wouldn't be good for business.'

It was Bashir's turn to nod.

'What if they can't get the mix right?' Yates asked.

'Then we take what we've earned so far and enjoy life. We've enough from our half already.'

Then Yates told Bashir about Crystal Meth, he'd heard about it, but didn't understand it.

'That was dreadful stuff, and the authorities were shit-scared it would take hold in the UK, but it never did.'

'Why not?'

'Not sure if I'm honest, but that was over ten years ago, so I guess the moment has passed,' she replied.

'What about your lieutenant in Preston?' Bashir asked.

'DC Jim Grantham?' Yates asked.

'Yes.'

'What about him?'

'Well, he had been busy helping to distribute the drugs when we were bringing in heroin, but now we've moved on, are you still going to use him?'

'Good question. I've not told him about this new stuff as I may have Preston covered by my local dealer.'

'So you are cutting him loose?' Bashir asked.

'I've told him that the heroin-runs have dried up, which is not entirely untrue, and it may reduce risks. He probably won't be happy, but that's my problem.'

Bashir could see the logic. He'd met Jim a couple of times. He was a weedy man in nature as well as stature and didn't like him. He'd made good money out of them and if they didn't need him anymore, it made sense to downsize. 'I hope he won't be a real problem though?' he asked.

'You leave him to me, I know him.'

'Okay,' Bashir said. They seemed quite close; he'd leave Jim to her.

Then came Yates' unasked question, who was the main man?

'I honestly don't know. I've told you before how I sold

some info to him through a contact at the Mosque, and then once I was on the hook, he just kept coming back at me for more. Threatened to blow me out if I tried to walk away. It was just easier to cave in and do what was asked.'

'I'd just love to know who we are actually working for, that's all,' Yates said.

'So would I. I only ever dealt with an intermediary who only ever referred to him as the boss man or the top man.' Bashir decided to turn the questioning back to Yates. 'Anyway, you've never told me who you've got knocking the stuff out at street level?'

'Yes, I have,' Yates said, 'I told you he's called Minty, and I trust him one hundred percent.'

'That means nothing to me.'

'Probably for the best. It can't hurt you. He's a dealer, and the dealing is my side of things.'

'Okay, fair enough.'

CHAPTER NINETEEN

By the time Cath had got to her feet, the new hoodie-wearing man was on her. Unshaven, scruffy, and with malice in his eyes. She instinctively looked around, the concourse was still busy, she was safe here. She put her hand in her pocket and felt the comforting contours of her mobile phone. She was about to pull it out as new hoodie came to a stop in front of her.

'If you're the filth, you is wasting your time,' the man started to say, with a slight lisp. Perversely, the imperfect speech made him seem less intimidating.

'I've got no gear and me mate you are following has no gear either,' he added.

The reason for his speech difficulties was obvious. The man was talking through blackened and rotten teeth. 'Look, you are mistaken, I'm not a police officer,' Cath said, finding her voice.

'Then why did you follow my mate in here then?'

Cath was starting to relax, and she noted that New Hoodie's stance had softened now he knew she was not 'the filth', as he'd put it. But she needed to engage with the youth, even if she was not entirely sure what she had witnessed between him and his mate moments earlier. She could pretend that she had not followed his mate into the station, but that would probably be a conversation-killer. In the split-second that she had, she decided to level with him. 'Okay, I did follow your mate in here, but it's not what you think. I'm trying to help, but I'll need your assistance to do so.'

New Hoodie didn't reply straight away, so Cath stuck her hand out – reluctantly – and told him her name, and that she was a reporter. But a reporter on his side. In the moment she had, she reckoned to tell him the truth would still mean 'filth' to him and frighten him off, so she decided to rely on her past credentials as a reporter for the *Manchester Evening Post.* New Hoodie stood in contemplation for a moment and ignored her hand. She was glad of the latter and quickly withdrew it, but the courtesy had been conveyed. He didn't introduce himself back, she noted, though that was not entirely unexpected.

'Here to help, how?' New Hoodie asked.

'There has been a rise in drug deaths, and I think there might be a bad batch of drugs going around. And if so, people need to be warned,' she said.

'I've not noticed anything.'

The guy was being protective, an addict's response. 'Look, I can tell you that there has been an increase in deaths related to cocaine use. Have you noticed any of your friends, having problems?' Cath said, immediately regretting using the word 'friends' as it sort of sounded a bit twee in this context. Like she was trying too hard to be sympathetic.

'I think you have got it wrong,' New Hoodie said.

'Not seen anyone with eye problems?' she pushed.

'Other than spaced out, no.'

'Not swollen and red, pupils too big and letting in so much light that it's painful?'

'Don't know who told you that, but it's bollocks. And you should drop it. You'll do more harm than good if you print anything.'

She pushed for an explanation. 'How will it make things worse?'

''Cause the gear round here is all good, and if you print something like what you're saying, the dealers will shit, and do one.'

'But these are the dealers in bad gear, so wouldn't that be a good thing?' Cath asked, feeling perplexed. She could understand an addict being protective of his normal supply, but not why he would be so towards the bad stuff.

'None of them would know who had the bad gear, see, most of them don't use themselves, so they'd all panic and close down. Then we'd all be in the proper shit,' New Hoodie said.

Now she could see his point. But knew how to reassure him, and said, 'Well, I might be able to help you there, but this is where I'll need your assistance.'

'How do you mean?' he asked.

'As far as I am aware, there is only one dealer in this bad drug, so if I could get to speak to him, maybe I won't have to report anything. Maybe, if I could just make him aware of my findings, it would all be over. As you say, the dealers don't generally use, so if he doesn't know about the unexpected side-effects, he would probably thank me.'

'Thank you?' New Hoodie asked.

'For saving his reputation and therefore his customer base,' Cath replied, almost through gritted teeth. But if the approach worked it was worth it.

'Do you know his name?' New Hoodie asked.

'All I know is that he is called Minty, and he works this patch.'

'Minty? Fuck me! I know Minty. Look lady, I'll tell him and sort it and you can drop it, yeah?'

'No offence to you, but I need to speak to him in person.'

'Don't trust me?'

'It's not that. It's just, well, I can see how difficult it might be for you to pass on such a message, and how he might not be too pleased. After all, it's going to cost him money, and it might affect your customer, stroke, supplier relationship.'

New Hoodie didn't respond.

'And I wouldn't want to do anything that would make life worse for you, believe me, I mean that. I saw a young man die at the hospital today, and I don't want to see that again,' she added.

There was no malice in New Hoodie's eyes now, but there was something in its place. Alertness on hearing her last comment. It was more than a general sorrow for having heard of a fellow addict's passing. She got the distinct impression that he knew the young man who had been rushed to hospital; but perhaps not that he was dead.

'So, if Minty just agrees to ditch the bad batch, you'll drop it?' New Hoodie asked.

'Yes, of course,' Cath lied.

'Okay.'

'Okay, what?' she asked.

'I'll take you to Minty. It's not far from here,' he said, then looked at his watch before adding, 'but we'd better get going.'

New Hoodie turned on his heel and started towards the exit without waiting for a reply. Cath had to run a few steps to catch up with him and could do no more than follow. Perhaps that young man's death would not be in vain after all.

CHAPTER TWENTY

Martin wanted to speak to the geographic inspector in charge of policing the Avenham district of Preston while Abdul's father's comments were fresh in his mind. He excused himself from Colin and found the office he was looking for on the ground floor. The sign on the door read: *Insp. Ian Laverty*, and someone was in. He knocked and entered to find a portly man in his fifties behind a desk. He introduced himself, as did Inspector Laverty, and then Martin outlined the reason or his visit. When he had finished, Laverty signified for Martin to take a seat, which he did.

'Michael Staining is the flag-abuser, and we know all about him. He is often getting himself locked up for being drunk and disorderly, and he probably hates us as much as he hates his neighbours,' Laverty said.

Martin was relieved to hear that he was known to the inspector.

'But can I ask why a regional organised crime unit sergeant was on the knocker in Avenham?' he added.

Martin should have expected this question and had to think quickly in order to hide the real reason for his visit, and said, 'Wrong address, looking for a witness from an ongoing job, but got the wrong street. But once there, the old man took the opportunity to unload.'

'I'm glad he was there, as that family have always blanked my staff when seeking witness evidence against Staining.'

'I don't think he would want to give direct evidence and probably wouldn't welcome a re-visit,' Martin added.

'No worries, we can use your statement of what you were told. It won't have the same weight as direct evidence would, but the hearsay thing was brought in to allow for this eventuality. People are scared and without such civil orders available to us it would be a nightmare,' Laverty said.

Martin said that he was pleased they were on with it and would sort out his witness statement ASAP.

'We are hoping to get him evicted by the council too, but that's always a harder one to obtain,' Laverty added, as Martin stood up.

He shook hands and thanked him for his time.

'Not at all, another arrow to aim at Staining is always a good thing.'

Martin headed back to his office and immediately cracked on with his statement for Inspector Laverty. Colin was busy in the office and returned thirty minutes later as Martin was finishing off.

'Nothing of note from the MFHs,' Colin said, as he entered the office.

'Yet,' Martin said.

'Early days, I know.'

'What was the script on the real robbery – if you'll pardon the expression?' Martin asked.

'They knocked over a sub-post office–cum–Spar shop in the Fulwood district.'

'Anyone hurt?' Martin asked.

'No, but the poor sod behind the counter was pretty shook up by all accounts.'

'Financially, that's a bit of a comedown, isn't it? From a

cash-in-transit van to a small sub-post office,' Martin said. He knew as far as the poor victims were concerned, there was no difference, but he was looking at it from the villains' point of view.

'There were two ATMs outside the premises, and guess who was in the back of the shop preparing to fill them with new cash cassettes,' Colin said.

Now it made more sense. But why not attack the van?

'I know what you're thinking, and it's odd. But we don't think the van was followed, so that means the villains must have laid in wait at the shop,' Colin said.

'But why not do the van, once the guard was out?' Martin asked.

'Well, here's the thing; it was the van's last drop,' Colin said, and added, 'so no point in doing the van.'

'Which means they had inside info,' Martin said.

'That's what Gary Falstaff reckons. He's staying on the job as we help on the murder side,' Colin said. 'Even though we are after the same people.'

'How much did they get?' Martin asked.

'Fifty grand.'

'This doesn't add up,' Martin said.

'None of it does, but which bit are you referring too?'

'The fifty grand is one thing, but why kill someone along the way?'

'I agree, it doesn't fit; we are looking at two different things; connected, but different,' Colin said.

'Any news on the deceased?'

'Not the car owner. He's in Southport, alive and kicking. His house was screwed a week ago for the car keys, and nothing else was taken but the motor,' Colin added.

'And I guess we are still waiting on the lab re that fireproof box?'

'Yep, and that's another twist which doesn't make sense. Anyway, grab the car keys; Rogers wants to see us in his office.'

Martin dropped his statement off with Laverty on his way out the building and twenty minutes later he was parking their car in the visitors' bay at Hutton headquarters.

Once in the chief's office, Martin expected him to ask Colin about the murder, but he didn't. He was on his favourite subject, Bashir.

'Gentlemen, the head of professional standards has been doing some background checks for me on Bashir and I wanted to share it with you face to face,' Rogers started, as Martin and Colin made themselves comfortable on the Chesterfields.

'He has been trying to sell some of our software systems to the Indians through some family contacts he has claimed to have over there. And as the systems involved were basic and non-sensitive stuff, the ACC above him agreed it, seeing it as a way to bring some outside revenue back in during these straitened times.'

'Do we know anything about these family connections?' Colin asked.

'Well, the ACC didn't overly pry about that, and to be honest, I'm not sure I would have done it differently,' Rogers said.

Martin didn't have to wait long for the 'but'.

'But, as the head of professional standards couldn't find any reference, anywhere, she went direct to the Indians via the Home Office. Whatever Bashir has been doing in Delhi, it's not been what he has claimed it was. Plus, we have proof that he has also been making personal visits there as well. Seven official ones, and three non-official.'

'If he had personal business, why wouldn't he do it whilst there on police business?' Martin said.

'Exactly, it's the first actual evidence we have that starts to prove the informant's information. Incidentally, have we debriefed him yet?' Rogers asked.

'He's gone to ground, his handlers think he's blown a gasket on this one and is done with us, but we are trying to find him,' Martin said.

'Wouldn't blame him. And that brings me onto the other thing,' Rogers said.

Martin and Colin just sat silently as the chief, continued. 'His day job here was head of IT development. He has a degree in computer sciences and was very good at aiding the implementation of new IT systems. He worked on the beta set up for the new CHAMPS database.'

Martin felt sick. He glanced at Colin who looked nonplussed, but Martin knew that CHAMPS stood for Chis Handling and Management Police Systems – the secure informant database. He jumped in, 'You said beta, sir?'

'Yes, in setting up and testing the system before it went live,' Rogers said.

Martin started to relax.

'But he carried his whole system's access over after it was rolled out in order to assist with any teething issues,' Rogers added.

Martin felt ill again.

Colin suddenly sat up and looked at Martin. He was catching up. 'So does that mean he would have had access to all the intelligence gathered by all registered informants?' he asked.

'Unfortunately, for a couple of weeks, yes,' the chief added.

'Would that access be audit traceable?' Martin asked.

'Not as such. He had the same access – albeit temporarily – as the authorising officer,' Rogers said, 'with one exception: he wouldn't have been able to see the informant's real profiles.'

'So he wouldn't know that Abdul was on the system?' Martin asked.

'Thankfully, no. The AO has assured me of that,' Rogers replied.

'Oh God,' Colin said. Martin and Rogers turned to face him as he continued, 'But he may have seen the intel talking about a police employee visiting India to import drugs?'

Martin felt as if he was really going to puke now.

'That's what I'm waiting to find out; the AO is doing a systems check now. I'm expecting her at any minute.'

CHAPTER TWENTY-ONE

All three men sat in silent contemplation. Martin was grateful Bashir would not have had access to the true identities of the informants; the scale of that level of compromise would have been unthinkable. Not just on all the police operations that were ongoing, but those going through the courts, too. Not to mention the risk to the lives of all the CHISs. When the police sign up an informant to work with them, they take on a duty of care to protect the informant's identity at all costs, and to ensure all risks faced are appropriate, and managed well with risk assessments and risk reduction strategies. No one here was suggesting that Bashir would have done anything with the informants' real identities, had he been able to access them, but the sheer thought of such a compromise made Martin's blood turn to anti-freeze. Such an infiltration had never happened in modern-day policing.

The more realistic damage was the bombshell they now faced, and that wasn't just the thought that Bashir had seen the intelligence naming him and talking about his trips to India, but what the hell else he had seen and digested.

Martin broke the silence as they waited for the

informant authoring officer to show. 'If he had read the intel on himself, then surely, he wouldn't have done that last run?'

'But what if he did it because he had?' Colin said.

'What do you mean?' Rogers asked.

'Well, the case *was* empty. What if he was testing the intel? Doing a dummy run to see if anything happened? And bingo, he gets stopped and searched.'

Colin had a point.

And God knows what else he has seen, Martin didn't say. They were back in unthinkable territory again. All the police operations including those using undercover officers were at risk, as were the undercover officers.

In what seemed like an eternity, eventually there came a knock at the door.

'Enter,' bellowed Rogers, and in walked a smartly dressed woman in her forties, who was quickly introduced as Detective Superintendent Kerry Danson, the officer in charge of authorising all CHIS activity for the force.

She joined them all at the Chesterfields as introductions were returned from Martin and Colin, and then she pulled a piece of paper from her handbag. 'Firstly, I want to reassure you all that Bashir had no access to the CHIS profiles, nor did he have access to their aliases. The only identifying marks he would have been able to see were their registration numbers,' she started.

'Which would tell him nothing,' Martin added.

'Quite,' Kerry said. 'And during the ten-day access he had after the system left its beta mode and went live, there were no undercover officers deployed.'

Martin let out a loud exhale, as did the other two. So far so good.

'What about his access to the intelligence gathered?' Rogers asked.

'It would have been very limited,' Kerry replied, and then went into detail to explain. Apparently, the old informants' database and the new CHAMPS system ran in unison as the contents of the former migrated to the latter.

'How long did that process take?' Colin asked.

'Twenty-two days in all. We had to run the migration programme at night, so it took a while. I've tried to establish what would have gone across while Bashir still had access, and as you can image, that is not easy to quantify. I've started with all the major level two and three operations ongoing, and I am convinced that they did not migrate until after the first ten days,' she said.

'How can you be so sure?' Rogers asked.

'Because I'd made a policy decision that all of the serious case investigations would not be transferred until the last minute, which on checking, was on day twenty-one and twenty-two.'

'Why was that?' Colin asked.

'I just wanted to make sure than any glitches were dealt with before we moved the really serious stuff onto CHAMPS,' Kerry added.

'If it was not inappropriate to say it, I would offer to kiss you, Superintendent,' Rogers said.

Kerry laughed but Martin noted that her cheeks had reddened slightly.

'But there is one exception.'

The mood suddenly dropped again.

'The intel collective is geo-sensitive, which means it prioritises any information involving Lancashire criminality over that being committed outside the county. The intel for outside, irrespective of its seriousness, would have been lumped in with all the day-to-day intel about street-level crime,' Kerry said.

She further explained that in the fullness of time any gathered intel for use by authorities outside of

Lancashire would be graded by the new system according to its importance so nothing urgent or serious was missed, even if it wasn't attached to Lancashire's own core objectives. But as a starting point, outside stuff was clumped in with the everyday minutiae.

She added that everything was sorted into order very quickly after migration so that nothing slipped through the net, and that individual intelligence officers were instructed to look after their own areas of responsibility.

'So, if I've understood you correctly, Kerry, none of our serious criminal investigations were at risk,' Rogers asked.

'No sir.'

'So the only intel Bashir could have seen, would be the likes of "who is nicking bikes in Burnley"?' Rogers added.

'Pretty much.'

'So there is no way he could have read the intel about his own actions?'

'No, sir. Definitely not.'

'And the out-of-force stuff, you mentioned?'

'We have no way of knowing if, and what, he may have had access to in that regard. But as we had very little in that folder anyway, at that time, the risk is very low. But I will warn the relevant intel authorities. I'll just say we've had a new systems glitch and leave it at that,' Kerry finished.

Kerry was duly thanked by all three of them and she quickly left them to it. It was about as good as they could have hoped for. It should have been much worse, if truth be known. Rogers called for refreshments, and they all iterated what had been said while they waited. After the tea arrived, Rogers did ask for an update on the murder and was just pleased that they had a named suspect in the frame.

'What about the deceased?' Rogers asked.

'The Home Office Pathologist is due to do the PM this

afternoon, and we are still awaiting the lab re the box,' Colin added.

'That box bit is strange,' Rogers noted, and added, 'are you doing a press appeal for the deceased?'

'Probably tomorrow, give the MFH angle chance to come good first,' Colin said.

'Fair enough,' Rogers said. 'I'll let you two get on then.'

Colin and Martin quickly finished their drinks and left but didn't speak until they were en route back to Preston. 'I think we've been very lucky there,' Colin said.

'I agree; I just hope that Kerry's information is as accurate as she has been told that it is.'

'She seemed certain about all the serious level two and three stuff. Her delaying decision on that would appear to have saved the day. Not that she could have ever known in a million years how it would,' Colin said.

Martin was about to voice his slight concerns re the out-of-force-stuff when his mobile rang, and the car's Bluetooth crackled to life. It was the communications room at Preston. 'How can I help you?' he asked.

'It's about your car, Sarge,' came the reply.

'What about it?'

'It has been parked at Blackpool North railway station for hours and the locals are asking you to move it if not still on official business.'

CHAPTER TWENTY-TWO

Bashir stood up and Yates did too. 'We all done now?' he asked.

'Unless there is anything else?' she said. Then added, 'When is the next run?'

'Not sure; the intermediary has said there shouldn't be too many more, as the boss man is close to setting up his own lab over here.'

'What happens then?' Yates asked.

'Not a question I've been bold enough to ask,' Bashir replied. 'Part of me will be glad that I don't have to go over there again when it does come to an end, but will our personal revenue stream come to an abrupt halt?'

He noticed that Yates had stopped listening and was looking over his shoulders. Before he could ask what was up, he heard footsteps on the stairs. Someone was coming. Bashir was not a brave man and instinctively moved backwards behind Yates.

Seconds later, a scruffy hooded youth appeared at the top of the steps and stood still.

'What the fuck are you doing here?' Yates asked.

'You said you were meeting your contact, I was just praying you were still here,' the scruff said.

Bashir relaxed, the youth and Yates obviously knew

each other.

'Yeah, a meeting you didn't need to attend,' Yates said.

'You don't understand,' the scruff said.

'This is Minty,' Yates said to Bashir, and then faced Minty, 'And this is my associate whose name you don't need to know.'

Minty nodded at Bashir and then said, 'We have trouble.'

'What sort of trouble?' Yates asked.

'A news reporter sniffing around.'

'After what?' she asked.

'Been looking into the drug deaths, from a "warn the poor users about bad gear" point of view.'

'How do you know?' Yates asked.

'I got warned first, earlier,' Minty said.

'By whom?' Yates asked.

'An addict blew her out for a free bag of Sky White,' Minty said.

'Which addict?' Yates asked.

'Doesn't matter, daft bastard went over this afternoon,' Minty said.

'Ah that one, I've been working on that,' Yates said.

'You said first?' Bashir said, speaking up. He hadn't wanted to interrupt but didn't want the 'first' comment to go unmissed.

Minty turned to face him and said, 'Yeah, then I was grafting at the railway station, and I'd just run out of my locals' stuff, when an addict said he'd been followed in by some bird.'

'What did you do?' Yates asked, regaining Minty's attention.

'I gave him a tenner and fucked him off. Then spoke to the bird who said she was this reporter. And in fairness she seems on the level, said she only wanted to warn users.'

'So where is she now?' Yates asked.

'Sat downstairs in the old taxi office,' he replied.

Bashir felt terrified, and Yates started to explode at Minty before she quickly lowered her voice and gave him the most vicious whispered bollocking he'd ever heard.

'I'm telling you she's not filth; I know the difference,' Minty said.

'You better be right; but why on earth did you fetch her here?' Yates asked.

Minty quickly outlined his plan. He said that she didn't know that he was Minty as she'd asked him about Minty, so he said he could bring her to meet him on the pretext that someone playing Minty could speak to her. He had someone in mind and that they would thank her for letting him know about the bad batch of gear and assure her that it was all done and that there would be no more. So there was no need for her to report her story. After all, she wouldn't want to upset the dynamics that the users and dealers worked to on the street-level drug market.

'And that's your plan?' Yates asked, with obvious venom.

All Bashir wanted to do was get the hell out of there and leave Yates to sort it, but he knew as soon as he reached the bottom of the stairs he would be on view, and the steel fire escape would make too much noise.

'Well, I had to think of something fast,' Minty said, and then explained that he had already texted a mate to meet him around the back for a little bullshit job worth ten free bags of Sky White.

Bashir could see this all going to rat-shit city quicker than Delhi-belly hits tourists.

'You really think you can reassure this woman, and that that will be the end of her interest?' Yates asked.

'Absolutely,' Minty replied.

Bashir thought that Minty was either stupid or a fantasist. He was sure that once the boss man had his own lab with the teething mixture problem sorted the sky was the limit. There was no need to risk importing large quantities of jungle grown cocaine. But irrespective of what their position with the boss would be thereafter, this reporter could kill Sky White off before business got going with a news warning. People wouldn't risk the new stuff and no amount of reassurance would work. They'd just go back to the jungle juice. 'We can't decide this on our own,' he said.

'What do you mean?' Yates asked.

Bashir leaned forward out of Minty's earshot and whispered his concerns in her ear. He then pulled out a cheap throwaway phone which he only ever used for ringing one person. 'I need to speak to the boss man's man,' he said.

Yates told Minty to get on with his plan and that he'd better make sure it worked. To go downstairs and keep this woman happy until his mate 'Fake Minty' arrived. As soon as he started down the stairs, Bashir dialled the number. He walked to the corner of the room as he made the call. The intermediary answered and Bashir quickly briefed him.

'If that bitch puts out a warning, the boss will see it and all hell will blow up,' the intermediary said.

'That's why I'm ringing you, to give you the heads-up and ask for your advice,' Bashir said.

'You sure this Blackpool toe rag can sweeten her up enough?' he asked.

'He reckons so?' Bashir replied.

'My first thoughts are to come to Blackpool and do the bitch. She can't say fuck-all then,' he said.

Bashir felt a Himalayan chill run through him. He knew that the people he was dealing with were serious people, and always expected they were capable of dishing out serious violence. It was one reason he'd always felt he had no option but to go along with them once they'd hooked him. But this was the first time he'd heard the man spell out any firm threat.

After a pause, the man continued, 'Having said that, it might draw more attention if we do her. The filth will no doubt start to look at what she was working on, who she had upset. It could still blow her story far and wide. End up with more publicity.'

Bashir couldn't believe what he was hearing; the man was actually rationalising whether or not to kill the reporter. He was looking at the pros and cons. Bashir had originally been given the man's number by an associate at the mosque but had never actually met him. He had always wanted to so he could see who he was dealing with. Now he never wanted to meet this guy, ever.

After a further silence on the line, the man spoke, 'It looks like we have no choice but to go with toe rag's plan. If he puts her off her public-spirited duty, then proper result. If he doesn't, then you're in the shit, as is your cop girlfriend.'

It had not occurred to Bashir that he or Yates was in danger. It wasn't their fault this reporter had started sniffing around; and Yates was not his girlfriend. In fact, the only reason they had a problem in the first place, was because the gear was not right. The man should be angry with those who made it, not them. He was about to point this out when the man spoke again.

'Make sure this is sorted, and ring me when it is, or the boss will have you two fuckers in his sights.'

The line was dead before he could respond. He considered ringing back, but then thought better of it. He dropped his phone arm to his side and turned to face Yates.

'You look like shit, mate. What did your man say?'

Bashir told her.

'Now hang on a minute—' Yates started to say but stopped as they both heard a banging on the back door, followed by Minty's voice from downstairs, in what

Bashir though was an over-the-top expression for their benefit, shouting, 'That'll be Minty, Cath, I'll just get him.'

Who the hell did he think he was shouting too? Cath being in the same room as him. He hoped Fake Minty's acting skills were better than real Minty's.

CHAPTER TWENTY-THREE

Loud banging came from a door at the rear and New Hoodie claimed it would be Minty in a daft, loud voice. Perhaps he was trying to reassure his guest before he opened the back door. Anyway, he scooted into the back and out of sight, and after a couple of minutes returned with another youth. And he wasn't what Cath expected. Not that she was an expert on what most street-level drug dealers looked like, but this guy looked no older than fifteen and eight stone when full. His complexion made a bowl of porridge look colourful. She relaxed further; this guy was only a threat to his own reflection.

He stood impassive in the centre of the room, and Cath stood up to join him. New Hoodie didn't introduce him as Minty, so she didn't use his name. As if trying to act as an honest broker, New Hoodie quickly iterated what Cath's concerns were. The guy then spoke.

'I didn't know the gear was bad, in fact, how do you know that the punters hadn't mixed it up themselves. They put all sorts of shit in stuff to make it last.'

It was a good point which hadn't actually occurred to Cath. She thought for a second and then asked, 'Won't toxicology show that up?' Both Minty and New Hoodie looked at each other, pained. She explained, and then

Minty spoke.

'They don't look that hard when it's an addict overdosing.'

Cath sort of knew that, so changed tack and asked, 'Have you ever seen anything affect the eyes really badly?' She then went into detail as to what she had seen earlier in the day.

'I can't say I have,' Minty replied.

'Me neither,' New Hoodie added.

'Look lady, the gear's all gone, I promise to warn my regulars so they can get themselves to A&E as soon as they feel any bad shit, and I won't be buying off that middleman again.'

Cath would love to know who Minty had bought his supply from but knew better than to ask.

'So do we have a deal?' Minty asked.

'I guess the public safety message no longer needs to go out, and I don't want to upset everyone if I don't need to,' Cath lied.

'So we all good then?' Minty said.

'As long as no other bodies turn up, yes.'

Minty nodded and headed back the way he'd come. New Hoodie followed him out the room and Cath stayed on her feet and awaited his return. This only took a minute.

'So we all good and done, yeah?' New Hoodie asked on his return.

'Yeah,' she replied.

New Hoodie said he needed to do some stuff upstairs before he left, whatever that meant, and added, 'And I've got a train to catch.'

She took the hint and said goodbye. Truth be known, she couldn't wait to get out of that place and gulp in some normal polluted air. She'd ring Martin once back in his car. It was only a couple of minutes away and it would be easier than trying to walk and talk. But as she sped back to the railway station on foot, she mused about the meeting she'd just had. Irrespective of the reassurances they had given each other, she was sure of a couple of things. Minty was a chronic addict, and therefore probably not the savvy user-dealer which New Hoodie had earlier described, so he probably wasn't actually Minty. And therefore, the whole thing was staged, which meant a third thing; they were hiding something. Oh, and a fourth; when she told them she would drop the whole story, a look of massive relief was evident on New Hoodie's face, not Minty's. In fact, Minty looked totally ambivalent.

CHAPTER TWENTY-FOUR

Martin had tried Cath's phone twice more with no response, so left a message. He was starting to feel concerned. He dropped Colin off and said he'd see him later, before he set the Satnav for Blackpool North railway station and then headed for the M55 motorway, which was thankfully clear, so he gunned Cath's little city car, which was surprisingly responsive. Thirty minutes later, the end of the motorway guided him onto an urban carriageway which in turn led him to the central area of Blackpool. He passed the town's football ground on the way. Ten minutes after that, he pulled up on a car park situated at the front of the railway station. He saw his car parked face-in at the end of the car park. He pulled across the back of it just as he noticed the vehicle's rear lights come on. He jumped out and saw Cath in the driver's seat. A mixture of relief and annoyance washed over him. Both feelings deeper than he would have expected. She must have seen him approach as she quickly got out.

'I've been ringing you,' he said, a little more firmly than he'd intended.

'I'm so sorry, my phone's been on silent,' she said, and then held up her hand with her phone in it. 'I was just about to call you back,' she added.

Martin's demeanour softened, though he'd no idea why her ringer would be turned off. But before he could ask, she explained. When she'd finished, his feelings of relief and annoyance were replaced with worry. 'Bloody hell, Cath, you could have been walking into anything?' he said.

'I know, but I made a judgement, and it was fine,' she said.

'Just so long as you are okay?'

'I am, but there is something weird going on.'

'I agree.'

If she thought that this Minty had put on a 'performance of appeasement' as she had put it, then there was obviously something darker to hide. He briefed her as much as he could about the robbery and murder, and that there was to be a press conference in the morning.

'Brilliant, I'll ring my mates in the press office; see if I can tag along.'

'We are not going to mention the body in the boot at this stage; we may have to later in the day, but we want to focus on the MFH appeal first.'

'This means you have a suspect?' she asked, with a grin on her face.

Martin couldn't hide a smirk back. She really should have been a detective.

'I can't confirm or deny that, Miss Moore,' Martin started, in his best official voice. Then returned to his normal one to add, 'But we owe it to the next of kin, whoever they are, not to publicise the circumstances of the deceased's passing until we know who he or she was, and we get a chance to do it privately.'

Cath nodded her understanding. Martin left her and went back to Cath's car and parked it properly so as not to block the car park. As soon as he got out, his own phone rang. It was Colin.

'You find Cath, okay?' he asked.

Martin said that he had and would explain later. Then Colin asked him if he was still in Blackpool. Martin said he was.

'Excellent, the local DI is tied up and they have another job coming in, I wondered if you could babysit it until the local DI can join you,' Colin asked.

'Yeah, no problem, what have we got?'

'It initially came in as a drug death, but from the first responders' reports, it looks more like a potential suicide job; a jumper,' Colin said.

'So you want me to make sure it was a jump and not a push, before the scene is all trampled on?'

'If you are quick, you can ask her yourself.'

'Sorry?' Martin replied.

'As of five minutes ago she was still alive. Not sure if she is conscious though, the paramedics are working on her as we speak.'

Martin quickly took the location from Colin and ended the call. He turned to face Cath and shouted, 'Got to dash, I've got a jumper,' and ran to the driver's side of his car and climbed in.

Cath ran round to the passenger side and got in.

'I haven't got time for this, what are you doing?' he asked.

'Coming with you,' she replied.

'No, I'm sorry—' Martin started to say.

'I am if you want these,' Cath said, holding up his car keys in her hand.

Martin hadn't time to argue, or to change vehicles. Seconds were precious. He just grabbed the car keys and said, 'Okay, but you keep quiet and just stick behind me, yeah?'

'Yeah,' she replied.

Martin reversed sharply out of the parking spot and put the car into first gear. He told Cath that she could work the Satnav as he drove in the general direction of the scene and then gave her the location. 'And put your seatbelt on, you'll need it.'

'I know where this is,' Cath said, as Martin drove out of the car park at speed.

'I've a pretty rough idea,' he replied. 'Head for the sea and turn left before we get wet.'

'Pretty much,' she replied.

It had been years since he'd been to Blackpool, but the Central Pier shouldn't be too hard to find. He knew they were on the north side of the town; hence the railway station's name and he also knew that the pier complex was close to the Tower, which was about as big a landmark as you could hope for. Martin went through two sets of red lights ignoring blaring horns from other cars and within minutes he had reached the promenade, and although he knew it was several miles long, the Tower looked close. He wasn't too sure why a jumper would choose a pier; it was a fair drop, but if you wanted to kill yourself, he could think of higher things to fling yourself off. Obviously one end of the pier was out to sea, so if drowning was your thing, then that made some sense. But Colin had said the incident took place at the beach end, which made less sense. Maybe it was just an accident. They'd soon find out.

Ahead, Martin could see several emergency vehicles on the frontage to the pier with their blue lights flashing. He pulled up and was immediately approached by a uniformed officer, so quickly drew his warrant card and told the officer that they were CID. Easier than explaining it further. The officer nodded and pointed to a space where they could park. 'Come on detective,' he said to Cath as he opened the car door.

On either side of the pier's frontage there was a set of stone steps leading to the beach which ran under the pier. All the activity was at the southern steps, so they hurried in that direction. At the top of them Martin could see the whole scene clearly.

On the sand close to the pier's structure lay someone face up. Two paramedics were working on the individual while two uniformed constables held powerful torches aloft to illuminate the victim; the natural light was fading fast. A further officer had a clipboard and was scribbling furiously. Stood next to her was a uniformed sergeant. He looked up and made his way towards the steps. Martin hurried down them with Cath behind him. They all met at the bottom, Martin quickly introduced themselves as detectives passing through and explained they had been asked to cover the scene. The sergeant nodded.

'Is she conscious?' Martin asked.

'Yes,' the sergeant replied.

'How hurt is she?'

'Bad. Too bad to move at the moment. They suspect spinal injuries, which they need to confirm, and then secure her before they try to move her. Air ambulance is five minutes away.'

'Surely, she's not done all that simply jumping off the pier?' Martin said.

'Not from Blackpool, are you, sir,' the sergeant asked, looking over Martin's shoulder towards the pier.

Martin instinctively turned to follow the sergeant's gaze and saw that atop the pier at the beach end was an enormous big wheel. Like a small version of the London Eye. 'That wasn't here last time I was,' Martin said.

'It's 108 feet above the pier itself. It's amazing she missed the pier deck if she did jump off that,' the sergeant said.

Martin nodded and then said, 'But she could have fallen, still?'

'Not from inside a carriage, they have a metal cage to stop that, but a small person like the victim could have climbed through if they were determined enough, but we don't know.'

'I suppose she could have climbed up the structure and jumped from that, too?' Martin added.

'Technically possible, but hard to do without being seen and stopped. She may just have come from the pier itself, and even though it's not that high, she might have landed badly.'

'Any eye witnesses?'

The sergeant shook his head.

'So we are none the wiser whether she jumped or fell, or from where?'

The sergeant shook his head again.

'Still, a tragic accident regardless, and someone is still critically hurt,' Cath said.

'Absolutely,' Martin replied. He could understand how dispassionate his conversation with the sergeant might seem to Cath, but it was just the way you dealt with terrible things. Observe, categorise and then deal with it. You couldn't do the last bit until you'd sorted out the first two. Sympathy and sorrow had to wait their turn until later when the time pressure was off. 'Can we have a quick word with her?' he asked the sergeant. 'Might sort it all out from a criminal offence point of view; while we still can.' Martin shuddered at how cold that must have sounded to Cath.

'Hang on,' he answered, and shot off to speak to one of the paramedics.

Martin turned to a shocked looking Cath, 'It's not what you think, I'll explain later.'

She opened her mouth but closed it again as the sergeant returned. 'If you promise not to get in the way and keep it brief. Don't bother with the obvious, we have her details,' he said.

Martin nodded and quickly made his way to the victim. He hadn't been able to see her clearly before, as the paramedics backs had been in the way. They were side by side; he looked through the gap between them. He could see a young woman laid on her back, in her twenties he reckoned. She was slightly built with grubby tangled hair. Next to her on the far side was a specialist stretcher which Martin knew was used to support the movement of patients with spinal injuries. The paramedics looked in no rush to try and lift her onto it.

He was about to ask whether she fell or was pushed, and if she fell, was it an accident, when he heard Cath scream behind him. Shocked, he turned to look at her, but she pushed past him and collapsed to her knees on the sand next to the young woman.

'Oh my God, I hope you are okay? Look, the helicopter will soon be here,' Cath said. Martin could see recognition clear on her face. And as if on spec he could hear the approaching *thump, thump, thump* of rotor blades. He glanced up towards the noise and could see a huge searchlight hovering towards them.

He turned back to the woman as she spoke. 'I'm sorry,' she said, to Cath, who was now stroking her face.

'Sorry for what?' Cath asked.

'Your card, he saw you give it to me and took it.'

Martin had no idea what she was talking about, but Cath obviously did.

'Forget that. I promised you I'd get you help when you wanted it, and I will,' Cath said, and then turned to face Martin, before turning back to the young woman.

'This is the man I was going to talk to; he can help get you into treatment. You didn't have to do this, Cath said.

'He's gone,' the woman said.

'I know,' Cath answered.

Martin could see tears on Cath's face.

'If it helps, I was with him at the end, he wasn't alone,' Cath added.

'That's nice, but . . .' the woman said, before she winced in obvious pain. 'But I'm no good without him.'

Martin whispered into the ear of one of the paramedics, 'Is there nothing you can do?'

He turned to face Martin, and whispered back, 'No, only a doctor.'

Martin struggled to hear him as the rotor noise suddenly became much louder as the whole scene was lit up further. Martin turned to watch the helicopter start to land about twenty metres away from them on the beach. A gale force wind came off the rotors and whipped the sand up. Martin raised his hand to cover his eyes and turned his gaze back to the young woman. She had turned her eyes away from the helicopter and away from the light. That's when he noticed her eyes. They were starting to redden and seemed to be enlarged.

Cath shouted, 'I don't even know your name?'

The woman said, 'It's . . .' but Martin couldn't hear what she said.

Then her head rolled to the other side, and the paramedic nearest to him shouted for everyone to stand clear. Martin backed off, as did Cath. A green jumpsuit-wearing doctor raced across the sand to the stricken woman, but Martin knew it was too late. He'd seen death enough times to recognise the lifeless look in the young woman's twisted gaze. He pulled Cath to him as she unleashed a wail of emotion and sobbed into his chest. He'd never heard Cath cry before, and even though he didn't fully understand why she did so now, he knew he never wanted to hear her cry again.

CHAPTER TWENTY-FIVE

Martin kept looking at the scene over Cath's shoulder and watched as the doctor stood and shook his head at the paramedics before looking at his watch. He was calling it, noting the time of death. Martin walked Cath back to the steps and told her to wait for him in the motor. She trudged off looking crestfallen. He then turned back to the uniformed sergeant.

'Your colleague knew the deceased?' the sergeant asked.

'Looks that way,' he answered.

'Must have been a hell of a shock then.'

'Looks like it hit her hard. Can I ask you to close the scene as soon as the medics have gone?'

'No problems.'

Martin went on to ask the sergeant to get a forensic tent to cover the body and maintain a scene log. He'd be back in ten. The sergeant shot off and Martin returned to his car and got in. Cath seemed to have calmed a little but still looked very upset. She then answered his unasked question and quickly brought him up to speed on the events of her day.

He was shocked, she'd been busy. 'So that apology at the end, re your card?'

'Her boyfriend must have taken it from her.'

'And given it to this Minty character,' Martin added.

'Looking that way, or just told him about me.'

Martin asked her if she was okay to drive. She said that she was. He set off and said he'd drop her at her car and suggested she went home and got some rest. He would be here for some time yet.

'One thing concerns me,' he said, as he drove.

'What?' Cath asked.

'Did you see her eyes start to bulge and redden?'

'I did, and that's bothering me too.'

'Christ, if this gear is bad or whatever, we could have corpses turning up by the barrow-load.'

'That's one way of putting it.'

'Did you believe this Minty geezer when he told you that the batch was all done?'

'Not a bit. They were just trying to silence me, stop me reporting on it.'

Martin glanced sideways at her as he drove and could see that she had regained more of her composure. He could see anger in her eyes now. 'I take it you are going to arrange a public health warning?' he asked.

'Damn right. I need to chat with Eleanor first, but I'm thinking just a short piece, a warning via our press office with a fuller report once I know more. We could even tag it on the end of your MFH press appeal tomorrow?'

'Good idea.' Even if this young woman's death was not homicide, he'd insist with the local DI when he arrived, that they made sure that a Home Office pathologist did the post mortem, and that they did a full toxicology test as well. The HO PMs were very thorough and didn't stop once the obvious cause of death was discovered.

Once back at the railway station car park, he made sure Cath was okay to drive back to Manchester. She insisted that she was. He could see that she'd recovered from her shock, so told her to take her time and text him when she was home. She said she would, and he said he'd see her at the press conference the following morning.

After dropping her off, he headed back to Central Pier just as the local DI was arriving. Martin quickly briefed him with what he knew before handing the job over to him but added that he wanted a full Home Office PM and toxicology doing.

'I thought we only did those for murders? This will just be a coroner's job,' The local DI said.

'The coroner will still need a full investigation of the facts.'

'I know, but it's not going to be an unlawful killing verdict. So we don't need a full HO PM.'

'Usually, I would agree with you, but if there is a bad batch of gear out there, we need to know about it.'

'Look mate, this is Blackpool, we get lots of addicts going over, so what?'

Martin was becoming more and more irritated by this guy and was struggling to hide his contempt. 'You might think it a bit of an inconvenience—'

'Well, actually it is.'

'Well, if you don't want to be further inconvenienced – several times over—'

'I suppose, if there is a bad batch out there . . .'

Martin turned to look at the victim once more as did the local DI. Her eyes now were fully red and enormous. Then blood started to leak from them. It was horrific. Martin turned back to the local DI and said, 'Did you see that?'

He nodded and added, 'I wish I hadn't.'

'Well, if that's what you want young children to find whilst playing in the park, you'll stop arguing with me and do as I ask.'

The guy nodded, and Martin was about to turn away again, when he spoke.

'Not being funny, but a HO PM and Tox will cost a

fortune; who'll pay for it?'

Martin had to stifle the animalistic desire to punch this runt in the face. He took a deep breath before he replied that the Regional Organised Crime Unit would. He didn't wait for a reply before he started to walk away. He shook his head as he did; the world of devolved budgets had driven these sorts of attitudes. He wondered how many criminals were on the loose due to financially driven shortcuts, by blinkered dickheads like this guy.

CHAPTER TWENTY-SIX

Martin was in the Preston office early, partly to beat the traffic, but mainly to help Colin prepare for the press conference due to be held at headquarters. Normally, Colin as DCI would do the press appeal on any major enquiry, but on this occasion, he asked Martin if he would front it. Colin said that as they were keeping the aim of the appeal on locating any missing from homes who might be at risk, it would look strange if a detective chief inspector fronted it. No problems, it made sense. 'When are we going live on all of it?' he asked. They couldn't sit on it forever.

'I've policy logged that if today's appeal doesn't work, then probably tomorrow we'll have to do a limited release. I don't think the wider public are in any danger, as such, but there may be witnesses we need to identify before it gets too old,' Colin replied.

Martin agreed. Who knows who may have seen the getaway car flying about? He suggested that they ask the local community bobbies to do a bit of informal digging, speak to folk in the area before they do a more structured house-to-house enquiry. Colin agreed.

Martin then brought him up to speed on what Cath had been up to, and her plan to arrange a limited TV mention to warn drug users on the back of their press appeal.

'Does she need a quote from us?' Colin asked.

'Not yet, but she has agreed to say that the police are aware and are investigating, which after last night's death in Blackpool, we can say that we are.'

'Okay, I'll give the Drug and Alcohol Action Teams the heads-up while you do the press appeal,' Colin said.

'Any news from the lab?'

'It's taking longer than expected but they have managed to open it and retrieve one document. The heat has bleached the ink, so they are going to try and recover that by way of indentations and residue left. I don't fully understand the processes involved, but I'm hopeful of something more concrete later today,' Colin said.

'Typed or handwritten?'

'It would appear to be typeface.'

'Shame,' Martin said, before he picked up his car keys and headed out.

Twenty minutes later, Martin arrived at Hutton Headquarters and ten minutes after that he was in the studio at the training school. Colin had given him a script and it was also loaded onto an autocue. There were about ten reporters present from various local and regional presses, Cath was chatting among them and clearly knew most of them. A regional TV rep and camera crew were there too. And albeit from a local perspective, they were probably more interested in the drug element. Cath's sergeant, Eleanor, had arranged the add-on; and had done well at short notice. But it did increase the stress a little. He manged a quick word with Cath before they went live. 'Didn't realise there would be an outside broadcast unit,' he commented. 'Just thought our press office would record something and then put it out later.'

'Be trickier live, but it'll give your appeal much more reach than some prepared video.'

'It'll certainly save me a load of time this morning. No endless re-runs. Just better get it right first time.'

'And the TV rep, Sally, is a top pro. Done stuff with her before when I was in the press office.'

Martin smiled before quickly asking her if she was alright after the events of yesterday. She said she was, and more determined than ever to get to the bottom of it. Martin didn't doubt her.

Five minutes later and he went through his prepared script about the appeal for the police to be notified of anyone who was missing, but not yet reported as such. Then came the questions. 'Did the police have fears for a particular individual? And if so, what were they?' Martin tried to keep his answers as generic as he could so as not to give too much away. Then he was asked by a local paper's reporter, Jim something-or-other, 'Is this in any way connected with the armed robbery which took place in Preston yesterday? We understand that the suspects have now been released from custody under investigation.'

Martin hadn't expected this and wasn't sure how Jim had made the link. He had to be careful, he couldn't say no and then have a further press appeal for witnesses in a day or two's time when they'd have to reveal the body in the boot. 'I'm not involved in the robbery investigation, so am unable to comment further on that,' he answered, truthfully; just. A get-out-of-jail answer for now.

Then Jim asked, 'I believe that there were a couple of drug related deaths over in Blackpool yesterday, I take it, neither of these are your missing from homes?'

A great question Martin thought, but one he could quickly discount as not connected. But Jim had cleverly put his link in with the question, and then he jumped on it just as fast.

'Can you tell us anything about those deaths, Detective Sergeant?' he asked. 'Two in a matter of hours is clearly a concern, is it not?'

Jim was astute, that was for sure. Martin glanced at Cath who was smirking at him. She was obviously enjoying his discomfort.

'Of course,' Martin replied, and added, 'any drug related death is a concern, and will be fully investigated on behalf of the coroner by the local DI.' He then took his opportunity to give them all the local DI's details. The guy would curse him, no doubt, but a press spotlight on him would not be a bad thing. It might help ensure a full HO PM and toxicology as promised. Jim seemed happy as he scribbled away on his pad. And it gave Martin a chance to ask for other questions. None came, which surprised him a little, so he thanked them all and wrapped his part up.

He then managed a quick word with Cath before she took centre stage with Sally. The other press all remained out of shot. Sally did a quick interview with Cath who was appearing on behalf of the police as an intelligence analyst.

'Should our viewers be worried?' Sally asked.

Cath gave a stock answer and then explained the red eye thing and quoted a Crimestoppers number for confidential contact but stressed that addicts should not take any new derivative of cocaine. The piece-to-camera interview only lasted a couple of minutes, but Sally seemed pleased with it. Martin had been watching from the shadows and approached as soon as it was over. 'Your false reporter guise is now well and truly blown.'

'Doesn't matter now, might encourage Minty and others to ditch the stuff.'

'That Jim guy was on his game,' Martin said.

'Yeah, he's from my old firm, but I don't know him.'

Martin actually welcomed press scrutiny, though many of his colleagues did not. Then his phone lit up, it was still on silent, but Colin's name illuminated across the screen. Martin answered.

'You done there?'

'Just.'

'Good, can you call in at Preston railway station on your way back?'

'Sure,' Martin said, and then asked, 'not another job?'

'Yes and no,' Colin replied, and then added, 'a dead body in the bogs on the main platform. Looks like another drugs death, and the local DI is en route. Can you just have a peep in case it's this bad drug thing that Cath is working on?'

'Will do,' Martin replied, and then ended the call. He turned to face Cath.

'I'm coming with you,' she said.

Martin realised that his loudspeaker on the phone had been turned on, and sighed before he asked, 'Don't suppose there is any way I can talk you out of it; just until we know what we are dealing with?'

'Not a chance.'

'Okay, but you'll need to keep out of the way while the local DI does what he has to do.'

Cath nodded and then walked over to Sally. He couldn't hear what she said but was relieved to see Sally's cameraman and sound recordist start to pack up a moment or so later, while making comments about getting back to their office. He didn't need them turning up at the railway station.

CHAPTER TWENTY-SEVEN

Martin knew that although railway stations were the remit of the British Transport Police, if the death at Preston station was homicide, then under an agreement reached between the BTP and the Regional Homicide Units, the regional detectives would do the investigation on their behalf and at their expense. He knew of colleagues who had copped these extra cases on top of their daily loads and knew that they all hated them. The transport police hated it too. They felt like they had been sold out by their bosses. But with the best will in the world, the BTP were not set up to efficiently run a murder. It would use all their resources and more. But jealousy and tensions on such enquires would always be high. And irrespective of whether it was homicide, the local DI would be here as soon as he could. The covering DI from the BTP could be in Cornwall.

Preston was a major station on the West Coast main line, midway between Glasgow Central and London Euston, and therefore always busy; that could be a help and a hindrance. There were several ways into the station, but Martin plumbed for the entrance at the front where the taxis and drop-off and pick-up places were. He parked close to main doors and Cath pulled in after him.

By the time he was walking through the entrance, she was right behind him. They were met by a uniformed sergeant who said they were the first to arrive. They were led to the toilet block which was on the concourse and ran between platforms three and four, just past the dining areas. Martin was glad to see that the approaches from both sides had already been cordoned off and noted a queue of passengers complaining to a stressed looking constable. All he could do was point them in the direction of a shopping arcade nearby.

As Martin neared, he heard one man say to the officer guarding the cordon, 'This is simply not good enough; can't you just move the body?'

This stopped Martin in his tracks. He turned to face the guy, but before he could speak, he carried on, 'How come you are letting them through?'

'Because we are here to help investigate how some poor soul has lost their life. And if all you have to moan about is that you are bursting for a wee, can I suggest you consider yourself very lucky; and take yourself, and your piss elsewhere,' Martin said, instantly regretting allowing this sad excuse of a human get under his skin.

'Well, I never,' the man exclaimed.

Too late to back off now, so Martin continued, 'Or, I'll instruct this officer to arrest you for wasting police time and place you in a cell, preferably one without facilities.' He turned away from him and carried on into the corridor of the toilet block before the man could reply further. The constable was grinning, and he heard the bloke stomp off in the opposite direction a moment later.

'That'll be another complaint, you smooth talker,' Cath whispered in his ear.

'He'll complain to BTP, and they'll have no record of me being here.'

'You hope.'

The corridor between the two platforms which

accessed the toilet blocks was clearly a thoroughfare. Martin stopped before they reached the cubicles and asked Cath to wait as he put on a pair of gloves and protective overshoes, in order to have a quick look. If the circumstances were as reported, he may need to put a full paper suit on; but hoped he'd be in and out in a minute.

He then carefully pushed the main toilet door open, taking care to use the top of the door so as not to disturb the area where hands would normally leave their traces. He could sense Cath trying to peek over his shoulder as she stayed behind him as promised.

On the floor, half in and half out of one of the WCs was a man in his twenties or thirties. He was laid on his side, keeping the cubicle door open. He was obviously dead, and by the look of him the paramedics hadn't even bothered to lay him flat on the floor to attempt any life-saving treatment. There was no point in disturbing the scene unnecessarily when he'd already gone.

Martin touched the back of the man's outstretched hand, and it was as he expected it to be: as cold as the floor. He'd been dead a while. Maybe he had been inside when he expired, maybe the paramedics had moved him, until they realised it was too late. He'd check later with them. If the guy had died inside the cubicle with the door closed, it would add to the whole drug overdose scenario theory. There were no obvious marks of violence. Interestingly, still grasped in the deceased's other hand was a vape. And more interesting still, was the man's face. Or to be exact, his eyes. The same not-of-this-world eyes he'd seen for the first time only twelve hours or so ago, in Blackpool. This problem *was* becoming worse.

Then Martin heard a muffled scream behind him and turned to see Cath in the doorway with her hand over her mouth. 'I thought I asked you to wait outside,' he said.

'It's him,' she said, removing her hand.

'Who?' Martin asked.

'The tramp who gave me Minty's details. He'd also been using Minty's drugs.'

That's three now and all inside twenty-four hours. And Cath seemed to know them all.

'Come on, lets backtrack our way out of here,' Martin said.'

'Look!' Cath pointed.

Martin followed her arm and saw a small white terrier come out of the cubicle; it must have been sat next to the deceased's head. The poor animal. 'I'll call the RSPCA,' he said. 'They'll take good care of it.'

CHAPTER TWENTY-EIGHT

Dan Manning was lying on his queen-sized bed in his spacious bedroom in the barn conversion he was currently renting on the north-eastern outskirts of Manchester. The place was rented in his girlfriend's name and his nearest neighbour was a mile away. Suzy was downstairs making breakfast whilst he was playing with his share of the money from the Post Office ATM job in Preston. After paying the rest of the firm, and the decoy team; what he was left with was not a lot but would cover the bills until he got his new project fully established. Then the sky would be the limit and he could sack the robbery business. He hadn't wanted to carry on with this one, but the lads had mouths to feed, so he'd let it run. Plus, it gave him the chance to have some fun at the filth's expense.

He turned the telly on but muted the sound as he stretched back and wished he could have been on the decoy run. He'd have loved to have seen the filth's faces when they realised that they'd been shafted good and proper. He'd have loved it even more if he'd been a fly on a dog turd as they discovered the burned-out motor from the real blag. He set off laughing to himself once more. He'd double-dicked them and they would be well pissed off.

In fact, he could have been on the decoy run, but for the little matter of being wanted for murder. He'd taken a call five minutes ago to say that the whole decoy team had been released without charge. They'd be well compensated for the inconvenience of a night in the cells, and for having their gaffs turned upside down by the filth. But according to Suzy, most of the missus' were a bit upset as the filth had done a proper job on their homes. Spiteful bastards. He might have to give the boys each an extra bung out of his back pocket to keep their grief-givers sweet.

The door opened, and in walked Suzy in her silk nightie carrying a tray of bacon butties and two mugs of tea. He could see her eyes widen at the dosh strewn across the bed. He knew it would excite her; it always did. It did him too, truth be known. And even though he'd not been on the real blag, he was still buzzing with that post-job high. It was better than drugs, not that he'd ever been tempted on that score. Gear was for morons, but morons who paid whatever they had to to get their next fix. He'd been a little pissed off when he'd received the call the previous evening from his man running the lackeys, but he'd been assured it was all sortable.

'Breakfast, or me first?' Suzy asked, as she joined Dan on the bed.

'Now that's a hard choice, babe. You know how hungry I get when I'm coming down from a buzz.'

'Okay, I'll let you off; butties first, then I want the hard choice,' she said, and they both laughed.

Dan sat up to eat his sandwich and un-muted the TV to watch the news. It was on a channel covering the regional stuff, some press conference at Lancashire pig headquarters. He listened as he chewed.

He half-expected something about the body in the car, he could barely wait until they got that box opened; he might even give Suzy a two-break after that. He'd been disappointed that there had been nothing about the job on the TV so far and was soon disappointed once more as some local DS banged on about some missing from home shite. He finished his food and took a slurp of his tea. He was about to turn the TV off as it was nearly party time with Suzy but noticed that she was still eating so he turned back to the TV. Some reporter was asking the DS, 'Is this in any way connected with the armed robbery which took place in Preston yesterday?' This made Dan turn the sound up, there had obviously been something in the media about the blag; he must have missed it. But then the plod said it was nothing to do with him. So the reporter asked, 'I believe that there were a couple of drug related deaths over in Blackpool yesterday, I take it neither of these are your missing from homes?'

Again, Dan listened intently, and again the reply was non-committal. No harm done. Dickhead users were always going over, no matter what or whose gear they were using, especially in Blackpool. The report came to an end, and he glanced at Suzy who had finished her breakfast. She climbed off the bed. 'Where are you going?' he asked.

'Steady on cowboy, I'm just going to clean my teeth, get the meat out of my mouth.'

A filthy retort flashed through Dan's mind, which he didn't say out loud. But smiled instead. He turned back to the TV as he waited. A Manchester TV news reporter was now talking to some cop civvie about the drug deaths in Blackpool. Cath Moore was her name; an analyst or some shite job – whatever the fuck they did. He was half-listening as he noticed the running tap in the en suite had stopped.

'I personally, saw both of the drug deaths in Blackpool yesterday; in fact, I was with both poor souls just before they lost their lives,' the Moore woman said. Dan turned the sound up. 'And as upsetting as this will no doubt be to the next of kin, family and friends of these two poor young people, of whom our deepest wishes go out to them,' the woman blathered on as he could hear Suzy preparing to leave the bathroom. It always pissed Dan off when they gave that 'our thoughts are with you' bag of bollocks. They never meant it. 'But I want to take the opportunity to warn all cocaine users out there; there is a bad batch of drugs doing the rounds, which led to both these fatalities. Obviously, the police have to conduct post-mortem examinations, but enquires so far have led me to believe that a new dangerous batch of drugs is out there, and I advise all addicts to be very careful. Why not seek treatment, this could be a good time to reach for help and to try and get off the drug merry-go-round,' she added.

'Jesus. Will this woman shut the fuck up?' Dan shouted, as a naked Suzy re-entered the room.

'Who?' Suzy asked.

Dan ignored her as he listened some more.

'One thing I have seen is that users affected start to have problems with their sight; light becomes painful, and their eyes swell up and redden. If you start to feel any of these side-effects, please stop and seek urgent medical advice,' she said.

'You ready, big boy?' Suzy asked, as she slid under the covers on her side of the bed.

'Are you fucking mad?' Dan yelled.' He then threw his empty side plate through the TV screen, sending shards of glass all over the bottom of the bed. Suzy screamed, and Dan jumped off the bed.

'Where are you going, babe?' Suzy asked.

'To sort this before it gets too late.'

CHAPTER TWENTY-NINE

Martin left Cath to head back to HQ. The unfortunate overdose incident was now a full BTP job on behalf of the local coroner. Martin would have a word with the BTP DI, later, and request full toxicology so they could compare the results with the young woman from Central Pier and her boyfriend. Once back in his office he quickly brought Colin up to date before turning his attention back to the murder. 'Have we had any responses from the press appeal? he asked.

'None yet, nor any reported through the normal channels,' Colin replied.

'The trouble is the deceased could be from anywhere. After all, Manning and his team are from Manchester,' Martin said.

'I've already actioned MFH enquires to be replicated in Greater Manchester and Merseyside for starters, but nothing is jumping out.'

'Let's hope the regional reach of Cath's TV address will help with that,' Martin added.

Colin nodded, and then told Martin that he had sent a team comprising of one DS and five DCs to Manchester and had told them not to come back until they had news of where Manning might be. 'The sooner we get our hands on that bastard, the sooner we can ask him who the deceased is,' Colin added.

Martin knew they were in a good position with regard to Manning, insofar as that they already had prima facia evidence against him for the previous murder. They could charge him and get him remanded into custody pretty quickly whilst they built a case against him for the second murder and the robbery. The custody clock would still run down, but whenever they stopped it, they wouldn't have to release him 'under investigation'; he'd go back to being on remand for the charged offences. They could ask the prison service to hold him at Preston Prison so access would be easier too.

Then Colin took a call, and Martin could tell instantly that it was a serious one. He paid attention, though Colin didn't say a lot until its conclusion.

'I see. We are on our way,' Colin finished with, before he ended the call. He then looked stony-faced at Martin, and said, 'That was the lab at Chorley. They've recovered most of the wording from the charred document.'

'What does it say?'

'He wouldn't tell me over the phone. Said, we needed to see it.'

Martin grabbed the car keys and followed Colin out of the office. It was mid-morning so traffic out of Preston was fairly light. They were headed to what had once been the regional, home office forensic science lab when they were publicly owned bodies, which had always been handy. They'd covered most areas of work, though some had specialised in certain areas. Ballistics, for example, had been the specialism of the Birmingham Home Office Forensic Science Lab. Years ago they had all been sold off, which meant you could end up dealing with any lab in any part of the country. Each job would be distributed differently, it was a nightmare. But the Regional Organised Crime Units had an unofficial agreement with each region's Forensic Science Service to try and keep serious crime exhibits local, if at all possible.

Twenty minutes later and they were on the outskirts of Chorley approaching the lab down a single-track lane. The only other premises at the end of it were the headquarters and training facilities of the Lancashire Fire and Rescue Service. Odd neighbours Martin always thought. The lab itself was atypical, sixties or seventies built, and looked more like a sixth form college.

Ten minutes later, they had signed in at reception and been given their visitors' badges. Dr Fenning would meet them shortly, the man on reception had told them.

'Didn't give you any indication at all?' Martin asked Colin again.

'I've already told you.'

'Sorry,' Martin said. 'Inflections in the voice?'

'Concern. Grave concern,' Colin replied.

A long five minutes later, a door opened on the north side of the central waiting area and in walked a small man in his fifties wearing the usual long white coat. He looked like a stereotypical medical doctor but for the lack of a stethoscope round his neck. But he was definitely their doctor as he made a direct line to them. Introductions quickly over, they followed Dr Fenning into his lab where there were several others working on several workbenches. Fenning led them to the furthest one in the open-plan lab and turned a TV monitor round to face them. It was blank.

'As you know, gents, the ink had lifted from the paper due to the heat, and the paper itself was close to collapse. Had our friends from opposite us not been so quick, there would have been nothing left for us to examine.'

Martin followed Colin's lead in smiling and nodding so as not to interrupt the good doctor's flow.

'It was a high-risk strategy by whoever left it, and notwithstanding the fact that they put one fire resistant

166

document case inside a larger one, the plan should have failed.'

'Why didn't it?' Colin asked.

'The centre of the heat was on the body, and although close to, there was a temperature drop. The case itself is probably good to 2,000 degrees and the use of two helped. But we are talking seconds here. A fine margin.'

Martin was impatient for Fenning to get to the point but knew that it would be rude to interrupt the scientist. It was always the same with them, they usually liked to walk detectives through the procedures, it was as important to them, if not more so sometimes, than the eventual evidential outcome. Martin inwardly groaned, as Fenning continued.

'As you are no doubt aware, we can get a lot back from the indentations in the paper, but the thinning of it by the heat did hamper this, so eventually I used a system of ionised air-washing and a chemical we have used for years in treating paper. I take it you are aware that there was no chance of DNA or fingerprint recovery?'

'Yes, thanks, we knew that bit, not that we would have expected our suspect to have been that slack,' Colin replied.

Fenning nodded and continued, 'The pink discolouration you will see is chemical residue.' He then pressed a button on the TV monitor which slowly illuminated. 'The original is being preserved in a sterile environment; here are the photos of it.' The doctor then stood back and allowed Martin and Colin to step in front of him as the monitor fully lit up.

Martin could see a yellow piece of A4-sized paper. The edges were uneven. The whole thing looked very brittle. It reminded him of when as a child, he and his brother used to draw maps of hidden treasure and then stick them in the oven to 'age them'. This looked exactly the same, apart from the red chemical residue. Then Fenning pressed a button on the monitor's remote and the screen scrolled down to a close-up of the recovered typeface. There were three lines, and it was crystal clear. As was its meaning.

THIS IS WHAT HAPPENS TO YOUR DIRTY INFORMANTS. I KNOW WHO HAS BEEN GRASSING ON ME AND THEY SHOULD BE VERY AFRAID. THEY WILL PAY A HEAVY PRICE. I'M GONE NOW. IF YOU COME AFTER ME, MORE WILL DIE.

CHAPTER THIRTY

The journey back to Preston had been a quiet one. A time for reflective anger. Martin's blood was boiling at Manning's arrogance. And he'd never seen Colin's chin so red from grinding his end-of-the-day stubble in. He knew it would soon become redder. Colin had managed to put a call in to Kerry Danson the Force Authorising Officer and without giving her the story, had said enough to persuade her to drop everything and to meet them at their office. The phrase, 'potential critical breach to CHAMPS' had achieved that. By the time they reached their office, each supporting a nitro hot cup of plastic coffee which required a spare polystyrene cup just to keep the burns on the fingers down to second degree, Kerry was already there waiting for them.

'That was quick,' Colin said, as they entered.

'The words 'critical' and 'breach' can have that effect on a gal,' Kerry said.

Martin asked if she wanted a brew, and when she said that she did, he gave her his, he couldn't be bothered going back to the machine. 'I'd give it a week or two to cool down first,' he said, as he placed it on his desk in front of her. He took a spare chair as Colin plonked himself behind his desk. They all sat in silence for what seemed like an age before Colin broke the impasse and told Kerry what had happened.

Martin just watched the colour drain from her face as she took in Colin's words. A moment or two passed before she responded. 'How close are we to ID-ing the body?' she asked.

'According to the lab there might be some DNA recoverable from the bone marrow, but they are not hopeful. There is some dried sludge in one of the femurs, but it's not been tested yet. It was a hot fire,' Colin replied.

'The body?' she asked.

'A burnt, blackened crisp; you should see it,' Colin replied.

Martin could see Kerry recoil at the thought.

'Teeth?' she then asked.

'Smashed with a blunt object post-mortem, but there will be some roots,' Colin replied. This was news to Martin. No good for a dental match but could hold some DNA.

'Just because Mad Manning has fingered some poor sod as being a snout, doesn't mean he's right. He could just be bigging his arrogant arse up, to put the wind up us,' Martin said.

'Or trying to make us alter what we are doing, to make us act differently,' Colin joined in with.

'How many sources do you have on the books reporting on Manning?' Colin asked.

Kerry didn't respond. Martin could see her inner torment, wrestling with what, under any other circumstances, would be a very inappropriate question.

'These are extraordinary events. Normal protocols need to be put to one side,' Colin added.

'Need to know, and we need to know,' Martin added.

'Need to know, backed up with a signed non-disclosure contract?' Kerry asked.

Martin and Colin nodded.

'Okay, but first, I don't get how anyone could access the serious level two and three intel before the last two days of the migration. I've double checked,' she said.

'Assuming any breach is from Bashir,' Martin added.

'If it's not Bashir, then who? Me?' Kerry spat.

Martin held his hands up and replied, 'Of course not. But it could be from somewhere else. A corrupt handler?'

'If a second informant was reporting on Manning, then that person would be handled by different handlers. And neither would be aware of the other's existence. Just me,' Kerry said, and then added, "I know who has been grassing on me and they should be very afraid" he bragged in the note, using the plural "they". So if Manning has access to CHAMPS, it cannot be from an individual handler.'

'Which leads us back to Bashir,' Colin said.

'But even if it can only be Bashir, how or why would he be involved with Manning?' Martin asked.

No one spoke for a moment, but then Martin answered his own question, 'Unless Manning is also involved someway in the drugs importation.'

'It just gets worse,' Colin added.

'But don't forget that Bashir's access was limited insofar as that the important stuff was not visible to him before his access expired,' Kerry said.

'Unless . . .' Martin said, feeling queasy at the thought racing through his mind.

'Unless what?' Colin and Kerry managed to say in perfect unison.

'Manning was an out of force target. Planning an armed robbery using Manchester villains. And even though it was a Lancashire investigation, what if the system pigeonholed the intelligence as "out-of-force" by mistake?' Martin asked.

'After all, he is wanted for a murder in Manchester,'

Colin added.

Kerry went white again, and asked if she could borrow Martin's terminal, which he quickly unlocked and then stood away from her to give her some privacy.

Three or four long minutes later, she closed down the screen and turned to face them both. 'Fucking bollocks,' she started with, which startled Martin, but only for a second.

'I'm afraid your hunch is correct. The intel on Manning had been put into the out-of-force folder by the system during the files' migration from the old hard drive onto CHAMPS,' she added.

'So Bashir could have seen it?' Colin asked.

'Absolutely, and as his temporary access was linked to mine with no audit trail, we have no way of confirming or denying it,' she added.

'So we have to assume the worst until we know different,' Colin said.

Kerry nodded.

They had to assume that Bashir had access to and had seen the intelligence relating to Manning. How much so, they had no way of knowing. And secondly, there is now a connection between Bashir and Manning that they knew nothing about hitherto. A plausible explanation being that Manning was involved with Bashir in the drugs importation somehow.

Then Martin turned to face Kerry, 'Okay,' he said, paused, and then added, 'time to declare how many sources you have reporting on Manning.'

Kerry didn't respond but turned back towards Martin's computer screen. After several minutes it was clear that she was going to be some time, so Martin pulled the spare chair over to Colin's desk and between them they wrote up their policy logs and agreed a number of urgent actions that needed doing pronto. Then Martin dialled the telephone number Abdul's father had given him. As previously, it rang straight to answer machine. He left a further message, imploring Abdul to call back as a matter of urgency. He was probably standing on his handlers' toes a bit but was working on the assumption that if Abdul did want out, and had gone away because of it, he might respond more favourably to a call from Martin rather than his ex-handlers. He noted that Kerry had finished pummelling his keyboard but was staring at the screen nonetheless; she was waiting for something.

Next, Martin rang the telephony unit and asked if they could track Abdul's phone. They said they would need Kerry's approval, so that shouldn't be a problem. Martin said that he had it verbally and would follow it up with the requisite paperwork ASAP. He saw Colin raise an eyebrow in his direction as the words left his mouth. The duty officer at the telephony unit said they could only try once the phone went live again. While it was switched off there was nothing they could do, but they'd let him know as and when anything changed, so long as the written authority landed today. When Martin came off the phone, Kerry was still staring at the computer screen whilst trying to sip some of Martin's coffee. He quickly ran the telephony request past her, and she just nodded her approval.

Then a *dinging* sound rang out from Martin's desktop, which surprised him as he hadn't realised it was fitted with speakers. Worth remembering. Then he watched Kerry blow out an audible sigh as she closed down the screen once more. Both Martin and Colin looked at her.

'Well, that's some relief,' she started. Neither man spoke. 'I was fairly sure that we only had the one source reporting on Manning and his robbery team, and the system quickly confirmed this, however, I couldn't be sure that somebody elsewhere wasn't also talking about Manning, so I've sent out an AO to All AOs Red Flag request.'

It had been a few years since Martin had been involved in the running and managing of informants and had no idea what she meant and said so. Kerry quickly explained that in exceptional circumstances any AO in the country could do a systematic search via all AOs' Urgent Mutual Access Network – or UMAD for short - to check if an individual was being reported on elsewhere. Martin smiled at the acronym. Normal system cross-checking should flag this up, but, if for example a CHIS had ceased to be authorised, then maybe not. Had Kerry's request hit a positive she would have received a 'wait' message and her mobile would have been rung by whichever AO had suddenly felt toe ache.

'So if I have this correct, the only source reporting on Manning anywhere in the UK is the one you have?' Colin asked.

'Confirmed,' Kerry replied.

'And even if Bashir saw the source file, he wouldn't know the identity of the source?' Martin added.

'Hundred percent, but that doesn't mean Manning couldn't have worked it out from the actual intelligence. Say, if a nickname was used and Manning only told one person about it or whatever. It shouldn't happen, we guard against it, but you can only guard against what you know about,' Kerry added.

'What do you mean?' Colin asked.

'Well, say the source refers to the target as TC – as in Top Cat, a friendly nickname – and thinks others do too; but they don't, and the target is only called TC by one person; the source,' Kerry said.

Both men nodded, Martin knew how hard it could be. CHIS's were trained to avoid such pitfalls, but it often happened, human nature. Kerry's was an obvious example, but it illustrated it for Colin's benefit.

'And we've no real way of knowing further, whether

that link or compromise has been made?' Colin asked.

'Afraid not,' Kerry said.

Suddenly feeling Kerry's pressure, Martin jumped in and added, 'But look on the bright side, Colin, we only have potentially one source compromised, and therefore only have one to protect.'

'Assuming of course that Manning wasn't correct in his belief that the body in the boot was indeed the true informant,' Colin said.

'An easy one to sort out,' Martin said, and then turned to face Kerry and added, 'You just need to ring the real source now.'

'Ah, that's where it starts to get tricky,' Kerry said.

'Why?' asked Colin.

'Because we've already lost contact with the source and don't know where he is,' Kerry said.

'Oh shit,' Colin said.

Shit indeed. Maybe Manning guessed right.

'And that's not the worst of it,' she added.

Both men turned to face her again. Martin saw her take a deep breath.

'Because the source reporting on Manning was our mutual friend, Abdul.'

CHAPTER THIRTY-ONE

'Oh bollocks,' Martin said, as he took in the news from Kerry Danson.

'Doesn't mean it's Abdul,' Colin said. 'He could have still fingered the wrong bloke?'

Martin didn't answer as he was already keying in the number he had for Abduls' father. It rang and was answered quickly. Martin used the guise that he wondered if the father had had a chance to speak to Abdul since Martin's visit. To see if he could add anything re their flag-abusing neighbour issue.

Two minutes later, Martin was off the phone and turned to the others. 'His wife apparently spoke to him on the number we have for him, but they can't say exactly when, other than that it was a couple of days ago.'

'So we are no wiser?' Colin said.

'They've tried since, but it remains switched off. I asked if that was normal when he "went away on business" and the father said it was if he went overseas. But then he quickly added that he did not know whether he was or not.'

'Passport?' Kerry asked.

'I asked that, but they just said he always takes it with him, even when he is not expecting to travel far, just in case.'

'They hiding something?' Colin asked.

'I'm truly not sure,' Martin said. 'Maybe they are just being protective.'

'So maybe he has just gone to ground for a bit,' Kerry said.

'Or maybe we have one dead ex-CHIS,' Colin said.

No one spoke for a moment or two, and then Kerry did. 'I'd better give the chief a bell.'

'Rather you than me,' Colin said.

'He'll probably want to see us all, so don't get too comfy,' she said, as she picked up the internal phone handset on Martin's desk and started to dial.

After listening to Kerry briefly outline where they were to the chief, there seemed to be a lot of listening and Martin noticed her cheeks flush slightly before she ended the call.

'What did he say?' Colin asked.

'Other than, he wants us all in his office ASAP, you don't want to know,' she replied.

They all left together, and Martin drove behind Kerry's car for the short trip to force headquarters. It gave all of them twenty minutes to collect their thoughts before they sat down with Don Rogers. He'd want answers and suggestions. The more Martin saw of the real Don Rogers, as opposed to his public persona, the more he liked him. He particularly liked his direct approach, but it also could be tiring. It kept them on their toes, which was clearly his management style. Rogers was an ex-guardsman and it shone through.

'The trouble is we have absolutely no way of knowing if the deceased is Abdul,' Colin said.

'Unless he turns up, or the DNA search comes good,' Martin said.

'And even if he does turn up, we still won't know who our deceased is,' Colin added.

It was a perverse situation they were in. If the body was Abdul's, then they could assume that Bashir had informed Manning that there was a source reporting on him, without realising that it was his own brother. And that Manning had somehow worked out that Abdul was the source, but without knowing it was Bashir's sibling. What a bizarre turn up that would be. He voiced his thoughts.

Colin added, 'Granted that Bashir could never have realised the source he was informing Manning about, was in fact his own brother.'

'Which has thereby led to his death, by his own disclosures,' Martin said. It was almost too weird to contemplate.

'Imagine how Bashir is going to feel, or react, when he finds out,' Colin said.

'I know. But until we have established the identity of the body for certain – assuming that it is Abdul – we can use this to our advantage before we know for sure,' Martin added.

'Go on,' Colin said, as he turned to face Martin.

'Well, he may have contact numbers or information about how to get in touch with his brother that the wife and father don't have.'

'Ah, this gets even more perverse,' Colin said.

'All we need is a cover story as to why we need to speak to Bashir's brother,' Martin said.

'We can do it on the back of your visit to his home address and the flag abuser stuff,' Colin said, suddenly sounding more positive. 'You can say that during your visit, the family let it slip in natural conversation that Abdul's brother worked for the police.'

'I think his dad did, if I remember correctly.' It was worth a go.

Both sat in silence as Martin indicated to leave the Longton bypass and then approached the gated entrance to headquarters. There was a queue waiting to pass the sentry and Martin could see Kerry's car two down from them. At least now they had something to suggest to Rogers instead of walking in empty.

Ten minutes later Martin and Colin followed Kerry into the chief's office. He was pacing the floor as they entered. Martin was last in and closed the heavy mahogany door behind him. As soon as it clicked shut, Rogers stopped in his tracks and turned to face them.

'If it takes us until we all retire, I want Bashir, Yates and Manning locked up. I didn't think I could be any angrier than when I had to accept that two of our own were bad. But this note thing has sent me into the stratosphere. The arrogant bastard. If he was an enemy combatant and I was still in The Guards, we, we, would take him outside . . .' Rogers said.

Martin could see him wrestling with a mixture of anguish and restraint as he forced himself not to finish his sentence.

'We are all fully committed, sir,' Colin said.

'And none of you will be allowed to retire until we do,' Rogers said, before he turned his attention to Kerry. 'Are we absolutely sure that Bashir could not have seen any other intel?'

'Not exactly,' Kerry started, and then quickly continued as Rogers's jaw started to open. 'But we know he could not have seen any level two or three intel on Lancashire operations.'

Rogers's jaw started to close. Then it grew wider again. Kerry jumped in. 'There were only a handful of "out-of-force" intel reports in the folder Bashir could have seen, and staff are working hard now to avoid any compromise. But the only intel in it involving the northwest region is the stuff about Manning, as he is normally a Manchester nominal. A glitch of the migration between the two systems which we could not have foreseen. Perversely, it was why Bashir had the temporary access, to help deal with such unintended issues.'

'You couldn't make it up,' Rogers said. 'Okay, plan of action?'

It was Colin's turn to jump in, 'As my sergeant, likes to say: "he has a Baldrick".'

'What?' Rogers said.

'A cunning plan, my Lord,' Martin added.

Rogers's grimace broke into a smile, the pressure eased a little. Then Martin outlined what he and Colin had discussed in the car.

CHAPTER THIRTY-TWO

It was late by the time Bashir arrived home after all the dramas in Blackpool, and as usual his good lady wife had shown her indignation of his late arrival with the usual amount of tactical silence. It suited him; it had been a trying day. He lived in a quiet cul-de-sac in Fulwood, a residential area of north Preston. The house was a modest three bedroom semi-detached, and he had no children. Another issue which, when raised, would cause his wife to have further periods of silence.

He had been quietly overpaying his mortgage for some time now, and although only ten years into its term of twenty-five, he had nearly paid it off. He was looking forward to the time when he could sell up and move away and live out the rest of his life in the manner that he thought befitting of him. Until then he'd have to carry on with his humdrum job and his outwardly unremarkable life. He was very aware of not raising any suspicion.

He also looked forward to the day when he was no longer in Manning's pocket. Not that he had ever met him, but he was fully aware of the maniac's reputation, and if his go-between was anything to go by, it was all justified. The intermediary himself was scary enough. And he knew that notwithstanding their reputation for violence and the stereotypical view that all nutters where thick; these two were different. They had carefully played to his greed, getting him to do the smallest of favours and then subtly upping the odds with each further request. He even tried to find the guy from the mosque who had first approached him on their behalf but was told he had gone back to Pakistan. He'd accepted that then, but now had little doubt that he had been all part of the setup. They had wanted someone who worked for the police and had access to IT systems, and he had ticked all the boxes.

It was when he was in too deep that they hit him with the importation jobs. He'd initially refused, but then they told him what would happen if he didn't comply; he quickly changed his mind. That said, he had become more relaxed with each run, until the last one when he nearly had a heart attack. But Yates had made a valid point, the new drug, this Sky White, had passed the test being moved around in the egg timer, and he had been paid very well by Manning over the previous runs.

He had toyed with the idea of legging it fairly soon, he had already amassed a decent amount; enough to sell up and disappear and have a comfortable life. His wife was welcome to join him, but he wasn't fussed if she chose not to.

He'd meant to catch up with his brother, Abdul, the other night and had failed again yesterday evening, so he'd dig him out at the weekend.

Now sat at his desk at police headquarters, he finished his reflections and turned back to his computer screen when the phone in his pocket vibrated. Not his day phone, the other one; the one which was usually on silent. He knew who was calling and swallowed before he answered.

'You told me it was sorted,' the intermediary started with.

'It is, I promise.'

'You not catch the TV news recently then?'

He hadn't and said so. Then he had to listen in silence as the intermediary told him about Cath Moore's TV broadcast. He hadn't known the reporter's name, but it rang a familiar bell.

'The top man is far from happy. This could kill our new market before we get established. And if that happens, it'll have all been for nothing.'

The bitch, she had been lying through her teeth when she'd promised Minty that she wouldn't report anything. 'But she promised,' he offered weakly.

'She's twirled you. She's not a reporter; she's semi-filth. And now there's been another death, in Preston. So that's three now.'

This was all news to Bashir, and he swallowed again.

'No one would give a fuck how many dickheads kill themselves normally, but if they all get linked back to our gear that your Blackpool knobhead is dealing for us, then this could be bad for business.'

'What's the top man said?' Bashir asked, nearly using Manning's name. He only just stopped himself, which would have put the intermediary over the top. He'd been warned long ago to never ever to use real names on the phone. You just never knew who was or who could be listening.

'She needs silencing, one way or another, but that's not why I'm ringing you,' the intermediary said.

Bashir swallowed on hearing this and felt terror rush through him as he realised where he had heard the name Cath Moore before. She was a field intelligence analyst, for God's sake. He felt physically ill.

'Why . . .? Er, what do you want me to do?' Bashir asked.

'The top man wants a face-to-face with you.'

Bashir's legs turned to jelly. The reason why he had

never met Manning and had always worked through this intermediary was for operational security, pure and simple. So why would Manning want to change that now. It could only mean one thing. 'Look, er, I'll get this sorted somehow, there is no need for Mr erm . . . I mean the top man, to do anything rash. You know you can trust me. I mean, why would he want to see me?'

'Don't shit your pants.'

'Don't forget, it was me who warned him about the informant, the one talking about—'

'Shut the fuck up, will you. Now get a grip.'

'Well, what does he want?'

'Just a favour, similar to what you've just mentioned. That's all you need to know,' the intermediary said, and then gave him the details of the meeting before he ended the call without pleasantries.

He'd only just put the burner phone back in his jacket pocket when a hard knock at his door nearly put him over the edge. 'Come in,' he said, trying to sound normal. The door opened and in walked a plain-clothed individual in his thirties. 'How can I help you?' Bashir asked, noting that his voice had returned to something similar to customary.

'I'm Detective Sergeant Martin Draker, and I'm after a favour,' the detective said. 'You alright? You look like you have seen a ghost.'

'Yes, I'm just busy, I carry a lot of responsibility,' Bashir replied.

'Okay, well it's about your brother, Abdul,' Draker said.

This took Bashir by surprise. 'How do you know my brother?' Bashir asked, trying to hide the trepidation creeping back through him.

'I just need to have a chat with him, and I'm struggling to get hold of him. I wondered if you might have a more appropriate contact number than the one that I've been

184

trying?'

Bashir's mind was swirling now, whatever did a DS want with Abdul? He asked his question without answering the DS's.

'Nothing to worry about, just need his number. You know, the one you use,' Draker pushed.

Bashir could feel heat in his cheeks and just hoped that they weren't too red. He took the opportunity to look down at his normal phone which was next to his keyboard as he spoke. 'Yes erm, of course, but can you tell me what it is about?'

'It's just about some anti-social neighbour in his street. I know he is working away, and I just need a quick chat with him. We are trying to build a case against the neighbour; I was just hoping that Abdul might have some info to add. I've talked to his wife and your father, who happened to mention that you worked for us, so as I was up here today anyway, I thought I'd pop in rather than ring you.'

It was all Bashir could do to stop himself from exhaling out loud as he kept his head down and researched his phone's contact list. Draker went on a bit further talking about some pain in the arse who lived a few doors down from Abdul who hated anything Asian. He vaguely remembered his brother mentioning it once, as if he could do something about it. He'd told him to call the normal police; he must have taken his advice. Bashir wrote Abdul's mobile phone number on a piece of paper and looked up for the first time in a minute as he handed it to the DS. 'I know he works away a lot, and is often incommunicado when he does, but if you leave a message, tell him I gave you the number and he should call you back.'

'What does he do exactly?' Draker asked.

Bashir wasn't too sure himself; he'd never shown too much interest in what his brother did for a living. He knew he drifted between things. 'Buying and selling this and that, I think. Not too sure what.'

'No worries.' Draker said. 'Thanks for this.' He put the piece of paper in his pocket and turned to leave.

'Oh, Sergeant?' Bashir called after Draker, who turned in the doorway to face back towards him.

'Yes?'

'Give him my regards when you speak and tell him I'll catch up with him at the weekend, will you?'

'Yes, of course,' Draker said, who then turned and left.

As soon as the door swung closed, Bashir exhaled audibly.

CHAPTER THIRTY-THREE

As soon as Martin walked back into the office his boss was on his feet, and asked, 'How'd it go?'

'Better than expected,' Martin replied.

'What, you've spoken to Abdul?'

'No, but we have a new number for him, so I have left a message referencing his brother Bashir. I'm hopeful he'll ring back when he can. I've made it clear I just want to talk about the anti-social neighbour, and that I'm not chasing him to work for us again. Though, I did mention that he is due some wages, but that all I wanted regardless of that was a minute of his time over the phone.'

'Fingers crossed,' Colin said. 'But which bit was "better than expected"?'

'I just asked for his brother's personal number at first and didn't answer when he asked for a reason.'

'Why?'

'Thought I'd let his guilt assume the worst, just for a few moments. Didn't want to push it too far but did keep my questions business-like and gave no reason at first.'

'How did he react?'

'Nearly shat himself.'

'Interesting.'

'That's what I thought,' Martin said.

'So when you gave him the excuse about the neighbour as to why you wanted Abdul's number, how did he swallow that?'

'My little misdirection helped sell it. Once he realised that I was only after Abdul's number because of the anti-social stuff, he lapped it up like a Greyhound drinking water after a race.'

'We'll have to just sit back and wait now,' Colin said.

Martin nodded as he plonked himself behind his desk. He really hoped Abdul would ring back soon. He knew it would put them back to the start as regard to identifying who the deceased was, and that regardless of that, some poor soul had lost their life in the most horrific of ways. He just couldn't help hoping it wasn't Abdul. He'd taken an instant liking to him when they'd briefly met, and the longer it went on with no contact, the worse it looked. He knew Colin had already made up his mind that the deceased was Abdul, and he sort of knew it probably was too, he just hoped it wasn't. But how they were ever going to identify the body officially was anyone's guess. That arrogant bastard Manning had done a proper job this time. He'd obviously learned from his mistakes when he'd killed his ex-girlfriend in Manchester, eighteen months ago; then, he'd left his DNA around the strangulation marks on her neck. No chance of any body-linking evidence this time.

Colin said he had to brief the enquiry team and issue some new actions. They had jointly agreed to keep back some of the more sensitive stuff, just for the moment. Normally, Martin would have argued vehemently against this, he was always of the opinion that if you couldn't trust your handpicked team, then who the hell could you trust. But the original intel from Abdul had stated that a local DC, Jim Grantham, who worked on the CID at Lea nick, in northwest Preston, was working corruptly with

Bashir, and they didn't know if he was alone. God, they could only hope so, he could have bent mates across Preston for all they knew.

He just hoped that when they eventually did give their team the fullest brief, they would forgive them and understand the need for total secrecy in this case. For Martin, it harked back to when he'd been a DC working on murders and was eventually given the full story by the SIOs when they'd held stuff back. It tended to rankle, and you'd lose some of your respect for those running the job. Who knew how one's enquires may have been unwittingly skewed by not asking a question you might otherwise have asked, had you known all the facts. Opportunities, often critical ones on murder inquiries, were easily missed this way. The Yorkshire Ripper jumped easily to mind. Even though that was more about an old-fashioned paper recording system failing to cross-reference things, but imagine if Peter Sutcliffe had had a known hammer fetish, and that had been held back from the enquiry team at the beginning . . .

He shook himself from his thoughts and left Colin to do the briefing while he checked in with Cath to see if she'd recovered from the revelations of the previous day, in Blackpool and at Preston railway station. He dialled her mobile and she answered quickly. He asked after her and she said she was fine. She sounded as if she was back to her usual self.

'Will I see you today?' she asked.

'Maybe later on, but I can't promise anything yet,' he replied.

'You know this "absence makes the heart grow fonder" or whatever, is all rubbish.'

Martin smiled before he responded, 'You sure about that?'

'I guess we'll find out. With your job, after six months I should be throwing myself at your feet every time I see you.'

Martin smiled again and asked where she was up to with her drugs research.

'The bastards who are pedalling that eye-popping shite need to be tied down and made to take it themselves,' she said.

'Granted, but actually laying hands on the bad guys is our job. I don't want you taking risks in that area, just because you are driven by recent events,' he said, and immediately regretted his choice of words. He hadn't meant to sound condescending in any way, he was just concerned. The following silence told him all he needed to know, so he jumped back in quickly. 'Sorry, I'm just being overprotective.'

'None taken,' Cath said. 'But without my intelligence package, those of you who do the laying of hands won't know where to lay them.'

'A fair point well made,' Martin conceded.

They both laughed, offence averted.

Then Cath carried on, 'Look, I'm pretty much deskbound for at least today. I'm trying to establish if any other drug deaths elsewhere in the country, have had this eye thing and gone unnoticed, and then been written off as "normal" drug overdoses.'

Very smart, and it was a line of enquiry that they had not thought to follow yet. God forbid that this Sky White, or whatever it was called, was more widespread. 'That's probably a very good question.'

'Probably?' she answered.

'Definitely, I meant.'

'Better.'

'I hope your research draws a blank; in the nicest possible way,' Martin added.

'So do I, but if there is any hint that it's more than local, we will need to go loud and proud on it, ASAP.'

'Totally agree. Will you give me the heads-up if it is

starting to look that way?'

'Sure. Look, I've got to go, the internet and my phone are waiting,' Cath said, before ending the call.

Colin came back into their office.

'You look glum?'

Martin iterated his conversation with Cath.

'Christ, we've been so focused; we've not stopped to consider the wider issues properly,' Colin said.

'I know.'

'And as the DCI, that's really my failing.'

'Don't beat yourself up; we are both guilty as charged.'

'She really should be a detective, that one,' Colin added. Martin could only nod in agreement. 'So what should we do next?'

'I have an idea. I checked earlier and discovered that Inspector Debbie Yates is off duty at midday. She will be booking off from Bispham police station north of Blackpool. Do you fancy putting your surveillance skills to the test? Unofficially.'

Now this did surprise Martin. Colin was usually a stickler for the rules. And perhaps Colin could see the uncertainty in his face as he carried on, 'It'll take a day to draw up the authority for an official surveillance, well, it will if I am writing it, and more over it'll take a week to organise a surveillance team as it will have to come from elsewhere in the region, for obvious reasons.'

'Granted,' Martin said.

'All I'm suggesting is that we are passing Bispham at midday and find ourselves behind the good Inspector Yates! Let's see where she goes without taking any risks. It might help justify a fully authorised surveillance should we need one.'

Martin jumped to his feet and said, 'Absolutely.' They both headed to the door and Martin turned back to face his boss who was right behind him, 'I'm loving the new you, Colin.'

Colin grinned and said, 'Don't get too used to it, but I do make the odd exception. And I'm getting a bit fed up with chasing all these bent bastards with a badge.'

CHAPTER THIRTY-FOUR

Manning was stood outside his rented Barn Conversion out in the sticks between Manchester and Yorkshire. An ideal spot for now as it was quiet and remote, but as picturesque as it was, he reckoned it would be pretty bleak in winter. Not that he planned to be here that long. He checked his watch again and then heard the sound of a car engine approaching and looked up. He could see Gazza behind the wheel of the dark blue Vauxhall Astra as he pulled over in front of him. He got in the front passenger seat and Gazza pulled away from the kerb. Manning had known Gazza since school, and now both in their late thirties, he'd never had cause to mistrust him. He was solid gold, and the only person he truly opened up to. 'Nice motor, small, nippy and instantly forgettable.'

'We aim to please, Dan,' Gazza said.

'Where'd you get it from?'

'Got a mate with a yard in Rochdale, this one's due for the crusher. He said once we're done with it that he'll kick his cabin door in and report it missing to the filth.'

'Nice one,' Manning said.

'Like I said, we—'

'—aim to please, I know. How much?'

'Two hundred of your hard stolen money,' Gazza said.

Both men burst out laughing. Then Manning pulled a baseball cap out of his pocket and put it on, pulling the peak down over his eyes.

'Which you want to do first?' Gazza asked.

'Let's try the tits with a gob, before we see Bash the Bishop.'

'At least if we miss her, we can try again after we've seen Bash the Bishop.'

'That's what I reckoned,' Manning said, and then leaned back into his seat and put one of his feet on the dashboard. 'How sure was he with the address?'

'Gave it large being head of IT, even accessed their HR systems whilst I was on the phone to him. Just handy that she lives in Manchester. He also told me that she used to work for the *Manchester Evening Post* before she joined the filth's firm.'

Manning nodded; Gazza had done good.

'He shat himself when I rang him back, then couldn't wait to give me what I wanted.'

Manning smiled and nodded, again.

They were soon down from the foothills of the Pennines and driving on main roads with far more traffic. Every time Manning saw a police car he slunk further down into his seat and dropped his head down. He also checked the speedo every time; a pull, followed by a pat down by some efficient filth was the last thing they needed. But he needn't worry with Gazza driving; nice and sedate.

An hour later they were outside the bitch's home address, but it appeared empty, so Gazza knocked on the door and after getting no reply, he tried a neighbour with a spurious reason. They struck lucky; apparently the neighbour had clocked her going out a while ago dressed up to the nines. And when the neighbour had complimented her, she'd said she was off to have a drink with her old editor mate at the Post. Gazza knew where the paper's office was and soon had them on Deansgate in the city centre of Manchester. A hustle and bustle thoroughfare with a mixture of high-end shops, pubs, restaurants and café bars; with a number of non-retail businesses weaved in too. Gazza pulled into a side street and stopped.

'It's just a bit further down, but there are few places to stop without drawing attention,' Gazza said.

'Can we keep the motor if we need to come back?' Manning asked.

'Yeah, for two hundred a day.'

'We'll give it a go now, you never know, but we can always go back to her gaff at a time of our choosing. It will scare her more there. Plus, I can't be arsed to sit around waiting.'

'Not a problem,' Gazza said.

Manning looked at his watch, it was 4.55 p.m. 'Come on, we can risk five minutes sat on Deansgate.'

Gazza nodded and did a three-point turn in the side street and drove them back onto Deansgate before pulling over on a double yellow.

'Just past that Costa coffee gaff, on the left,' Gazza said.

Manning lifted the peak of his cap up slightly so he could get a clearer look. The shop next to the coffee shop looked as if it had been closed down, but the one after that had MANCHESTER EVENING POST painted on its opaque front window. Above it was the words, *News and stories from the community, that YOU can trust.*

At the stroke of five, a blue glass door next to the opaque main window opened and several men and women, mainly women, left.

'The last one, that's the editor,' Gazza said. 'Seen her photo in the paper.'

Manning leaned forward and took in as much as he could. He'd remember her again, she was top totty, but the others were forgettable. 'Can't see the tits with a gob, can you?'

'No.'

'It's not the fit one at the end, is it, next to the top totty? It has a look of her,' Manning said, suddenly leaning closer to the windscreen.

'I've only seen her on TV briefly, like you Dan, and I'm as sure as I can be that that is not her.'

'Hmm, I guess.'

Then Gazza pulled his smartphone out and played with it for a minute before showing Manning the screen. He looked at it; it was an online news story repeating the details from the earlier broadcast with a photo of the police analyst, Cath Moore, next to it. She had a similar look to the fit one walking away from them, but Gazza was probably right. It wasn't her. 'Come on, let's do one; time to go and see Bash the Bishop.'

'Do you want me to ring my mate re the motor?'

'Yeah, but tell him it's a hundred a day after today. And if the cheeky bastard doesn't like it, I'll cut his balls off and torch his yard.'

Manning was soon regretting coming all the way into central Manchester at five o'clock on a workday. He also regretted not making the meeting with Bash the Bishop until much later. As it was, it would be six-thirty at least before they reached the motorway services. Gazza texted Bashir while they were crawling along the M602 out of Manchester to tell him that they'd be late and then commented that it wouldn't do any harm. It would keep the little shit nice and nervous, and that was true. Just how he liked people to be when he wanted something from them. Eventually, they passed the one-mile marker board for Charnock Richard services on the M6 in Lancashire. Manning had relaxed after they'd left Greater Manchester but didn't want to go as far as Preston. He was wanted in both cities. 'I know you have done all the dealings with him, but he's never met you, has he?' he asked Gazza.

'No, I never even gave him a name. He sometimes calls me the intermediary.'

'Well, you may as well stay in the motor then. There's no reason to expose you, too. Just tell him to park up, pull his rear-view mirror to one side, and if he doesn't keep looking forward, I'll maim him.'

Both men laughed. 'Don't suppose it matters long-term if he sees you either?' Gazza asked.

'Not really, but it'll add to the tension.'

Two minutes later, they pulled onto the main car park of the northbound services. There was also a hotel here, near to an exit that led onto some residential streets; a great place for any meeting, which was why Manning liked the location.

'There he is.' Gazza said, and pointed. At the edge of the car park, well away from the service station customers' cars, was a lone motor parked face-in near to, but not on, the hotel's car park. No man's land. Gazza parked their Astra directly behind Bash the Bishop's car, three spaces back, and kept his engine running and headlights on, blinding any view to the rear Bash may have had via his mirrors.

'This won't take long,' Manning said, and pulled his baseball cap down once more and reached for the door handle. He was about to open it when Gazza put his hand on his arm. Manning turned back to face him, 'What is it, mate?'

'I was just thinking, as he's never seen either of us, so as not to put you at greater risk of exposure, why don't I be you? I can alter my voice; you can tell me what to say.'

Gazza was a top bloke, but Manning wanted to judge Bashir for himself, and Bash shouldn't see him properly if he did as he was told. 'I wouldn't expose either of us normally, but – no offence – I want to hear him, sense him, and judge him, before I ask my next favour.'

'Think he might be a grass himself?' Gazza asked.

'Hopefully we've got rid of the filthy grassing bastard that was shafting us; I just want to make sure that there are no more. Hence my favour.'

Gazza started to nod as if he'd caught Manning's drift, and said, 'Pointless asking him to find any other grass, if he's one, too?'

'That's what I was thinking,' Manning said.

'With you now.'

'And if he is a grass and we need to off him, it should be me who makes that call,' Manning said.

'Fair enough.'

'Plus, as soon as we can get the recipe for Sky White from the Indians, we won't need Bash to do any more runs for us,' Manning added.

'So his shelf-life will expire then, anyway,' Gazza said.

'Exactly, we can bin his Blackpool girlfriend too. No need for any more field tests once the gear is right.'

'So you want to maximise him while we still have him,' Gazza said, nodding again.

'Got it in one. He's fried either way; I just want to make sure I can trust him before I give him his final grass-finding task.'

'Never considered that he could be a double agent, nice one, Dan.'

'To be honest, I don't think he's got the balls, but I need to make sure.'

'And what if he is?'

'Another reason I like this spot for a meeting is that there is no CCTV between the services and the hotel. So if he is, only you and I will be leaving.'

'I'll flash you if there is any drama approaching,' Gazza said.

'Cheers. It shouldn't take long,' Manning finished and then got out of the car and started to walk to the one in front.

CHAPTER THIRTY-FIVE

Earlier in the day.

As Martin and Colin headed out of Preston Central police station, they passed uniformed Inspector Laverty, the Geographic Inspector for the Avenham district of Preston. It was the guy Martin had spoken to about the flag-abuser, Michael Staining. 'Hang on, Colin, just had a thought.' Martin said, bringing them both to a halt. 'Ian, you got a sec?' he shouted after the officer.

Laverty spun round and smiled. Martin and Colin approached. Martin quickly introduced Colin and then asked, 'Just wondering how you are getting on with Staining? And was my statement any help?'

'Your statement will go a long way to supporting the anti-social behavioural restraints and eviction strategy, thanks for doing it so quickly. As regards, to Staining himself, he seems to have gone a bit quiet for the moment.'

'I suppose that is good,' Martin said.

'Good in one way, but bad insofar as flying in the face of the picture we are trying to paint of him to the CPS, and ultimately the courts. I mean, don't get me wrong, if he was to remain quiet and alter his behaviour; I would be over the moon. But in my experience his sort has peaks and troughs. Very reactive and unpredictable, you think you are getting through and then something sparks them off again, and it's the neighbours who have to bear the brunt.'

'I see; a lull before the next storm?'

'Can be. My staff have been around several times in order to talk to him and put him on notice in no uncertain terms what we will do, or plan to do, if he doesn't behave. It can prove to be powerful evidence against him in securing an order when he's been officially warned and chosen to ignore it.'

'Can't bleat to the courts that he promises to change his ways if they are lenient with him, if he's already had his chance, I guess,' Martin said.

'Exactly. And the fact we can't get a reply at the door means to me that he realises we are on his case, and he is therefore avoiding us. I'll send someone round daily, and who knows, that might actually work.'

'Love your optimism,' Martin said.

'Cheers. Anyway, I'd better get on,' Laverty said.

Then Martin asked the question he'd really stopped the inspector for. 'Couldn't ask you a small favour, could I?'

'Sure, fire away.'

'Well, as you know I was in the street originally wanting to speak to Abdul on another non-related matter.'

'Yes, of course, it's when his father opened up to you.'

'Well, I can't seem to get hold of Abdul; he seems to be working away. I just wondered if you could ask your staff to keep an eye open when they are in the area or doing the daily visits to Staining's house. If they see that he is home, I could do with knowing, day or night.'

'Not a problem, consider it done,' Laverty said, and then he turned and hurried off.

Once out of earshot, Colin said, 'Nice one, worth a try.

But you know what I think?'

'I know, Colin, you think he is never coming home.'

Traffic to the Fylde coast was fairly light at this time of day, and Martin and Colin reached Bispham a bit early. They found the nick near a roundabout and sorted out a good vantage spot in order to see the vehicles coming on and off the station's car park. That done, they had a drive around the area to get their bearings. Bispham seemed very similar to Blackpool in so far as that it was full of hotels and B&Bs and food outlets. It didn't have all the amusements or places of entertainment that the centre of the resort boasted and seemed to be interwoven with residential areas as well, though they seemed to be inland. Whereas the commercial side for the tourists were nearer the sea. Martin found a fish and chip shop close to the front and he and Colin filled up, not knowing when they would get their next chance if Yates took them on a long drive. Martin hadn't had fish and chips from Blackpool since he'd been a kid, and they were every bit as good as he remembered. In fact, this chippie, which looked quite old and traditional, still served its food wrapped in old newspaper. It had been many years since Martin had experienced that. It seemed to enhance the taste of the food somehow. Though he knew he was looking back through rose-tinted glasses.

At 11.50 Martin moved the car to the pre-arranged spot and turned the engine off. 'What if she goes straight home and stays there or goes for a drink with her staff in a local for the afternoon?' he asked.

'Then we sack it as she's obviously not up to anything naughty,' Colin replied.

They sat and watched a number of private cars arrive at about five to the hour, each driven by a cop wearing a civvies coat over a uniformed shirt. The next shift. And at five past the hour several similar cars left, driven by similarly-clad officers. But no Yates. By 12.20, Martin was starting to feel uncomfortable.

'Look,' Colin said, as he pointed at the windscreen. Martin did and could see a grey Ford Mondeo on an '18 plate leave the car park and pause by the road. The female driver looked left and right, and then straight at them. It was Debbie Yates. The road was clear, and she took off with purpose and was soon at the roundabout, where she took the first exit heading in the general direction of Blackpool. Martin had to respond quickly to hit the roundabout before she was too far ahead. But he hadn't wanted to go too quickly and be up her backside, either. Always a difficult balance to achieve on mobile surveillance; keep the target in sight, but without blowing yourself out.

As far as Martin was aware, Debbie Yates, even though she'd been a detective, was not surveillance trained, and in any event, there was no reason to suspect she should be looking in her mirrors for a tail.

'She's not going home,' Colin commented.

'How do you reckon that?' Martin asked.

'Because she's not wearing a civvies jacket over her uniform.'

Martin had been concentrating on his driving and joining the traffic as she had left the police station, so had not had a chance to look at her. Now they were settling down behind her, he could only see the back of the top of her head jutting around her seat's head restraint. 'She's changed out of her uniform?' Martin asked.

'Defo. Dark blouse, and no jacket. Surely, if she was going home, she'd wait until then to change out of her uniform,' Colin added.

Very true, and it explained her delayed departure. Maybe they would drop lucky today, after all.

Martin stayed several cars back from Yates who settled down into a steady drive. She wasn't rushing anywhere. Something about the whole demeanour of her driving told Martin that she was going on a journey but was in no great hurry to get there. He voiced this.

'How the hell can you tell all that?' Colin asked.

'After years of doing surveillance as a DC, I've got a sixth sense. An ability to read a driver's mind-set, away from the obvious.'

'Like if they are legging it?' Colin said.

Martin laughed and said, 'That's always an easy one to read.' And the more Yates settled down into her drive, Martin settled down into his. Twenty minutes later, it was clear they were headed out of town. Inland, east. And twenty minutes after that, they joined the start of the M55 motorway towards Preston, which then joined the M6, from where she could go absolutely anywhere.

CHAPTER THIRTY-SIX

Bashir hadn't been in the car park long when he saw a motor pull up a couple of spaces behind him. But before he could see it properly it had turned its headlamps onto full beam so he could see nothing in his door mirrors. He had already moved his interior mirror to one side as instructed. All this cloak and dagger stuff was adding to his nerves. And the way they turned up so quickly after him led him to believe that they had been here for a while. The text that said they were delayed in traffic was obviously made up to add to his tension. This wasn't necessary as he couldn't imagine it being much higher. Other than when that drug dog came sniffing at Delhi airport.

Then he heard the rear passenger door behind him being opened and someone get in and close the door.

'Keep looking ahead,' a rough north Manchester accent said, as a large hand gripped the top of his head.

'Yes, Mr Manning,' he said.

'And don't use my name, it's a bad habit to get into,' the man said, as he released his grip on Bashir's head, but he had effectively confirmed that he was Manning.

'Absolutely. Is everything okay?' Bashir asked, as he rubbed the excess sweat from his palms onto his trousers.

'I hope so. Why do you ask?' Manning asked.

'It's just that I normally go through your mate, and then that is only ever over the phone.'

'As you probably know by now, I have got rid of the grassing bastard you helped me identify,' Manning started. Bashir felt a dread run through him. He'd passed the intel he'd seen on CHAMPS about someone talking to the cops mentioning Manning's mate planning a robbery. The intel never mentioned Manning by name, just one member of his gang. He couldn't remember the man's name now, but the intermediary had given it to him to look out for. But he'd no idea exactly how the named man's robbery preparations had fitted in with Manning exactly, other than the intermediary was obviously interested in him. For all Bashir knew, the guy could have been a rival to Manning. He had just assumed the latter. 'I thought you were only interested in the guy in the intel, the one planning the robbery?' Bashir said.

'You are not paid to think, that's my job. Joey is one of mine, and knowing the filth were looking at him allowed me to throw in a decoy while I did the real job, but that's not why I'm here,' Manning said.

Joey: that was the name, Bashir remembered, but still didn't know what Manning meant about getting 'rid of the grassing bastard', so he asked him.

'I managed to work out who the grass was, so I offed him.'

Bashir felt ill. He'd no idea how on earth Manning could have worked out who the informant was. Even he didn't know. Notwithstanding that he'd had the same access to CHAMPS as Kerry Danson, the AO, for a short time anyway. 'What did you do to him?' Bashir asked weakly.

'Burned the fucker. You not heard about the body in the boot?' Manning asked.

Bashir nearly retched. He'd heard titbits around headquarters about a body found in the boot of a burned-out car after a robbery in Preston but had no access to the details. He couldn't believe what he was hearing.

'Erm, I hadn't heard much, just canteen talk; it's not gone public yet, I don't think. Oh God,' Bashir said.

'And trust me, the fucker was still alive when the car was torched,' Manning said.

Bashir should never have become involved, not for all the money in the world. That said, they had tricked him; for that first small innocuous favour he had been paid a ridiculous amount of money. Then they had him; there had been no going back. He had tried to get out after the severity of the favours started to ramp up, but the intermediary told him in no uncertain terms that his bosses would be told about all his misdemeanours if he did. That had terrified him into submission at the time. But he'd had no idea what terror really was; not compared to what he had just heard. Now he knew what Manning was really capable of. He was in far too deep, but with nowhere to go. What a greedy, arrogant fool he had been.

'So, you can see what I think of dirty grassing scum, and what happens to them.'

Bashir was struggling to retain any kind of calm but knew he had to dig deep to sound as normal as he could. He was petrified that his fear might come across as if he had something to hide. As if he wasn't on-side in some way. Which of course he wasn't now, well, not freely. He swallowed and then replied, 'Yeah, well I guess they shouldn't be grasses then,' frantically hoping that his words didn't sound as hollow as they were.

Manning behind him suddenly roared with laughter, and he felt a heavy hand pat his right shoulder.

'Good man, that's what I wanted to hear. See, I need to make sure there are no other grasses out there talking about me. As you know, when we scale up with Sky White it's going to be massive. The biggest. Global even, possibly, so I need to know my foundations are solid before I start to build,' Manning said.

'Yeah, but what's that got to do with me?' Bashir asked, suddenly starting to feel even more nervous, if that was possible.

'I need to know I can trust you,' Manning replied.

Bashir's heart nearly stopped, and it was all he could do to stop himself from turning round to face Manning in some instinctive need to look at him as he sought to convince him of his loyalty. 'Of course you can trust me, look at the intel I brought you, look at the drug runs I've done, and the sourcing of Yates to help you road-test the gear—' Bashir said, almost tripping over his own tongue as he rushed to get his reassurance out. Until the return of Manning's heavy hand cut him short.

'Okay, Bash, don't shit yourself. I'm happy with you, and I'm happy you'll never shaft me as you now know what I could do to you if you ever did.'

'Absolutely,' Bashir hurriedly added, as the hand left his shoulder once more.

'And I'd start by having some fun with your missus while you watched.'

Bashir coughed as he had to suppress vomit which raced up his throat. He only just managed to stop the ejection and cringed as he swallowed the foul-tasting fluid. 'You've more than made your point. Can I go now?'

'Nearly, Bash. Now I'm happy you are solid, I need to ask that favour, I need to just check that all is well before the next phase.'

'Yes, sure, anything,' Bashir said, frantically keen to get this whole thing over with.

'Good man, now listen up.'

***

Five minutes later, Bashir was driving off the services car park to re-join the M6 northbound towards Preston. He was driving at normal speed whilst fighting the urge to drive as fast as he could as if his very existence depended on it. He drove onto the main carriageway and satisfied himself that Manning's car hadn't followed him. There was no reason why it should as Manning had left to return to Manchester. It was just Bashir feeling extra paranoid. He gave himself a couple of minutes to calm a little more as he repeated all that Manning had said to him in his head. He'd always thought that he could leave at some point but had no idea when that would be. It was clearly Manning's gift to give. All he could do for now, was to go along with everything Manning wanted. But herein lay his first problem.

The favour he'd just agreed he could do.

He'd bigged himself up too much to the intermediary in the first place, now the 'The Head of IT' was paying for that conceit.

He used his Bluetooth to call Yates as he approached junction 29 at Bamber Bridge, just south of Preston. He activated his nearside indicator as he did. The phone rang several times and Bashir was preparing to leave an urgent but cryptic voicemail, when she picked up.

'Hi, didn't expect to hear from you today,' Yates said.

'Debbie, I need to see you right away. I'm in the shit, we're in the shit. I need your help,' Bashir said.

'Calm down, whatever it is, I'm sure we can sort it. Where are you now?'

'Just coming off the M6 south of Preston.'

'Perfect, you're in luck. I'm in Preston at the mo. Tell me where you want to meet up.'

Bashir did and ended the call. Then he put his foot down, he couldn't help it.

CHAPTER THIRTY-SEVEN

Martin couldn't quite believe their luck; Yates had taken them straight to a modern town house at the north end of Preston, close to where the M55 and the M6 merge. He'd let her drive down the residential cul-de-sac on her own to prevent them from being noticed. Under his directions, Colin jumped out on foot as soon as Martin had cleared the junction in hope of seeing which house she approached; if any. She could be picking someone up for all they knew.

Martin turned the car around and Colin was back in a couple of minutes.

'She's parked up and gone in number thirty-three. And guess what?'

'What?' Martin asked.

'You won't believe this. She was met at the door by Detective Constable Jim Grantham.'

'My God,' Martin said. 'What great evidence of their collusion and knowledge of each other. In fact, it's the only real evidence we have putting those two together. Circumstantial against the main offending, but it's a start.'

'It gets better.'

Martin turned to Colin, who was grinning. 'By the way Grantham greeted Yates on the doorstep, they are far more than associates.'

'Even better. I'll find a good spot to park up, where we can see the front aspect. This will be worth waiting for.'

Four hours later and Martin was starting to become unsettled, plus he was bursting for a wee. 'Do you think she is there for the night?'

'Starting to think that myself. We can't wait here forever.'

'I was hoping she was going to come back out with Grantham and do some drug related business while they were together,' Martin said.

'Me too, but she might be there for purely personal reasons today. And the longer it goes on, the more it looks like that. Plus, if they do take off together to do some dirty business, we are one car on our own, we'd probably blow it.'

'Sadly, you are right. This needs a fully staffed surveillance team from out of force with all the kit they have to do it properly. Even if we missed them doing something today, there will be other days,' Martin said.

'At least our impromptu observations will justify the authority for a full surveillance,' Colin added.

'I'm still loving the new you,' Martin said.

'I've already told you not to get too used to it.

Martin started the car engine and knew that the next time Colin caught him out telling a tiny little white lie for the greater good, Colin's bollocking would have to be scaled down to avoid an accusation of hypocrisy. Not that he would ever say so out loud. He was just about to drive away when Colin said, 'Wait! Look,' and pointed down the cul-de-sac.

Martin followed Colin's finger and could see a man and a woman head towards Yates' car, with a determination in their step. 'Looks like they are on a mission.'

'Doesn't it. We going with them?' Colin asked.

'Be rude not too, but we'll have to be mightily careful, and I'll let them run at the first sign of trouble,' Martin said.

'I'll let you be the judge.'

Yates' car reached the junction, and barely slowed as it turned right, passing Martin and Colin's position. Yates was driving and Grantham was the front seat passenger. Martin let them go for about twenty seconds before he pulled onto the road behind them. He then did what was called a 'boot lid follow', where you held back as far as you dare, just keeping an eyeball on the target car's boot lid as it traversed around bends, and even then, only just. The idea being that you could still follow the target but without actually being in their rear view; or as little as possible. But by the way Yates was driving, Martin could tell that her rear view was the last thing on her mind, she was going for it; whatever *it*, was, heading for the motorway to join the M6 southbound. Fifteen minutes later, they left the motorway just south of Preston at junction 29 in Bamber Bridge, turned right at the roundabout and then a hundred metres later, right onto a retail park and into the car park of a Burger King.

Martin was confident they hadn't been spotted. If he was choosing a route for a single-car surveillance, he couldn't have picked a better one, irrespective of the focused way Yates was driving. He drove onto the car park twenty seconds after Yates and was relieved to see her ignore the drive-thru lane. She parked her car and rushed into the restaurant with Grantham in tow. Martin pulled into a space near the exit, but with a line of sight on Yates' car. He then turned to Colin. 'Wonder who they are rushing to meet?'

'Unless they are just very hungry?'

Two gags in as many days, Colin was on a roll.

'Let's find out,' Martin said, and then opened the glove box and pulled out two radios and earpieces. He passed one of each to Colin and quickly explained how they could turn two normal police radios into makeshift covert ones. He set the radios to a spare set-to-set channel and they each put one in their inside breast pocket. He told Colin that he had set the mics to whisper mode so that they should pick up their speech through their jackets. They would still have to reach in and press the transmit button, but to do so slowly and not make the fatal mistake of trying to talk to your coat lapel. 'Use a menu to hide your lips if you need to speak. I'll sit separate to you, so we can double our chances.'

'Where shall I sit?' Colin asked, as he put his earpiece in.

'As close as you can. We need to pick up any conversation we're able. I'll sit at the opposite side, or as close as possible before someone else does.'

'Got it,' Colin said, and they left the car and made their way to the entrance.

Colin walked in first, which was a godsend as it turned out as it gave Martin cover that he hadn't known he'd need. He looked to his right and could see the backs of Yates and Grantham as they took a seat at a window table at the front of the restaurant. Already seated there was Bashir. That was a surprise. It just got better. But very conscious that Martin had met Bashir earlier, he swiftly did an about-turn and headed back to their motor. He called Colin over the radio to tell him that he was on his own, and why. Colin whispered an acknowledgement.

Back in the motor, Martin grabbed a clipboard from the rear seats and started to make some notes of the surveillance so far. It would have to do as a log and should be fine to use in court if they ever needed it. Four or five minutes passed and then Martin's phone rang, it was Colin. 'Yes, mate, how's it going?'

'Hello darling,' Colin started.

'Hello sweetie,' Martin couldn't resist saying back.

'Look, I have a podcast due to go live, which I forgot about before I came out; can you monitor it for me, and take notes of any salient points? I'll be home in a little while. Just waiting to meet a business associate in Burger King,' Colin said, and then ended the call without waiting for a reply.

As soon as Martin put his phone down, his earpiece crackled to life. He could hear a lot of background noise and the sound of the odd chair being scraped along a titled floor. He could also hear voices in the near distance. He turned his radio volume up to maximum and strained to pick up as much of the conversation as he could. Most of it was just about discernible bar the odd interruption from elsewhere.

Martin wrote down exactly what he could make out.

'Bloody hell, Bash, you need to calm down and go through it again. Slower this time,' a female voice said.

'Don't call me Bash, that's what Manning called me,' a male voice with a hint of an Asian accent said.

Then Martin received a text from Colin confirming who he was listening to. Yates, Bashir and Grantham.

'He threatened me and my wife if I ever grassed,' Bashir said.

'In what way?' Yates asked.

'In the same way he killed the other grass. But fuck knows how he found out who it was. Even I don't know,' Bashir said.

'Killed who?' Yates asked.

'The body in the boot. Manning claims that he was the author of the intel I passed on,' Bashir replied.

'Jesus,' A male voice with a local accent said. Martin knew that this could only be Grantham.

'But how was I to know he would do that? How was I to know he'd somehow be able to work out who the author was?' Bashir added.

'Look, I want nowt to do with this. Knocking a bit of

gear about is one thing, but this! Come on Debbie, let's do one,' Grantham said.

'In a mo. What does he think about us?' Yates asked.

'Didn't mention you two, but said now he's happy with me, he wants to make sure that there are no other grasses about, before they scale up to the next level,' Bashir replied.

'And how does he propose to do that?' Yates asked.

'Wants me to access the secure database again, and check,' Bashir replied.

'And your problem is?' Yates asked.

'I'm not sure I can gain access now.'

'Can't you just pretend, and tell him all's sweet?' Grantham asked.

'Yeah, but what if there is one and he finds out? What will he do to me?' Bashir asked. 'He'll think I'm in collusion with whomever.'

'Can't you gain access one last time, on a pretence, then tell Manning that that is the last time you can do it?' Yates asked. 'Say your access has expired or something, he won't know.'

'Or just say your access has already expired,' Grantham said.

'I've kinda already said that I can do it,' Bashir said.

'Why the fuck did you say that?' Yates asked.

'I was scared, you weren't there,' Bashir replied.

'Okay, okay, back to plan A. Find a way for one last go, then tell him you can't do it again, even if you wanted to,' Yates said.

'I suppose, I could dream up some maintenance related reason. That thick cow Kerry won't question it,' Bashir said, with an added confidence back in his voice.

'Don't get cocky, that's what has led you here. You get cocky, you get sloppy, and you put us all at risk,' Yates said.

Then the transmission ended abruptly. Martin read

back his notes and couldn't believe what a goldmine of evidence they represented. He glanced up and saw Yates and Grantham returning to their car and Bashir heading to the one in front of it. He kept his head down. Seconds later the passenger door opened, and Colin got in. Martin was aware of two cars driving past them, towards the exit.

'Which one should we follow?' Colin asked.

'Neither,' Martin replied, as he risked a look up. He could see the rear of both cars as they drove away. 'We've pushed our luck enough today.'

'Fair enough,' Colin said. 'Did you get it all?'

'I think so, until the transmission ended abruptly.'

'My finger was killing me trying to keep the transmit button depressed, so I jammed it open; until it failed. But they said their goodbyes after that, so you should have all that matters.'

Martin passed Colin the clipboard and asked him to write down any additions or amendments needed while his memory was fresh. 'I can't believe what we've just heard.'

'Neither can I. Rogers will have a boner that'll last for days when he hears all this.'

'Colin, stop with the gags, that's my job.'

Both men roared with laughter, which Martin knew was as much about a release of pressure as anything else.

'And I can't wait to see Kerry Danson's face when she reads the transcript,' Martin added.

CHAPTER THIRTY-EIGHT

Manning and Gazza left the motorway services via the hotel access road and re-joined the southbound side. There were steel vertical posts in the road, but they were down. In fact, Manning had never known them up, another reason why he liked Charnock Richard services as a meeting place. Gazza had asked him how it had gone with Bash the Bishop, and he filled him in as they headed back towards Manchester.

'Sounds like he shat himself,' Gazza said.

'Reckon he did. I'm as sure as I can be that he would never cross me. And he never saw me, either. Not that that really matters, long-term,' Manning said.

'And he can get back into the filth's scum database, no probs?' Gazza asked.

'Said he was head of IT so it wouldn't be a problem,' Manning replied.

'Yeah, he's given me all that la-de-dah over the phone before; never too sure how much was bull.'

'He came up with the intel on Joey; but I guess we'll find out,' Manning said.

'He might be a bit more reluctant now he knows we offed the grass.'

'I'll off him if he doesn't.'

'Do you think there are any more?' Gazza asked.

Manning was about to comment further when his phone rang. He looked at the screen, it was his partner. He took the call. 'How's it going out there?'

'Getting there and it should be all good,' came his reply.

'What about the field test problems?' Manning asked.

'The Indians reckon they can easily sort that, just need to tweak the formula and all should be good.'

'Do we need more field tests over here?' Manning asked. 'There's plenty of dickheads to try it on.'

'Thankfully not. As we are happy with the strength, and its similarities to the real stuff being the same, if not better, there shouldn't be a problem once they've removed the adulterant that was causing the eye problems. They say they'll test it with some locals just for that single issue and then we should be good to go.'

'You alone?'

'Yeah, fire away.'

'You still good to go about nicking the recipe?'

'Everything is in place here, no sweat. Just need to know that we are all secure at your end?'

'As you know we have taken care of the problem, or to be exact, who you reckoned for it,' Manning replied.

'Had to be that bastard. Paid me too much attention.'

'Not doubting you, but to be on the safe side, I'm having further checks done.'

'You using Bash the Bishop again?'

'Yeah, only just left him.'

'I'll be glad when we're done with that conceited idiot.'

'If the egg timer hadn't passed the test, we already would have been.'

'Well, it did, but as things are panning out, we won't need him or the egg timer on any more runs. Once these idiots have perfected the recipe and I've nicked it.'

'Just need him on his current task,' Manning added.

'You don't think we have another rat, do you?'

'To be honest, no. We've had no further intel since the robbery job, I'm just securing all bases before you come back with the goodies and we go mega.'

'As you say, best to be on the safe side. Look, I gotta go.'

'Don't have their curry again, you'll only get the shits,' Manning said, and then ended the call.

'All good, Boss?' Gazza asked.

Manning told him that it was and filled him in on the other half of the phone call.

'The Indians are going to be mightily pissed off once they realise that we've nicked their recipe. They have a long reach over here,' Gazza said.

'That's the beauty of the plan. They won't know. We copy their set up and cancel our orders. We can say there are still problems with the eye shit thing, and the users aren't buying it. They'll soon drop us and seek to establish it elsewhere. Then we set up our own lab and knock it out here regardless,' Manning said.

'But what if they do and come looking for us?' Gazza said.

'Then we go to war. But it'll be war on our turf.'

'Fair enough, Boss.'

They soon passed over the boundary between Lancashire and Greater Manchester, so Manning pulled his baseball cap low again and settled down into his seat. He could see the one-mile marker sign for the M62 and noted that Gazza was preparing to take the exit and head east, back towards Manchester and then the open hills above Rochdale.

'Just need to sort our little irritation out, and confirm that there is no more scum, and then it should be easy life time,' Manning said.

'Where to now?'

'You can drop me at the barn, and then see what you

can do to find the tits with a gob.'

'If she turns up at home, do you want to be on it, or do you want me to sort it?'

Manning thought for a moment, then said, 'I'll leave it with you, unless you need me. I could do with finishing some unfinished business from this morning.'

'Fair enough.'

'But it might be worth trying some of those poncy wine bars near to the newspaper office. Be easier, and safer than spending hours watching her house; less obvious,' Manning said.

They joined the M62 headed towards the M60, the Manchester orbital ring road – the northern version of the M25 – from where they would pick up the M62 eastbound once again.

After a few minutes, Gazza spoke again. 'If by chance I do see her, and manage to follow her on her own, do you just want me to follow her home first? Or . . .'

Manning looked up. 'If you get the chance to run her over. Do it. Just make sure the motor's sorted.'

'There's a jerry can full of petrol in the boot. I used to be a boy scout,' Gazza said.

Both men laughed and then Gazza asked, 'Just so I'm clear; how bad do you want it?'

'Dead. And make sure. They'll never link it. It'll just be a tragic accident with a stolen car.'

'You got it, Boss.'

'And it'll save us a hundred in extra rental,' Manning added, and both men laughed again.

CHAPTER THIRTY-NINE

Martin and Colin headed back to Preston to grab something to eat before the canteen closed for the evening. En route Colin rang the Chief's bagman and was able to arrange a meeting in Rogers's office for just over an hour's time, between them and Kerry Danson. Colin carefully re-read Martin's notes and made a couple of annotations to the makeshift surveillance log and as soon as they arrived at Preston, they both went through it once more and when they were happy, they signed it. It would act as a joint pocketbook in any future court proceedings. Martin was just glad that he had pretty much managed to capture it all accurately. He was also amazed at how well Colin had done, and at how well the whisper mode on his radio's mic had picked up the conversation. 'You must have been sat on their knees?' he'd quipped.

'Pretty much, but you did say to get in close,' Colin answered. But then explained properly. Bashir, Yates and Grantham had been huddled around a small table. Colin had started off on a bench seat at the next table with his back to them. But he had felt conspicuous and noted that they dropped their chatter volume. And Colin's finger was killing him as he did a Nelson impression while trying to look at the menu one-handed. He saw a matchstick on the table. He said it looked as if someone had used it at a makeshift toothpick before discarding it. Martin said, 'Urgh.'

Colin went to say that he used it to jam the transmit button in the down position and then threw his jacket over the bench seat. He then moved to the other side of the table so was not breathing down their necks. But his Jacket was right next to them.

Martin was impressed, 'That was inspired on-the-hoof thinking; you sure that you are not surveillance trained?'

Colin laughed and then said, 'That's why I rang you to say I was waiting for a business associate. To explain why I was sat on my own with no food.'

Martin had noticed that Colin had been nearly shouting down the phone.

'The only trouble was, having moved away a bit, I couldn't hear too much of the conversation. I've underlined in the log the bits I did hear. I was desperately relying on you to pick it all up and note it down. And thank God you did.'

'Teamwork, partner, teamwork,' Martin said. Colin was grinning widely, Martin could tell he'd enjoyed being back out in the field, and to be fair, he'd done a first-class job. Pivotal in fact.

They finished up and headed over to headquarters which only took fifteen minutes at this time of day and were soon in Rogers's office. As usual, the chief was pacing up and down as they waited for Kerry to join them. No point in going over it all twice. Five minutes after Martin and Colin had arrived Kerry rushed in, and they all crowded around the coffee table by the Chesterfields.

Both the chief and Kerry sat in silence as they told their tale; until Colin read the 'thick cow' remark.

'The cheeky arrogant, bastard,' she said. 'We'll see

who will or will not question it.'

'Excellent, that's what I like to see, Kerry, passion. We'll hang them for this,' Rogers said.

'By the balls,' Kerry added.

'I have to say, gents, you've done a first-class job here,' Rogers said.

'It was Mr Carstairs who did all the hard work when it mattered,' Martin said.

'A joint effort,' Colin added quickly.

Martin noticed that Kerry had suddenly gone quiet. Then Rogers asked, 'And those verbal's, are all lawful?'

'I made the notes contemporaneously and Mr Carstairs and I debriefed them together at our earliest opportunity, which in any event was within an hour. We accept that some of it is hearsay, but Bashir was relating what Manning had said to him in first instance,' Martin said.

'It will get challenged by any defence, no doubt, and may even be subject to a Voir Dire hearing with the jury out to ascertain its admissibility,' Colin said. 'We have to be prepared for that.'

Then Kerry came out of her machinations and spoke, 'I've just been wrestling with that as an authorising officer,' she started. Martin, Colin and the chief all turned to her. 'Had you been operating within an approved *directed surveillance* authority, then there would be no problem legally and the defence could challenge all they want.'

'But?' Martin said for her.

'But you weren't. You were operating on the hoof, and there is a way to grant a retrospective authority, but we need to do that sharpish. One question though,' she said.

'Yes,' Colin and Martin said together. A little too anxiously, Martin thought.

'What the fuck, were you both doing at Bispham nick at the exact time that Inspector Yates drove out of the station car park?'

'Easy,' Martin jumped in, 'We were there just to try and identify what vehicle Yates was using so we could arrange for a fully authorised surveillance team in the coming days.' He didn't look at Colin, and he knew that this was not the first time he had lied in front of the chief. The only difference being that this time, Colin couldn't bollock him afterwards.

'And follow Yates to Preston?' Kerry asked.

'Not at all, we were heading back ourselves on the M55 and found ourselves behind her, so we obviously held back.'

'And then followed her to Grantham's and then to the meeting at Bamber Bridge?'

Martin fell silent, it was getting tricky now.

'I'm only asking what a defence barrister will ask,' Kerry said. Martin realised this.

'Okay, our interest was piqued when she left the motorway and when we saw her go to Grantham's home address,' Martin said.

'Okay,' Kerry said.

'Advice, Kerry?' Rogers asked.

Kerry cleared her throat and then replied, 'We prepare the retrospective authority, based on what Martin has just told us, and if the CPS are happy to use the conversation in evidence, then we're all good.'

'You mean it could be thrown out as inadmissible?' Colin said.

'I'm afraid so. So we plan for the worst. We may not need to use it in evidence, or certainly not have to rely on it. Let's assume it will be thrown out and the jury will never see it.'

'Go on,' Rogers said.

'So we use it as intelligence, and seek to corroborate all the information by other means which would thereafter be standalone evidence. Used as intelligence, it tells us what we need to know and which direction to aim our enquiries in order to convert it into evidence,' she said with a flourish at the end.

'Brilliant,' the chief said.

Martin exhaled.

'And I know exactly how we should do it. Then we'll see who the thick cow is?' Kerry finished with.

The journey back to Preston was a quiet one, as both Martin and Colin fell into contemplation. As soon as they were back in their office, they sat down to take stock. 'I should have realised the flaky ground we were on, Colin. I was just on such a high after what you'd managed to achieve in the Burger King.'

'We both should have, and we both were. But let's see where we are. Okay, the information about Manning killing the informant in the car boot was always going to be hearsay.'

'Agreed,' Martin said.

'We have all three together acting in a joint enterprise, with Grantham admitting to "knocking a bit of gear out".'

'True, and we know they're about to scale the drugs side of thing up,' Martin said.

'We have confirmation that it was Bashir who sold confidential intelligence, leading to the informant's death,' Colin said. 'And we both know who that is, even if we can't prove it yet.'

Martin nodded his reluctant acceptance of the latter.

'And Kerry's plan is a good one,' Colin finished.

Martin was about to reply when the ringing of Colin's phone interrupted them. He watched Colin as he took the call. He listened wordlessly and then thanked the caller and ended the call. He looked up at Martin, expressionless.

'What is it, Colin?'

'That was the lab; toxicology is back on the three drug deaths you requested. And as they were fast-tracked, they rang me to confirm the cost, and to give us the results. The three bodies all died of heart failure brought on by the same toxic substance.'

'Yeah, we gathered that, they had all taken Sky White,' Martin said.

Colin nodded and then continued, 'The toxic substance referred to as Sky White by us is a chemical cocaine substitute. And as it's brand new, it's not yet listed as a controlled drug. It's not covered by the 1971 Misuse of Drugs Act.'

Martin realised straight away what his boss was saying. 'It's not illegal to buy it, sell it, or supply it. Oh shit.'

Colin was just shaking his head. And then added, 'Drug-wise, Manning, Bashir, Yates and Grantham have done nothing illegal.'

CHAPTER FORTY

Martin and Colin had decided to call it a day as it was approaching seven o'clock. The mood had become even more sombre after the phone call from the lab. They were both tired and decided not to debate things further until the morning. Fresh start and all that, though it wouldn't change the facts. Martin went back over the entire day as he headed down the M61 towards Manchester. At least the rush-hour traffic had passed its peak now. It was still busy, but he was able to maintain a steady fifty. It freed his concentration up a little as he regurgitated the salient facts. Sky White was not a controlled drug, though thanks to the toxicology evidence linking its abuse to three deaths, it should be fairly soon. He knew that there was a legal backdoor to the Misuse of Drugs Act to enable new drugs to be added to the controlled lists. Spice the zombie drug was a recent example; he just wasn't too sure how long the process would take. But irrespective of that, it wasn't illegal by that act's virtue now.

The thought that what Bashir, Yates and Grantham had done was legal was really depressing. Manning was another issue; they had a rock-solid case against him for the earlier murder of his girlfriend the previous year, so could do him for that while they tried to build a case against him for murdering the informant and committing robbery. Martin still wasn't too sure why Manning had gone to all that trouble with the note thing. As if they would back off hunting him down. It made the opposite true, not that there was much slack in their desire to nick him anyway. Maybe, it was just arrogance. Villains like Manning thrived on their inflated egos. Martin always liked to think that the extremely arrogant ones were all subconsciously compensating for being deficient elsewhere. And in the males' cases – as the vast majority were male – they were all pencil dicks. He smiled at the thought, as he always did; it brought them down a mental peg.

Once Manning was lifed-up for the former murder, they would ensure they proved the latter offences. Then his life sentence would become a longer one. That said, they had to catch him first. It was a huge pity they hadn't known in advance about Bashir's meeting with him. It was undoubtedly a rare opportunity, but that chance had gone.

Returning to the Sky White issue, there might be a chance of prosecuting their three for conspiring to administer a noxious substance. The police still used and relied heavily on an old Victorian piece of legislation that had stood the test of time in The Offences Against the Person Act of 1861. It was where all the assault offences such as actual bodily and grievous bodily harm came from. But jumping into a far corner of Martin's memory was a little used section within the Act relating to administering a noxious substance to a person. It was undoubtedly intended to cover acts such as poisoning, which had apparently been commonplace in the Victorian era, but if the constituent parts needed to prove the offence fit their Sky White circumstances, then there was a real chance they could use that archaic offence. At least they could charge them with something, even if it was not as heavy a sentence-attracting offence as they might have wished for. The parameters for its commission would no doubt be tighter than with The Misuse of Drugs Act, but it was a possibility and Martin started to feel better.

He nearly rang Colin but decided to leave him in peace until the morning. He could do with researching it further before he mentioned it, and a call to run it past CPS as a working hypothesis wouldn't do any harm first, either. But what was definitely still in play was Bashir's selling of intelligence to Manning. Even though, as Colin had pointed out earlier, if they lost the admissibility in court of his admission picked up by Colin's makeshift bug, then all they could prove was that he had access to the information. They couldn't prove that he had passed it on or had even seen it. This is where Kerry's plan came in. He'd never met Lancashire's Authorising Officer before, but he was mightily impressed with her, she was razor sharp, and he particularly loved the way she swore in front of Rogers and seemingly got away with it. Especially, in front of junior officers, like Martin.

He realised that he should be paying more attention to his driving as he was now on the M60 and couldn't remember turning off the M61. This was a worry. Driving a well-trodden route on autopilot. He cleared his mind and slid a Blues CD into the car's player and settled into the rest of the drive home. He was only twenty minutes away now.

Then his phone rang, it was Cath. 'Hi stranger, I was going to call you when I got home.'

'You on your way now?' Cath asked.

'On the outskirts of Manchester, nearly.'

'Brilliant, you fancy joining me for one. I'm in a wine bar round the corner from my old office.'

'Yes, sure.'

'Loads to tell you.'

'Me too, but you first.'

'I'll tell you more when I see you, but I have found three more deaths in the Northwest which have been written off as normal addict overdose fatalities, but each had the enlarged red eye thing going on. I think the problem is worse than we thought.'

Martin quickly told her that the three deaths they knew about were now being officially linked to Sky White, confirmed by toxicology. It wasn't a bad batch of normal cocaine cut with a toxic additive, but a new chemical cocaine substitute, one that's never been seen before. And with one hell of a side-effect, as they knew. Plus, the scientist who did the work is worried it might be more addictive than crack cocaine.

'Shit. Well, if it helps, Eleanor and I have already cobbled together a short news release to go out later, just to raise awareness with no definite links disclosed yet. Just a public health thing, until we know more.'

'Thanks for that. Are you going to do a cameo again?'

'Yes, the press office thinks the same face representing the force might provide continuity and therefore add to the seriousness of the message. It might also give us more intel if it leads to more addicts coming forward.'

'Help you provide a more structured map of areas of most concern,' Martin added.

'Defo, and just might save some lives with any luck. But that's not the only reason I rang you, I could have told you all this later.'

'What is it?' Martin asked.

'Well, you'll probably think I'm mad, but I finished early so I could have a catch-up with my old newspaper editor, and get them involved in the drug story too,' she started.

'Hence the wine bar,' Martin said.

'Absolutely, and a few of the reporters joined us for a swift one, too. Anyway, it thinned down to just Judy and me, so we walked around the corner to the Gin and Sing bar.' Martin knew it. 'And I saw this guy which I didn't really see, if you know what I mean?' Martin didn't. 'Anyway, Judy left, so I went back to the last bar, as I must have dropped my lippy in the loos; I'm back in Gin and Sing now and the same guy is here.'

Martin wasn't too sure what she meant, but her diction had quickened, and he sensed that she was ill at ease. This made him feel unsettled. 'What's this guy done?' he asked.

'Well, that's why I might just be being paranoid, nothing as such.'

Martin trusted Cath's instincts and said so before qualifying his last question to, 'What do you *think* he's done?'

'I think he's following me. In fact, I'm sure of it. I wouldn't have noticed but for dropping my lippy.'

'Where is he now?' Martin asked, as his heartrate started to rise.

'Just sat watching sport on one of the bar's TVs. But he keeps glancing over.'

'Perhaps he fancies you?' Martin asked, perversely hoping so.

'It's not that kind of a look.'

Martin told her to stay exactly where she was, not to go to the loo, and not to look at the guy again. If he makes any move towards her, to go straight to the bar and grab one of the bar staff and say he's pestering her before ringing the cops. To stay calm, as it might still be nothing. He'd be with her in ten minutes. He ended the call and noted that she'd sounded nervous but not frightened as such. A good sign, but Martin put his foot down, nevertheless. He could be there in five if he tried hard. He knew the bar, and also knew it had security staff on the door. If Cath did as instructed, should the guy approach in a hostile way, he knew the door staff wouldn't take any risks. The guy would be out in the street before he knew what had hit him.

CHAPTER FORTY-ONE

Cath felt much better as she ended the call to Martin. She prided herself on her sassy confident nature, but there was something unclean about this guy sat across from her. He was in his late thirties, white, and looked rugged. The sort of look a man who had spent a lot of time outdoors had; but a lot of villains seemed to sport the same appearance. She decided to make as many mental notes about the guy as she could, in case she needed an accurate recall later. He'd seemed to be of average height but looked stocky. He had the shoulders of someone who bench-pressed a lot of weights; on anyone else it would have looked attractive.

She'd first noticed him after they left the other bar. She nearly mentioned it to Judy but shook it off as just a bloke on the pull. She wished she'd told Judy now, as she would have stayed with her. She next saw him when she entered the Gin and Sing bar; he was the next person to enter after her, which was when she started to take notice. He was wearing tatty blue jeans, and a black jumper that looked baggy. Not like it was the wrong size, but loose through age. He had stubble and unkempt mousey hair. A scruff who looked out of place in a wine bar.

But she'd ignored him again, until she realised that she had misplaced her lipstick. She knew she had used it in the last bar, so after ordering her drink, she'd asked the barman to watch it for five while she legged it back. It wasn't a particularly expensive lipstick, though good ones weren't that cheap, but she liked the shade. Fortunately, it was still by the side of the wash basin in the ladies. She'd collected it and then headed straight back to the Gin and Sing. That's when she'd become concerned. Alone at a table near the entrance to the ladies as she left was the baggy jumper-wearing man.

Minutes later, she was back in Gin and Sing where she retrieved her gin and tonic and found a table. A minute after that, baggy jumper man was back. That's when she'd started to freak out a bit and had rung Martin.

As she was nervously waiting for Martin to land, the G & T was going down too fast, so she started to sip it. She was dying to glance over at baggy jumper man but resisted the urge. She checked her watch and guessed Martin would be here soon. She was sat with her back to baggy jumper man as he'd now taken up a position behind her. She had an idea. Time to put the lippy to work. She took it out of her bag together with her compact and reapplied her lipstick. She could clearly see the guy in her little mirror; he was sat at a table at the other side of the room near to the bar's second exit. And he was staring at her.

She snapped her compact shut and put it back in her bag with her lipstick and carried on sipping her drink. Several long minutes later she heard someone approach her from behind. Her heart nearly stopped as she felt a hand on the back of her chair. She steadied herself, they were in a public place, what the hell could he do to her in here? Normally, she wouldn't have felt so unsettled, even if she had convinced herself that she was being followed, and she had, but there was just something dark about this guy.

She tried to regain her resolve as she turned to address the owner of the hand, and nearly collapsed when she saw that it was Martin. He must have come in via the other door. She jumped to her feet and hugged him. But as she kissed him on the cheek, she saw baggy jumper man leap to his feet and hurry towards the exit. 'Martin, he's legging it,' she said, and pointed to the door Martin had obviously just come in through. She quickly described him as Martin turned to look, and then he told her to stay put. She watched him race across the pub and out the door. She wondered what he would do or say once he caught the guy. After all, he'd not actually done anything. But he'd mark his card and no doubt make him identify himself, and that would do for now. She headed to the bar to refill her glass and order a pint for Martin. She'd just returned to her table when he came rushing back in looking huffed and puffed. She hoped he'd not been in a fight.

He sat down and took a long slug of the pint as his breathing returned to normal.

'He was too quick, which means he was definitely up to no good,' he said.

'What do you mean?' she asked.

'I mean he'd vanished into thin air. It's only twenty metres to the first side street, so I reckoned he'd gone that way, so I legged it there, but there was no sign of him. Didn't think that he'd had enough time to go the other way to Deansgate, but he must have, so I legged it that way, but you know what Deansgate's like. It's busy 24/7. Like Oxford Street in London.'

'What about the door staff?' she asked.

'None there,' Martin replied, and then as if on cue, Cath noticed two door staff walk past as they gingerly escorted a young woman from the bar. She looked wasted and was complaining all the way.

'This means he must have run full pelt to Deansgate. There was no way he could have walked in the time he had,' Martin added.

'And people don't run for no reason,' she added.

'I'm afraid not.'

'Do you think he recognised you? You used to work in Manchester before you joined the regional organised crime unit.'

'Not sure, but he certainly acted like someone who might have.'

Martin emptied his glass and said he'd get another, but had to nip to the car first, which he said was outside on double yellow lines. She knew that he kept an official looking – although homemade – laminated card in his glove box which was covered in police crests and the words 'CID: Detective on Scene' or similar written on it. He'd be sticking it on the dashboard to ward off any passing parking attendants.

He was soon back and asked if she was okay.

'I am now, but just super curious to know who the hell that was, and what he wanted?'

'I think if he'd meant you harm, he would have done so by now. Could have easily grabbed you between bars and dragged you to the side street I first ran to.'

'But the door staff would have seen that,' she added. Martin didn't respond. She reckoned he already knew that, was probably just trying to reassure her. When he eventually spoke, he said, 'You pissed anyone off recently?'

'Probably in Blackpool, but not in Manchester. I don't work down here, as you know,' she replied, trying to put a smile back in her voice. But when Martin didn't laugh, she felt unsettled again.

'What are you working on apart from your research into these drug deaths?'

'Nothing, just them,' she replied. It was a mystery. She

quickly finished her drink as did Martin, and then he said they'd have to get going. He didn't want to risk more than two drinks or push his luck with the local parking enforcers who were legendarily enthusiastic in their work.

They left the bar and Cath could see relief on Martin's face that his car hadn't been towed away. 'One day that ruse will fail you,' she said.

'I know,' he replied, as they both got in the car.

'I think I should crash at your place tonight, just until we work it out,' Martin said, with what Cath realised was still a sombre demeanour.

'Sure, I was going to ask you to anyway. And thanks, but as strange as all that was . . .' she said, before pausing to choose her words.

Martin spoke first, 'Very strange.'

'Indeed, but you seem deeply troubled. Is there something you're not sharing?' she asked.

'Sorry, no,' Martin said, and then looked at her with a smile back on his face.

'Well, what is it then?' she pushed.

'You really should have been a cop.'

They both laughed. 'Might do one day. We'd work well, and I do think we'd make a good interview team,' she said.

'And you'd definitely be the one playing "bad cop".'

'So, give,' she said.

Now she detected a real grin on Martin's face as he said, 'Sorry, it's nothing too sinister, I'm trying not to worry you more. It's just that the guy looked familiar. It might be nothing as I only caught a fleeting glance of the side of his face as he left, but it chimed somewhere in my head.'

'Thought so; he had villain written all over him.'

'Come on, we can chat it through later. Let's grab a Chinese takeaway on the way, I'm starving.'

'Good shout and it's my treat,' she said.

CHAPTER FORTY-TWO

Manning was lounging around in the front room of his barn conversion on his own, having a beer or two, and cleaning and oiling one of his sawn-off shotguns. Things only let you down if you didn't look after them. He'd never had a gun fail him in his life. His girlfriend had gone out for the evening with her stupid mates. He couldn't stand them even though he'd only met them once. He made instant assessments of people, and they were all fuckwits. All they waffled on about when he had met them was makeup, clothes and something called *Love Island*. To be honest, they could all be Suzy clones, which was why he enjoyed a bit of peace when she was not home. Outside of the bedroom, he had little interest in her, and if everything went to plan, he'd soon be on a Caribbean island somewhere, where Blighty and Suzy would be a distant memory.

It frustrated him that he could not put himself about like he used to, well not since his ex-girlfriend had got on his tits so much that he'd had to off her. All her own fault, she never knew when to leave it. At least Suzy didn't pry; she didn't seem interested in where all the cash came from, it was the spending of it she excelled in. In fact, he might have to have a word with her about that; she might draw some unwanted attention.

He'd almost set everything up over in Yorkshire; a bunch of spotty, failed chemistry students were about to make more money than their mates who had passed their degrees, and now only earned peanuts making cold remedies of whatever. Gazza was in charge of them and when everything was sweet, he was going to re-locate him east of the Pennines to be hands-on. In fact, Manning wanted Gazza to run the entire UK business while he tanned his toes, he hadn't told him yet, he was saving the surprise. Gazza would become a very wealthy man.

All they had to do was make a serious inroad into the UK cocaine market, from the dickheads to the Hooray Henrys, and they would be fabulously rich. That was the beauty of cocaine; it was a drug of choice that transcended social boundaries like no other. The widest possible market. And in recent years its use and abuse had grown massively. It was a very good time to get involved in it with their replacement product, which would be more addictive and give a greater high, once perfected. Crack cocaine, the concentrated version, however, was still a niche market. It seemed to stay on the sink estates and never reached the middle or upper classes. Manning didn't know why, but he had never been a user. Alcohol and pussy were his sins of pleasure. But who knew, maybe they could steal some of the crack market too? The all-round potential of Sky White was mesmerising.

All he needed now was for his partner to escape from India with the recipe for Sky White, and for the new market to remain viable and plentiful. It was feasible that even if they didn't get the recipe they could still go ahead. Gazza had told him that the head Beaker over in Yorkshire reckoned that with some decent kit and a bit of time, they should be able to reverse engineer the drug. But he didn't trust the Muppet lookalike, or his fellow

239

failed boffins that far. Just look at the problems he'd had so far with the field testing of the prototype: red eye and death. He was reassured by his partner that the Indians, who were the real experts after all, had now fixed the issue and were testing the new formula. He was very aware that if he let Beaker and his mates have a go, and something worse happened, it could kill his entire business plan overnight. It would have all been for nothing, and he didn't really want to add several more murders to his tally.

There was just the market-threatening issue that needed sorting, along with the security check he'd put in place with Bash the Bishop. He was sure the security thing would be okay; after all, when it got out what he'd done to the one informant they knew about, it would act as a very powerful deterrent. That was the real reason for the note. Without it, the cops might have suppressed the fact that barbeque man was a grass, but the note would come out at the coroner's inquest, or so he'd been advised. Regardless, it was fun. He'd have loved to have seen the filths' faces when they read it. The further check he was doing was just tradecraft; better to be safe than nicked.

As for the market threat issue, it was currently in Gazza's hands. Once the tits with a gob was stopped, then he'd start to get excited. He'd ring Gazza for an update in a while. Then his phone rang. He thought it might be Gazza as he'd just been thinking about him, but it was his partner. He muted the TV and took the call. 'You got the shits yet?' he started with.

'I love my curry back home, but even *I'm* not tempted over here,' his partner said.

'Always were a delicate little soul. Anyway, how's it hanging?'

'To the left as always, thanks for asking, but getting back to business, our friends over here have fixed the problem with the product and are getting very excited.'

'Until we shaft them.'

His partner laughed before continuing, 'Yeah, and it'll be my arse they are chasing.'

Manning knew this and had great respect for his partner in slime and said so.

'Hopefully, they won't know I've copied it, not for a long time, and only then, when we've gone global, by which time there'll be fuck-all they can do. Plus, I have an idea.'

'Go on?'

'I've been building up a great rapport while watching their team in the lab closely, and I'm hoping I can pour some sugar in their petrol tank, so to speak, before I do one.'

'Brilliant, but don't take any unnecessary risks. Your first priority is to get the hell out of Dodge once you have the script.'

'Will do, but if we can give them a second issue with the recipe to keep them occupied it would help explain why we suddenly cancel our mega order.'

Even better, Manning thought. Then he returned his partner to the initial problem. 'Have they finished field testing the fix?'

'That's why I'm really ringing you tonight instead of tomorrow; they have fully tested it and its perfect. No red eye, no light sensitivity, and definitely no deaths.'

'That's absolutely brilliant. We are close now, very close,' Manning said.

'I know mate, all the hard work and scheming will have paid off. Just one question from this end.'

'Manning knew what it was before it was asked. 'No need to ask, we are on it as we speak. By this time tomorrow it'll be sorted.'

'The subtle way?'

'By far the preferred option. But worry not, my

Korma-loving mate, if for any reason that way fails, I'll sort it myself; and that won't be subtle.'

His partner laughed and then they said their goodbyes.

Manning reached for another beer and unmuted the TV; the regional news was due to start.

CHAPTER FORTY-THREE

Martin called in at Cath's local takeaway and then raced to her home so they could eat the food hot. She'd suggested ringing for a home delivery, but Martin didn't like doing that. It always took ages to come and often the food was warm, at best. Plus, they were nearly passing the place on their way to her flat.

After they had eaten, he could tell she was starting to feel better. She looked more relaxed. Food often did that; he had found at times of stress.

'That Chow Mein was lovely,' she said.

'Ages since I've had a Chinese takeaway,' Martin said.

'Be a while again, unless we are at yours.'

'How come?'

'Because the house will stink for a day or two, at least.'

She was clearly more comfortable now as she was grumbling. Martin just smiled, but he was still trying to place the guy in the bar, baggy jumper man as Cath called him. It had only been a glimpse, but he was definitely familiar. And if that meant he was a villain, then that was not a good thing. And why exactly was he following Cath? She had taken the food cartons away and had reappeared carrying an empty bottle of wine, interrupting his thoughts.

'I don't suppose you'd be a real sweetie?'

Martin had to laugh; sweetie being a name Cath would never normally use. 'Seeing as you have asked so nicely,' he said, and picked up his car keys from the coffee table.

'Lazy sod, the offy is only round the corner.'

'I may as well go to Asda, cheaper and I'll be quicker.'

'You may as well stock up then.'

Martin raised an eyebrow.

'Hey, I paid for the food,' she added.

'Fair point, I'll grab a few bottles. I won't be long,' Martin said, and headed out of the flat. In truth, he wanted to take the motor as it would give him a chance to have a nose around. Just in case baggy jumper man was about. He'd been very careful when he'd driven from the Gin and Sing bar and was as sure as he could be that they had not been followed. Though, he had no idea what, if any, car baggy jumper man would have access to. Nevertheless, he'd seen nothing suspicious in his rear-view mirrors, but he also knew it was not an exact science.

Cath hadn't lived in the flat long; it was a typical modern professional person's flat, close to the centre of Manchester, tucked away on a quiet side street. One side of which contained old, terraced housing, all freshly painted in pastel colours, many of which were split into flats. On Cath's side of the road, the old houses had been demolished and replaced with the modern purpose-built flats with city living as their obvious theme. A row of parked cars lined both sides of the road, and Martin had been lucky in being able to park right outside Cath's flat, he just hoped the space would still be there on his return. He did a quick recce around the block but saw nothing of note. He then drove to Asda and bought two bottles of rosé and two bottles of cabernet sauvignon. Ten minutes later he was back at Cath's having done a further recce and again having seen nothing out of place, but his parking space had gone so he had to park opposite and a bit further down.

Two glasses later and they were both far more chilled. Cath told Martin all about the research she'd done, and the details of the additional deaths. 'I'll get straight on it tomorrow and try and arrange retrospective toxicology,' he said.

'Will that be possible?' she asked.

'All depends on what samples were taken at the original post-mortems, such as blood, and whether they have been kept.'

'What are the chances?'

'Not sure to be honest, it's a slightly unusual one. I suspect that they will keep all samples until the coroner's hearing at least, just in case he or she orders a fresh examination, for whatever reason,' he answered.

'And if the coroner's already decided on the cases?'

'Then we are probably stuffed, but I don't know. In non-suspicious cases the coroner reports on their findings fairly quickly, but I doubt that's been done yet, so fingers crossed,' Martin said.

Then Cath asked about his day, and he knew he had to be careful about what he told her but was able to reassure her that they were actively investigating the drug supply side at Blackpool and had made good progress.

'What about the murder?' she asked.

'I can tell you that it's linked.'

'Come on, Martin, I'm dying to know more.'

'You know I can't, yet.'

'Yet?' she seized on. 'That means you will be able to at some stage.'

Martin grinned, and then looked up at the muted TV, and saw that the regional news was about to start. 'Look,' he said, pointing at the set, 'let's watch you now that you're getting famous.' He unmuted the TV as Cath turned to look at the screen and they both settled down to watch. The headlines came on first and Cath's report was the second item. She took the remote from Martin's hand and turned the volume up.

The anchor first gave a sixty-second potted history of events in Blackpool and Preston over the last couple of days which then linked into a quote from the previous broadcast. Then it cut to her update recorded a few hours ago with the anchor saying, 'And now to the Lancashire Police spokesperson who has been instrumental in identifying this terrible problem, for an update.'

Then Cath's face filled the screen as she spoke to the camera, 'From our enquiries of today we have found other drug-related deaths which lead us to believe that there is a bad batch of cocaine on the streets, which can prove fatal.'

Then the broadcast cut back to the interviewing correspondent, 'Thanks for that, Cath, this is very worrying. Are the health authorities fully aware?'

'The police are actively investigating, and we are linking in with some of our statutory partners, such as drug and addiction treatment workers, as well as the NHS, so hopefully the message should get out quickly.'

'How widespread do you think this bad batch of cocaine is?'

'I was led to believe yesterday, that it was gone, but two of the deaths which we believe are linked, only happened today, and as it appears to be fast-acting, the worry is that the two who died today probably only bought the drug today, such is the "hand-to-mouth" and "day-by-day" nature of drug abuse.'

'And finally, Cath, what should users of the substance look out for?'

Cath replied, 'If any cocaine user starts to feel discomfort with their eyes such as sensitivity to light, seek medical attention swiftly. But if past that and their eyes start to swell and turn red, they should dial 999, as death may not be far away. I've witnessed it for myself, and it's horrible.'

'Thanks so much for that, Cath, and now back to you in the studio.'

Martin grabbed the remote and turned the TV volume down, before turning to face Cath, 'Hey that was spot on, well done.'

'Thanks, it seemed okay, and we've got the message out.'

'Hopefully the contact number which flashed up on the screen will be red hot tomorrow, now the balloon's gone up a bit,' Martin said.

'If it saves one life.'

Martin nodded.

CHAPTER FORTY-FOUR

Manning had just finished cleaning, oiling and loading his sawn-off shot gun when the news started. He put the weapon down on the table in front of him and picked up another beer. He always kept his weapons loaded, and close to hand in the house.

Five minutes later he was apoplectic. He couldn't believe what the tits with a gob had just said. It was hard to evaluate how much damage she had just done. She obviously doesn't know that Sky White exists, or if she does, she hadn't mentioned it, yet. She had tied all the problems to a bad batch of normal cocaine. But even so, anyone with the symptoms she so kindly described would know that they had bought Sky White and not usual cocaine. This was a disaster. Manning wasn't sure how many cokeheads watched the news, but if they kept repeating the story in further bulletins, or worse, added to it, the damage could be catastrophic. And if they named it or explained that it was a cocaine substitute it could be game over.

It took a further five minutes before his anger had subsided enough for him to use the phone. He called Gazza who picked up straight away.

'Have you seen what that bitch has done now?' he

started and then went on to explain what he'd just seen whether Gazza had or not. 'And it'll cost me a new Ultra HD TV.'

'Why's that?' Gazza said.

'Because I've just shot the fucker.'

'Very Elvis.'

'No time for jokes, Gazza, you won't laugh if I shoot you.'

'Sorry, Boss.'

'Where the fuck is she now?'

Gazza then gave Manning a quick update on how he'd followed her between the bars but had to do one when the geezer turned up.

'Why?' Manning asked.

'He had filth written all over him.'

'Recognise him?'

'No.'

'Recognise you?'

'Didn't give him the chance.' Gazza went on to explain how he'd managed to follow them back to her flat. But didn't hang around as the geezer went in with her. He'd only just arrived home himself.

'What about the filth geezer?'

'Reckon he's giving her one.'

'Living there?'

'Hard to say.'

Manning paused as he mused over his options. As much as he wanted her sorting as soon as possible, he didn't want to bring any more attention to what she'd been working on. Plus, there was always a chance lover-boy would still be there, making it more difficult. 'It can wait until tomorrow. She can't do any more harm before then, plus it'll be much sweeter that way,' Manning said.

'And attract no questions.'

'Exactly.'

'Till tomorrow then. I'll bell you with the good news,

once she's had the bad.'

    'Excellent. And remember to make sure she's dead.'

CHAPTER FORTY-FIVE

Martin stirred as Cath rose and didn't glance at the clock until she returned with a mug of tea a few minutes later. It was 6 a.m. 'You're an early bird, considering you polished off two bottles of wine,' he said.

'Loads to do. I want to dig deeper into the drug deaths. I'm worried that it could be even more widespread than we know.'

'A jolly thought.'

'Come on lazy bones, you've got to get to Preston too,' she said, as she yanked the quilt off him.

By 6.45 a.m. they were showered, dressed and fully toasted-up. 'I do wish you'd get some proper bread,' he said, as he brushed the last crumbs from the sides of his mouth.

'Light bread is good for you,' she said.

'It's bread with the bread taken out.'

'Come on, you have to drop me first, don't forget. You can moan in the car,' she added.

Martin followed her out the front door. Cath was ahead of him and about to walk down the four or five steps to the pavement. It was raining and the light wasn't too good. She turned on the top step, and said, 'I'll just grab my brolly, it's behind the door.'

Martin stood back as she did, and as she was about to set off back down the steps, he remembered that he'd left his keys on the coffee table and said so.

'I'll see you by the car,' she said.

'It's opposite and down a bit,' Martin shouted after her. She raised her left hand, thumb up. He dashed back into the lounge, grabbed his keys and was back by the door a few seconds later. He could see Cath pause on the pavement as she put her brolly up and then fiddled with her ear. He closed the front door and approached the top step.

Then he heard a car engine racing, and instinctively looked to his right towards the sound. Cath seemed not to react to it, having already glanced to her right just before Martin heard the noise. She was now crossing the road with her head stuck under her brolly. It was one of those semi-transparent plastic ones you were supposed to be able to see through, so you could put your head into it and give your shoulders protection from the elements.

Martin glanced back towards the approaching noise and could see that it was coming from a dark coloured Vauxhall Astra that looked like it had seen better days. The car was racing down the street towards Cath. She still hadn't reacted. 'Cath,' Martin shouted, as he leapt to the bottom of the steps. She didn't seem able to hear him.

He glanced towards the ever-nearing car just as the driver accelerated.

Martin now saw this for what it was and sprinted the few metres into the road to its centre where Cath was still obliviously ambling across. Martin hit her hard; a rugby tackle by someone who had never played sport, wrapping both arms around her midriff as he did so, propelling her to safety. She swept through the air then landed between two parked cars.

The car was a couple of metres away from them, at most. He could smell its engine. A hot oily scent invaded his nostrils as the screech of its exhaust assaulted his ears.

The Astra hit one of the parked cars that was providing a safe space and careened past Martin. He felt his trailing right foot glance off the driver's side bodywork as he cleared the road and landed on top of Cath.

His right ankle hurt, but he knew he was okay, just; it had been a glancing blow. He quickly got up, hoping to see the car's registration number, but all he caught were sparks as the Astra continued bouncing off parked cars further down the street. The driver rounded the bend at the end of the road and was gone.

Martin quickly turned his attention to a shocked-looking Cath who was now stood and rubbing her left hip. He could see that she had earpieces plugged into both ears. She slowly pulled them out, and Martin could hear faint music, until she pulled her phone out of her pocket and switched the sound off.

'Are you okay?' she asked.

'I'll live. You?' he asked.

'Same as you. My God, Martin, I think you just saved my life.'

'I reckon I did. But by God that was close.'

'I missed what exactly happened. What was it, a drunk driver or something?'

'I only wish it was, Cath. But someone just tried to kill us both. And it was you they were after first.'

CHAPTER FORTY-SIX

Martin insisted Cath be taken to hospital in the ambulance for a check-up, and she agreed as long as he came too. Truth be known his ankle was throbbing and he was limping on his right foot slightly, but he was certain there was no lasting damage. He managed to have a quick word with a local detective at the scene before they left and made sure that he knew that what happened was no traffic accident. He said he'd get their written statements done later, but for now they had both Cath and his verbal accounts. The guy from the corner shop also came forward as a witness, having been brought out from behind his counter by the sound of the offending vehicle playing pinball with the parked cars, including his own.

At the hospital they had a long wait before they were both cleared to leave with just a few bruises and swellings. They had been lucky. The triage nurse bandaged Martin's right ankle and it was feeling better now the painkillers were starting to kick in. Martin said he would be okay to drive and that he would take Cath with him to Preston; she could work from there rather than headquarters, thankful that his car had been one of the few that the maniac missed. She had initially argued until he reminded her that their assailant knew where she lived and may know where she worked. They needed to change both until they fully understood what was going on. They first called back at her flat and she packed a small case of essentials which they dropped off at his place, where she would stay for the foreseeable.

Martin went into full anti-surveillance mode until they were clear of his place and on the motorway. He'd already cleared it with Colin that she could work from their office in the short-term. Once they settled into the motorway journey, Martin voiced what had been really troubling him since the incident. 'I'm so sorry, Cath, but I reckon he must have followed us back to your place last night from the gin bar. It's my fault.'

'You can't know that, so don't think it. He might already have known where I lived, and even if he had followed us, you had no way of knowing which car to look out for.'

Typical Cath, and even though what she said was fair, he still felt responsible. 'If I get my hands on that scumbag . . .'

'You'll arrest him and follow procedure; or risk losing your job,' she said, finishing his sentence for him. Martin wasn't too sure about that.

He then took a call from the detective he'd spoken to earlier, who informed him that the motor involved had been found burned out behind some garages about a mile from the scene. There was nothing left of it, accelerants had been used. The driver had obviously come prepared.

'You know, if you hadn't been there, I'd be dead now. I never heard the revving engine until the vehicle was on me. By then, I was hurtling through the air, courtesy of your good self, Cath said.

'Those ear pods should come with a health warning. And it was the least I could do, seeing as it was probably my fault he was there,' Martin said.

'You're missing the point.'

Martin paused as he indicated for her to exit the motorway at junction 31, the central Preston approach, and then said, 'Go on.'

'Think it through. The car was found burned out, so he had accelerants on board ready to light it, once the job was done.'

'This probably confirms that he followed us back to your place last night and then came back this morning to attack you.'

'And if you hadn't been there, not only would the car have hit me, but it would have appeared as a tragic hit and run. The driver only lost it when he tried to prevent your intervention.'

'Meaning?'

'Meaning, he wanted it to look like an accident. 'If he wanted to silence me for whatever reason, why the subtle approach?'

Martin had no idea but hadn't really thought it all through yet. It looked like Cath had. She went on, 'If I was openly attacked, putting your detective's head on, rather than my boyfriend's, what would you ask first?'

Martin thought for a second and then said, 'I'd want to know why. An accident doesn't need a motive, but an attack does. They wanted it to look like an accident so the question of why wouldn't be asked.'

'You're catching on, detective. And where would you look first to answer the question?'

'Your private life and professional life,' he replied. 'And assuming they weren't after me, as I came second, and I know your private life personally, that can only leave your professional life. They didn't want your death to be linked to it.'

'And we both know what I've been working on to the complete exclusion of everything else,' she said.

'The drug deaths.'

'My broadcast must have pushed them over the edge, especially as I promised Minty that I was going to drop it.'

Martin knew she was right. His first thought was to arrange the finding of the scumbag she had spoken to, and his mate, whichever one was actually Minty mattered not. He would get on with it as soon they reached his office. But this must mean that this new chemical cocaine was potentially a far bigger threat than they'd first thought. Not that Colin and he had had time to evaluate fully what the lab had told them yet. He hadn't worked out how all the pieces fit together, but he would. It was time to level with Cath on what the lab had told them, it would help her to make sense of it all, but she'd have to keep it to herself for the moment.

'So Sky White isn't just a new form of cocaine, or a bad batch mixed with whatever, it's a totally new compound?' Cath said, after Martin had finished bringing her up to speed. He just nodded.

'And it's totally legit?' she added.

'As a substance, yes, for now.'

'Unbelievable,' she said. 'So what do we do?'

'I can't tell you all of it yet, but there is believed to be a bent official involved, and for God's sake don't let Colin know I've told you. Not yet anyway.'

Cath nodded.

'And there is a plan to nab him being put into place today. If it works, it will hopefully give us evidence on Manning.'

'Will it lead you to him?'

'Not sure yet, but it might. Or certainly point us in the right direction.'

'Well, if it doesn't, I may be able to help.'

Martin wasn't too sure what Cath meant, so said, 'Well, for now, you can work from my office on your research into just how big this is, as in how many deaths there have already been.'

'I intend to, and I'll arrange a further TV update to keep the warning fresh. Drive him to make a mistake, perhaps.'

'That'll really piss Manning off, and hopefully make him show himself,' Martin said.

'If your plan doesn't work, I have a sure-fire way of making him out himself,' Cath said.

Martin really didn't like the sound of this, but asked anyway, 'What do you mean?'

'I'll be your bait.'

'Excuse me?'

'I'll do a further TV update from somewhere public. But make sure that it's done live, and that it is advertised in advance. Give Manning a chance to come to us at a time of our choosing.'

'No, Cath, it's not happening. It's far too dangerous.'

'Better make sure your Plan A works then.'

CHAPTER FORTY-SEVEN

Bashir arrived at police headquarters early as he wanted to sort out the CHAMPS thing as quickly as he could to satisfy Manning and get him off his back. He hadn't slept much as he'd been churning over the advice from Yates and Grantham. He reckoned he could access the database one last time and then he could tell Manning that it couldn't be done again. If there were no other informants reporting on Manning, then that should be all he needed to hear. And to be honest, he doubted he could get back in after today, so he wasn't even lying. The system had not been 'live' for long, so his one-off chance today was a good one, as it had occurred to him during the small hours as he had lain staring at the ceiling. Get today out of the way and he could relax a bit more; he might even find time to look up his errant brother, Abdul, if he was home. It did annoy him that it was always he who seemed to make the effort.

By half seven, Bashir was at his desk and had brought up the CHAMPS database on the force internal intranet. He typed in his access codes, and as expected, a dropdown box appeared in red stating that this password had expired. He then typed in his 'Head of IT' username which he had not used previously. It gave him universal access to most of the other police systems, and a further dropdown box appeared questioning the reason for his login. This was a very good sign. It had occurred to him in the night to try his Head of IT approach rather than the mirrored access he'd initially had, courtesy of the authorising officer, Kerry Danson.

Bashir clicked on a link which read, 'Engineer's Urgent Access' and then the system brought up a number of options. Bashir chose the installation menu which he was mightily relieved to see still there. He knew it was a temporary list of options for use with any teething problems for the migration from the old software onto the new. It would disappear after Kerry Danson had signed off that the new system was fully functioning. This was the bit he couldn't have known. Had she already given CHAMPS the full thumbs-up, he would have been stuffed. He let out a huge sigh and took in a large gulp of fresh air. He knew that his backdoor access could disappear before his eyes at any second, but he was just relieved to be in.

He worked quickly searching 'All Accounts' for any mention of Manning or Joey. The 'All Accounts' access was normally limited to the Authorising Officer only, so he was conscious of getting in and out before Kerry arrived at her desk and logged on. She'd never know he'd been on the system at all once he'd gone. He wasn't a normal user, so the system didn't store his footprint. He glanced at the office clock as he worked; it was now ten to eight. He wanted to be gone before eight, before Kerry was at her desk, just in case she decided to make checking in with CHAMPS her first task of the day.

Several hits came back, and Bashir quickly read through them, he was relieved to see that they all related to the stuff he had already passed on to Manning, there was nothing new. Though, his relief was mixed with guilt when he realised once more how those disclosures had led to someone's awful death. He shook the thought from his mind as he backed himself out of the system and felt a huge weight lift from his shoulders as he logged off.

He closed down the thumbnail icon completely and sat back in his chair. He then sent a quick text to the intermediary's phone stating that he been allowed one last access as Head of IT and that there was nothing new across the entire system. He had only just placed the burner phone in his pocket when it beeped a response, which read, *Noted. M will be pleased.*

Bashir put the phone back in his coat and leaned into his chair. He felt his neck click as the tension lifted.

Then his door burst open.

In walked Kerry Danson and a detective who identified himself as Colin Carstairs – and they looked like they were on a mission.

'Knocking first is usually the polite way, but as you are here, how can I help you?' Bashir said.

'Why have you just accessed CHAMPS again?' Danson asked.

Bashir nearly fainted but put on a brave face and denied it. He knew his visit would leave no audit trail, and now he was logged off, that was the end of it.

'Don't lie, Bashir, I know you have just been on the system, so I'll give you another chance to tell the truth,' Danson said.

'I've no idea what you are—'

'Searching all accounts for any mention of Manning,' Kerry interrupted him with.

Bashir nearly fell off his chair, how could she possibly know? He caught his breath, and said, 'Oh, you mean just now? Sorry, erm, I just wanted to do a final systems check.'

His words sounded strained to him, so God knows how weak they must have seemed to Danson and Carstairs, but he was trying to meet them halfway. It was a panicked reaction.

'Glad you said that,' Carstairs said.

Bashir turned his attention to the detective as he continued, 'See, we knew someone using your codes and passwords had just accessed the system via your terminal, we just needed confirmation that it was you, and not someone else using your codes.'

Bashir dropped his head on the realisation that he had just hung himself.

'We've had an authorised bug on your computer watching every keystroke your terminal has made,' Danson said. 'Just needed to prove that it was you. Now comes the fun bit. Colin, will you do it? I should retain my independence as a witness from here on in.'

'Be my pleasure,' Carstairs said, before turning to face Bashir full-on once more. 'Stand up.'

Bashir did as instructed, but his legs were turning to jelly.

Carstairs continued, 'Mohammed Bashir, I'm arresting you on suspicion of malfeasance in public office. You do not have to say anything . . .'

CHAPTER FORTY-EIGHT

Martin received a text from Colin as he'd been driving, but as his iPhone didn't allow it to chime through while mobile, he hadn't seen it until he was walking Cath to his office. It read that Colin couldn't ring him as his car's Bluetooth would have put the call through his speakers, and Colin knew Cath was with him. But as soon as Martin had settled her in their office, he was to get to the chief's office ASAP. He smiled as he read it and guessed that the trap had worked. He explained to Cath that he had to shoot off and she said she didn't need babysitting, just a desk, a phone and a desktop, so she was good to go. He brought her a brew and then explained where the canteen was if she needed anything else. He texted Colin back to say he was leaving Preston and would be with him soon.

En route his phone rang via the car's Bluetooth, and it was Colin who double-checked he was alone before he quickly briefed Martin on the morning's events.

'I bet you enjoyed arresting him yourself, Colin, sorry I couldn't have been with you.'

'It's been many years since I've had the pleasure of feeling a collar; forgot how much fun it was. But why I'm ringing is to divert you to Leyland police station, south of

Preston. They have opened the defunct custody suite there due to the sensitivities of the situation.'

'Makes sense.'

'And Bashir, for now, has elected to be interviewed without a brief.'

'That's a surprise,' Martin said.

'His arse proper dropped out, and I want to get at least one interview in, however quick, before he catches his breath and regains his confidence.'

'Be with you in ten,' Martin said, and ended the call. He knew exactly what Colin was saying. Often when someone was arrested – who was not used to being so – they would be in a state of shock and often feel a primeval instinct to actually tell the truth; but it never lasted long. As soon as Bashir caught his breath, as Colin put it, he would be fully lawyered-up and 'no commenting' all the way, no doubt.

Ten minutes later Martin walked into Leyland police station and into an eerily quiet custody suite. They got Bashir out of his cell, and the custody officer asked him again if he wanted a brief. Martin held his breath. Bashir confirmed that he didn't but understood that he could stop the interview anytime he changed his mind. Martin and Colin had previously discussed strategy for this first interview and knew when they dropped the Big Bertha on him everything would change.

In the interview room, they sat Bashir on one side of the table and Martin and Colin on the side with the door behind them. They quickly did the admin and got the tapes running. Colin led and went through the events immediately leading up to his arrest, followed by asking who he had texted on the phone they took from him, and what it had meant.

Bashir came out with a load of fantasy and then Colin cut to the point. 'We've been monitoring you for some time, and we know that – prior to today – you have accessed intelligence relating to Daniel Manning's associate, Joey.'

Martin was watching Bashir intensely as his attention in turn was focused on Colin. Martin saw it in his eyes, a definite reaction to Colin's question. Martin knew that they were not going to mention the drug stuff at this stage, and as Bashir had been arrested for malfeasance only, they didn't have to. They were sticking to Bashir's unlawful disclosure of sensitive information, for now.

'There must be some mistake, I have only ever been checking the IT systems, if I happened to cross over pages mentioning these people, it is a pure coincidence,' Bashir said.

'Twice?' Colin said. Bashir didn't reply. 'And who is this M that will be pleased?' Colin pressed. Martin watched Bashir swallow hard, but he didn't answer. 'Don't suppose M is Manning by any chance?' Colin added. As expected, still no reply. Martin knew that Colin's words were digging in deep by the lack of response. Bashir had gone from arrogant denial to silence. The next bit had to be timed just right. Too long, and Bashir would ask for a brief and the interview would end there and then. Too soon, and he wouldn't be as vulnerable as they wanted him for the maximum effect. Not that the bombshell wouldn't do that at any time due to its nature, but it was what they intended immediately after that, that was really the key to everything. They needed to get their hands on Manning, first and foremost. Bashir's fate was secondary as much as Martin despised him. He glanced at Colin; it was good cop time.

'Look, Mohammed, we get it, we understand that Manning is a maniac, a very scary one,' Martin said, noting that he had Bashir's undivided attention. 'We realise that you have no doubt been manipulated. Things have happened that you have had nothing to do with.'

'What do you mean?' Bashir said, with a sudden

weakness in his voice. Martin knew he was ready.

'You passed on the information about Joey planning a robbery,' Martin said. Bashir didn't answer but didn't deny it. Martin continued, 'And you probably thought not much of it. I can understand that. But it led to two robberies; one a decoy and one for real.' Still no reply from Bashir, but he was hanging on Martin's every word. 'And in the real one, someone lost their life.'

'If you are referring to the body in the boot thing, I heard about that, but it has nothing to do with me,' Bashir said, suddenly showing more confidence.

'But if Manning worked out whom the informant was, and killed him . . .?' Martin said, leaving the comment unfinished.

'Even if I had access to the information you mention, I have no idea who the informant was, that part of CHAMPS was never available to me,' Bashir said.

'We know Manning has been threatening you, putting you under pressure to comply with his demands,' Martin said.

'Rubbish,' Bashir said, and started to sit upright in his chair.

Martin glanced at Colin; it was time.

'"Do as I say, or I'll start by having some fun with your missus while you watch,"' Colin said.

The words hit Bashir hard. His face went ashen. Colin and Martin had decided not to reveal that they overheard the conversation, not at this stage, just in case it was ruled inadmissible, but to use a line from it. Bashir would have no idea how they knew this; Yates or Grantham could be a double agent for all Bashir knew. But the remark had worked like a body-blow that ex-boxer Ricky Hatton would have been proud of.

'If you want us to believe you had no idea the leak would lead to a man's murder, then you have to work with us. Tell us the truth,' Colin said.

'I'm listening,' Bashir said.

Got him.

Now for the bombshell, and Martin really wasn't looking forward to this bit. He and Colin had tossed a coin, and he had lost.

'The guy who was murdered, the one in the boot of the burned-out car.'

'Yes, what about him?'

'I'm really, truly sorry to have to tell you this. And believe me, there is no other way we can do it.'

'Do what? What is this?' Bashir said.

'We have very strong reasons to believe that the deceased is your brother, Abdul.'

CHAPTER FORTY-NINE

Bashir sat back in his chair, stunned as Draker's words took root. He churned them around in his mind for a second or two to make sure he had heard correctly. He could tell by the sullen look on both the cops' faces that he had. Then the realisation of it hit him. Involuntarily he let out a howl of anguish. His head dropped into his hands as he wept uncontrollably. After a minute or so, though it could have been five or more, he wasn't sure, he felt a hand on his shoulder. He looked up; it was Draker.

'We've stopped the interview, I'm so sorry to have to break it to you this way. We'll take you back to your cell. Give you chance to get over the initial shock. We need to ask a favour, but it can wait.'

Bashir didn't know what Draker was talking about, but he was going nowhere until he knew more. He shook Draker's hand away, and looked up, quietened for a moment. Then spoke. 'Wait. How can you be so sure it's Abdul?'

'We've turned the tapes off, we can't interview you now, well, not about why you are sat here,' Draker said.

'I'm interviewing you. Tell me how you know.'

'There was information left by the killer saying that the deceased was the informant, and we've been unable to trace Abdul since,' Draker said.

'What information?' Bashir asked, the thought that it might not be Abdul had given him renewed positivity.

'We can't tell you, but take our word for it,' Draker said.

'Well, Abdul was no grass, so there must be some mistake. Whoever the poor sod in that car boot was; informant or otherwise, it can't be Abdul,' Bashir said, and then noticed Draker and his boss, Carstairs, glance at each other. 'What?' he demanded.

'Look, normally we are not at liberty to disclose anything about informants, but . . . as he is no longer with us . . .' Carstairs said, leaving his sentence unfinished.

Bashir was struggling to keep up. Even if Abdul was an informant, who he was not, why would anyone want to kill him? Instead, he asked, 'But you haven't formally identified the body, I'm guessing?'

He saw Carstairs shake his head, but he then added, 'Not enough tissue left to do so, I'm afraid.'

'So it may not be him,' Bashir said, with added hope.

'It's him, it has to be him,' Draker said.

The certainty in Draker's voice unnerved Bashir. He weakly asked why.

He watched Draker take a deep breath and then glance at his boss once more before he spoke. 'Because Daniel Manning was, we suspect, behind the robbery. He torched the car or ordered it so. He was responsible for killing Abdul in the boot.'

'You've still not said why the body has to be Abdul?' Bashir said.

'Abdul was the informant who told us about "Joey" planning the robbery. Joey is one of Manning's gang members, in fact we think he was on the decoy robbery, and Manning has claimed to have worked out who the informant was. So you can see why it has to be your brother in the car boot. I'm sorry, Mohammed,' Draker

269

said.

Bashir sat back again, his mind racing even faster than before as he took in what Draker was saying. He was stunned to learn that his brother, with whom he spoke intermittently, was a police spy. And not only a spy, but the very one whose information Bashir had passed on to Manning. He strained to remember all the details of the intelligence. Then it hit him, it talked about the planning of a robbery in Preston – cash in transit - but even though he couldn't remember any other details, it was all starting to fit.

Then he recalled, once, ages ago, foolishly bragging to his brother about having Grantham in his pocket and making a fortune out of doing drug runs to India. What an arrogant fool he'd been. He calmed himself and strived harder to remember the intelligence report he had initially intercepted, the one he'd passed to Manning, the one he'd speed-read this morning. There had been no mention of Jim Grantham, or Bashir, or drug runs. Bless him, his brother may have been a police spy, but he had obviously kept what Bashir had told him to himself. Blood was thicker than water, even if they didn't get on too well most of the time.

Then the locomotive hit him.

It was his fault Abdul was dead. Unwittingly, but his fault, nonetheless.

How the hell was he supposed to know that the grass informing on Joey was his own brother? And how the hell had Manning managed to identify him? The wave of guilt that hit Bashir was a tsunami. He burst into tears again, and sobbed, 'Oh my God.' He saw Draker and Carstairs share a further look. Then the next train came along.

Manning must have known that Abdul was his brother, but that hadn't stopped the ruthless bastard killing him.

He rocked back in his chair a third time as a blend of

emotions cut through him. Sorrow, guilt, anger, then hatred; unadulterated, white-hot hatred.

The one emotion, however, that had hitherto crushed and directed his every waking moment, was gone. The fear was no more. The terror he had of Manning, the overwhelming constraining dread of the man, vanished. Only to be replaced with an even stronger urge: revenge. He didn't care what happened to him now; he just needed to avenge his brother's death. The fractious relationship he had with him was irrelevant. It was a matter of blood, family, and honour.

Having regained his equanimity once again, he looked Draker in the eye, and said, 'I'm ready.'

'Ready for what?' Draker replied. 'To go to your cell?'

'I'm ready to hear what you want of me. And I don't care what it is, as long as it means getting Manning.'

CHAPTER FIFTY

Martin and Colin grabbed a quick lunch at the café in Tesco which was opposite the police station. The nick no longer had a working canteen, just vending machines. Cuts. The morning couldn't have gone much better. Colin had put a quick call in to Rogers's staff officer to arrange an early afternoon meeting.

As soon as they arrived at headquarters, they were met at reception and taken straight to the chief's office. His door was open, and he was pacing inside, waiting for them. As soon as they entered, they were joined by Kerry Danson who rushed in just after them.

All four took a seat at the chief's long conference table.

'Come on, tell us how the interview went, the suspense is killing me,' Kerry asked.

'Well, it couldn't have gone any better, but that's because your plan worked a treat,' Colin replied.

'It didn't take long for Bashir to go hunting online, and I can confirm that he was only allowed access to the original text he saw about Joey etc. All the extra stuff naming him, and DC Grantham and the drug-run intel had been safely quarantined and can't be accessed without my codes together with my deputy's,' Kerry said. Then she turned to face Martin. 'Forgive me, I should have asked how you and Cath are?'

'Both okay, thanks. My ankle's a bit sore but there's nothing broken,' Martin said.

'Any idea who was behind the wheel?' Rogers asked.

'I only got a side-glimpse of the driver, and only for an instant, but it looked a lot like the guy who followed Cath the previous evening,' Martin replied. He noted the raised eyebrows from Kerry and the chief, so quickly filled them in.

'Relevance?' Rogers asked.

Martin told him.

'The press angle should form part of our strategy going forward,' Rogers said.

'We intend it to,' Colin said. 'Apart from the obvious public health concerns, if we can damage, or even kill the new market for Sky White before it has a chance to take hold, then all the better.'

'How did you manage to turn Bashir so quickly?' Rogers asked.

'Yeah, give,' Kerry added.

Martin sat back and took a sip of tea that had been waiting for him and let Colin fill them both in. Adding at the end, that Bashir is happy to plead guilty to his offences as long as he can help nail Manning.

'Will he give Queen's evidence against Manning?' Rogers asked.

'He will, and we've told him that he will get a lighter sentence himself for doing so,' Colin added.

'If he gives evidence about what he said to Yates and Grantham, then your overheard conversations should be admissible too, hopefully,' Kerry added.

'It's starting to come together nicely,' Rogers said. 'But what about those toe rags, Yates and Grantham?'

'We can nick them at any time. Bashir will be released later on police bail before anyone misses him. He's under strict instructions to act normal and avoid any contact with Yates or Grantham unless approved by Martin,' Colin said.

'Can we trust him?' Rogers asked.

'He's been told that the deal is off if he breaks the rules, and that he could face a charge relating to the murder of his brother if he does. He's onside now, driven in part by his own guilt that his unlawful disclosure indirectly led to Abdul's death,' Martin said.

'So we just need to get our hands on Manning?' Rogers said.

'We do, but we have to be careful,' Colin said.

Rogers and Kerry looked on with the same question on both their faces, so Martin jumped in to explain. 'We did a thorough non-PACE intelligence gathering interview with Bashir once the formal interview into his alleged malfeasance offence was over. And during that chat, he let it be known that Manning was not only determined to flood the streets with Sky White, but he wanted to produce it himself.'

'How the hell is he going to do that?' Kerry asked.

'This is getting even more serious; can you imagine the potential damage they could cause with an unlimited supply of the stuff?' Rogers added.

'Exactly,' Colin said to Rogers.

Turning to face Kerry, Martin continued, 'He doesn't know how or by whom, but Manning intends to steal the recipe for Sky White from the Indians.'

'He must have someone out there, working for him,' Kerry said.

'That's what we reckon,' Martin said.

'The Indian cops?' Rogers asked.

'As soon as we get back to Preston, I'm going to ring Sub-Inspector Aadi Das and put him on notice,' Colin said. 'You can see how we need to delay nicking Manning until we have the other side sorted, or the recipe for Sky White will just end up being produced by someone else. Plus, we have no idea who is working for Manning out there.'

'Understood and agreed. Add my acquiesce to your policy log entry, Colin,' Rogers said.

Colin nodded, and then they moved on to the press strategy, and how that could help flush Manning out as and when the time was right. Rogers asked if the press would play ball with them, and Martin said he hadn't run it past them yet, but Cath's view was that there wouldn't be a problem.

'What about Abdul's family, have they been informed yet?' Rogers asked.

'No, and Bashir is under strict instructions to say nothing. It's not in his interests to, as that's when all the difficult questions will follow as to how Abdul ended up in the boot of a burned-out getaway car. That will lead straight back to his door. He'll have to face it at some stage, but the later the better as far as he's concerned.'

'Sorry to ask, but aren't we under a moral obligation to inform Abdul's next of kin, as soon as we can?' Kerry asked.

'We are, when we have finally officially identified the body, which we haven't yet,' Colin said.

'But what if we can never do so? I believe the body was in a pretty rough state,' she added.

'Then we are duty-bound to tell his wife that we strongly believe that the body is his,' Colin replied.

'Timescales?' Rogers asked.

'We are still waiting on the lab; they are still trying to extract DNA from what was left. It should buy us enough time,' Martin added.

The meeting then came to a natural end and Martin and Colin headed off towards Preston. Colin would ring the Indians and Martin would speak to Cath re further press releases. Then they would put in place their plan to snare Manning, once they had thought one up. There was no way he was letting Cath use her Plan B.

CHAPTER FIFTY-ONE

Daniel Manning didn't blame Gazza, as he'd been at pains to explain. It would have all gone sweet as, if that cop hadn't stuck his nose in. He could see the worry in Gazza's eyes as he entered the lounge at the Barn, but Manning had been with Gazza too long, and he'd had an hour to calm down since he'd rung with the bad news. Plus, he couldn't afford to keep replacing his TVs.

'To make it worse, she was oblivious, must have had ear pods in. Sorry, wrong thing to say,' Gazza said.

'No, you did your best,' Manning said, as he paced the room in contemplation. 'In fact, you did well to nearly mop them both up.'

Gazza just nodded from his armchair. 'Motor?' Manning asked.

'Burned out.'

'Good. What about the cop?'

'Here's where we have a plus.'

'Go on.'

'He's the same cop who was in the bar last night,' Gazza started.

'Dirty dog is obviously giving her one.'

'Here's the good bit; he looked familiar, not just as filth, but something else, and it's only just occurred to me why, on the way here.'

'Who is he?'

'He's the same cop who did that TV appeal for some daft bastard who'd gone missing, the one where drug deaths were first mentioned, and the tits with a gob did her first TV report of it.'

'Good work, Gazza. I recorded it so it's still on my Sky box, we can go over it, find out who he is?'

'We also now know where to find him, so if we follow him, we find the tits with a gob,' Gazza said. 'Just in case she doesn't go home.'

'Be too risky to try there again,' Manning said, as he picked the TV remote up. Then his mobile rang. He looked at the screen; it was his man in India. He threw the remote to Gazza and told him to find the news clip while he answered his phone. He wandered into the kitchen away from the noise of the TV and took the call. 'Didn't expect to hear from you today, which means news; just hope it's of the good kind.'

'That it is, my little fat friend,' the caller said.

'A few extra pounds don't make me fat, Chapatti Chops,' he answered.

'As in Rome, plus there's nothing else to eat over here.'

'Not progressed from the Kormas then?'

'It's not compulsory to love hot curry, like you. Anyway, talking about a few extra pounds, we are about to make a million extra.'

'You've got the recipe?'

'Have I, and more.'

'So you did manage to sabotage theirs, too?' Manning asked, suddenly feeling elated again.

'Did I. And if they try to start up again, it won't work at all. Their recipe is now fatally flawed.'

Manning was uber-impressed with his business partner. The bloke was a star.

'How have *you* got on?' the man asked.

'The lab is all ready to rock 'n' roll in Yorkshire, G's going to run it, and we are just awaiting your recipe to get fully operational,' Manning replied.

'What about your little problem?'

Manning didn't want to share the bad news at his end, so said, 'We know where she lives, drinks, and works, so a cinch. It's in hand.'

'Well, I've got a little extra surprise for you.'

'Go on.'

'I've made excuses as to why I have to return to the UK, while they get our mega order together. But not only will they soon discover the flaw in a day or two, but I've paid a local to firebomb their lab in three days' time.'

'You really have outdone yourself, mate.'

'I'm hoping they will put the fire down to the flaw, which is a volatile one, so I'm told, but if not, I'll be long-gone anyway.'

'How did you manage it?'

'Can't go in to too much detail until I see you, but I traced an ex-lab rat they fired and gleaned what I had to do. In fact, he's going to be the local fire-starter.'

'No one is more loyal to a cause than someone with a grudge,' Manning added.

'Plus, he has no idea who I am, so two and two won't make four. But as I say, I'm not bothered if they do. I'll be far away.'

'If we need extra insurance, we could always arrange an "anonymous" call in to them after the fire, and blow the fire-starter out,' Manning added.

'Hadn't thought of that, and I thought I was a bad bastard; you're the worst.'

Manning roared with laughter at the compliment, and then asked when they could expect him back.

'On the first available flight I can get,' he replied, and then they ended the call.

Manning went back into the lounge, just as Gazza was

switching the TV off.

'You sound like you're in a better mood,' Gazza said.

'Too true. Listen to this,' Manning said, and then quickly told him about the news from India.

'It's all coming together nicely now. I'd better get my bag packed and my passport ready to cross the Pennines,' Gazza said.

'You find the clip?' Manning asked.

'Eventually, hidden among the porn. And I was right, it's the same mush.'

'The last thing we need is the tits with a gob winding her pig boyfriend up and getting him interested in the drug deaths,' Manning said.

'My thoughts too.'

'Who is he?'

'Detective Sergeant Martin Draker. He works on the regional organised crime unit from Preston,' Gazza replied.

'Oh God, not him.'

'You know him?'

'Shit, must have missed the name when I first watched it, was only half listening to the news until that newspaper reporter started asking about the drug deaths. Only then I tuned in proper,' Manning said.

'So who is he?'

'Never actually met him, but he was the lead investigator chasing my arse over my ex's death.'

'Christ, what are the odds of that?'

'I know, and with everything at a critical stage, we need to act fast, even if fast means unsubtle. Our man in India will soon be our man in England, we need to sort this before he gets home.'

'What do you have in mind?'

'Did she turn up at work this morning?'

'I rang pig headquarters pretending to have information for her about the drug deaths and was told that she is working from Preston police station and that I should ring there.'

'Nice one, Gazza,' Manning said. Gazza was a star. So they now know where she is working from: Preston pig shop with Draker. 'We need to stop this before it gets any bigger.'

'What do you want me to do?'

'We need to off them both.'

Gazza didn't reply, but Manning could see reticence on his face, so asked why.

'Not a problem, for me, I'm just bothered it might bring a world of shite after us.'

Manning knew where he was coming from; it was a huge balancing act. Hurting, or worse, killing a cop was not to be done lightly. They would come after them in a way that was a thousand times more dogged than they had come after Manning up until now. That said, they wouldn't know who'd done it. And a DS would have a thousand enemies, different again to the analyst who may only be working on the one job and didn't piss half as many people off.

Gazza broke his thoughts, asking, 'Another accident?'

'No, we've lost that chance now. Plus, we need to get them together, then the police will be chasing down a long list of suspects, especially if we leave no clues.'

'That's true I suppose.'

'And getting them together might not be as hard as it sounds whilst she is working from Preston. They might even figure it was him you were aiming at this morning and not her. She could be written off as collateral,' Manning said.

'I can see that. Look, I'd better get my arse up to Preston and start watching the nick.'

Manning didn't answer; he was churning something over in his head.

'But if I get a chance to do him on his own, do you

want me to take it, or wait until he's with her?'

'If we get the chance to do them together, happy days. But if he pops up on offer first, we have to take it. We need to close this down fast. As soon the recipe is with Beaker and his mates, we will be rolling the distribution side out twenty-four hours later.'

'That quick?'

'Yes, so if we still want a market to distribute into, we have to move fast and do what's needed,' Manning replied.

'Not a problem, I can see that, but the "we" bit is worrying me, Dan. You need to keep your face well away from all this.'

Manning didn't respond straight away; it was what he had been chewing over. Every bit of tradecraft he knew agreed with Gazza. He should stay well away, but every bit of his psyche wanted the pleasure of tagging along. 'You're probably right, Gazza, but let's work up a plan first.'

CHAPTER FIFTY-TWO

By the time Martin and Colin had finished briefing Cath on the backstory to the whole drug saga and answering her hundred questions, it was almost mid-afternoon.

'The chief is happy for you to work with us now on all areas, as the murder and robberies are too interlinked with the drug stuff you've been working on,' Colin said.

'Brilliant, I don't usually get to work with an operational team. Once I hand my intelligence package over to a team to do the investigation bit, it's the last I see of it, should be fun.'

'That's where the trade-off comes,' Colin said, and went on to explain their press strategy to help infuriate Manning and flush him out.

'I can get Eleanor to speak to the press office and schedule a rerun of the last news bulletin straight away, while we work on a new release to give the press to follow on with,' she said.

'That would be brilliant,' Colin said.

Cath got straight on to it and Colin said he'd give Sub-Inspector, Aadi Das, in India a ring. Martin said he was late for his pre-arranged meet with Bashir, so hurried off.

It was a short walk from the police station to the city centre, where Martin had arranged to meet Bashir in a local coffee shop. He needed to give him strict instructions and keep him on the right path. Apart from his evidence against Manning being crucial, both Colin and he suspected Bashir had a lot more to tell them, even if it was only used as intelligence. As Martin walked past the new Crown Courts, he kept thinking about the thug who had attacked him and Cath. The more he thought about it, the surer he was that the driver was the guy from the gin bar; it made total sense. And the more he recalled the guy from the gin bar, the deeper the feeling of familiarity he had about him. He shook off his thoughts as he approached the café; Bashir was seated at a window table, waiting.

He spent the first ten minutes reassuring him that the CPS had been spoken to and they were happy that he would get an appropriate reduction in sentence commensurate with the help he was now giving the police. But he had to be clear on two things: one; that he had committed serious breach of trust offences and would undoubtedly receive a prison sentence. And two; the amount of any reduction in that sentence was entirely in Bashir's hands. Bashir nodded his understanding. He then reached into his pocket and passed a piece of paper with a number written on it to Martin.

'I only ever dealt with an intermediary, until I met the main man at the motorway services, though he was very careful to ensure that I never actually saw his face. This is another telephone number that the intermediary uses, it's different to the one on my burner phone from this morning, I thought you should have it, but don't expect either to be switched on. He only uses them when he wants to speak to me, or he is expecting a reply from me,' Bashir said.

This is a great start.

Martin then asked why the man had two burner

phones. Bashir said he didn't know, just guessed that he was extra cautious. He then went on to unburden himself, clearly wracked with guilt over his brother, Abdul's, death. He openly told Martin that he had been a pompous and arrogant man. 'A braggart.' Which Martin thought was an example of his pomposity using such an awkward old English word.

'See, I'm doing it again,' Bashir said. 'I can't help showing off.'

He then explained how he had first been approached for a minor favour in return for an inordinate amount of cash. Then the favours grew in severity, and the threats came flying in when he tried to get out. It was like joining the Mafia.

'That's how they snare you. You were probably targeted from the off as head of IT, and the potential access that it could give,' Martin said.

Bashir smiled weakly. Martin knew at some stage, they would have to nick Bashir on suspicion of the drug runs he had done to India, but he also knew that they had no direct evidence to prove it. They would have to interview Bashir under caution, and unless he was daft enough to admit the offences, it would most likely lead nowhere.

'I know I don't merit anyone's sympathy, and totally deserve what's coming to me, but I am truly sorry. And not just because of Abdul's death, and not just because I've been caught. I've been a greedy arrogant fool and I just want to try and help repair some of the damage by helping as much as I can,' Bashir said.

'That's really good to hear.'

'It was only when I met Manning the other day that I truly realised how evil he was, and as scared of him as I am, I am incandescent with anger at how he killed my brother without a second thought. He is a monster and must be stopped.'

Martin nodded.

'And now I want to tell all I know about Inspector Debbie Yates and DC Jim Grantham.'

Thirty minutes later and they parted company. Everything Bashir had told him about Yates and Grantham would have to be written up properly into a witness statement at some stage and would provide worthy evidence against them both. It would be tainted by the fact that Bashir is, or will be, a co-accused, and therefore challengeable by defence barristers, but it should ensure that they got them both to a jury in the first place, which was half the battle. Though Martin noted Bashir had been selective, leaving out the bits that involved him, but he must know that that would have to come at some stage. He was just glad that was not now; he didn't want his hand forced to arrest Bashir for the drug stuff. Not yet anyway.

Martin walked back to the nick with a spring in his step, and couldn't wait to tell Colin and Cath. The meeting had gone better than he could have hoped. He glanced at a white transit van which was parked opposite the nick; it had a guy in blue overalls reading a newspaper in it. His arms were covered in white paint. He'd noticed decorators on the ground floor of the police station on his way out, they were clearly taking their time; as most contractors did when working for the police. It had often wound Martin up how much builders and the like took the piss when working on a public contract.

As if to prove his point, as he passed through the station's reception, he saw two more sat on trestle tables having a brew. His mind turned back to the background nag he couldn't' shake off, the gin bar guy. Then he walked past Gary Falstaff, the DI who had run the surveillance on the decoy robbery, and they exchanged nods. This in turn made Martin think about that job, and the fact that those who'd been arrested were released with no charge.

Then it hit him. Martin rushed to Gary's office and arrived just as he was sitting down. He asked to see the mugshots of the decoy robbers, and Gary swiftly obliged. There he was, Gary Cradshaw, aka Gazza, with known links to Dan 'The Man' Manning. Bingo.

CHAPTER FIFTY-THREE

Martin quickly brought Colin and Cath up to speed on his meeting with Bashir, and the identifying of Gary Cradshaw.

'That's fantastic news re Cradshaw. We need to find him straight away,' Colin said.

'Must admit, I feel safer now we know who he is,' Cath added.

'And he has known links to Manning,' Martin said.

'Turning to Bashir, I'm glad he's not thrown himself on his drug-related sword just yet,' Colin said.

'So am I, but it'll come. Though whether we can prove enough to link him directly to the deaths will be another matter. But it's good that he is grassing up Yates and Grantham. As and when we get them in the cells, we can play all three off against each other and see what we end up with,' Martin said. 'Anyway, how have you two got on?'

Colin replied first, and said he'd spoken to Aadi in Delhi, who said that their investigation had gone quiet, with little or no movement. Though, they had picked up an incoming from a UK registered mobile on the last batch of telephone billing they had intercepted, but it was not known to them, or the UK, apparently, having already done the relevant checks. They were monitoring its location which had not moved out of Delhi since they became aware of it.

'Sounds like Manning definitely has a man over there?' Martin said.

'Probably trying to arrange further importations, too, in addition to their own home-grown aspirations,' Colin said.

'Let's hope any new stuff isn't flawed like the first batch was?' Martin added.

Then Cath joined in, 'On that, the press office has spoken to regional TV and they are fully onside and will arrange a rerun of last night's broadcast but will also add a link that a fuller programme will be coming soon.'

'Excellent, public warned, and Manning wound up. It's a win, win.' Martin said.

'I could still put myself—'

'Not a chance, Cath. No way. In fact, I reckon you and me should stay in a local hotel tonight, just to be on the safe side.'

'He's right, Cath,' Colin said. 'And as far as we know, Manning might have Martin's address too.' Then Colin turned to face Martin, 'On the last point, I've just arranged with the chief to grant authority for you to carry a sidearm for self-protection.'

Martin nodded and said he'd draw a weapon from the armoury before they finished for the day.

'And before we do finish, we need to sort out an armed surveillance on Cradshaw, and check the new number Bashir gave you,' Colin said.

'I'll arrange the surveillance, if you sort out the firearms authority,' Martin proffered.

Colin nodded and picked up his desk phone.

'And I'll do another ring around all the hospitals in case there have been any more deaths before the bulletin rerun goes out,' Cath said.

It didn't take long before Martin was able to establish that Cradshaw's last known address in Oldham was in fact his current address. When he and his mates had been arrested on the decoy robbery, they'd had to give a proven address in order to get police bail pending further enquires, or so they had been told by Gary Falstaff's detectives. A smart move. And according to Gary, the address given by Cradshaw was one which their surveillance team had logged during the many background surveillances they had done when investigating the conspiracy to rob in the first place. Gary had also readily agreed to provide his surveillance team from 6 a.m. tomorrow. They knew the target, knew the address and area, and had a very personal and vested interest in nicking him. The latter was the only bit which Martin had to debate with Gary. Even though Cradshaw could be arrested on sight for his attack against Martin and Cath, as Gary was keen to do, Martin argued that they should hold off. Just follow him and hope he leads them to Manning. If he didn't, then they could reassess things. Gary eventually agreed and promised he wouldn't nick Cradshaw without running it past him or Colin first.

Colin sorted out the firearms authority for the surveillance team and Martin went with Gary to brief them. It would save time in the morning; the plan was to have the surveillance plotted up on Cradshaw by 7 a.m. Martin thanked Gary again. He checked his watch as he walked back into their office. It was 4.55 p.m.

Colin was on his phone, and he kept looking at Martin as he listened to the call. He thanked the caller and put the phone down, and then said, 'That was the lab. They've managed to recover DNA from one of the femurs from the deceased.'

'That's excellent, but it means that we will now have to tell Abdul's wife, and request something with his DNA on it to cross-match it against,' Martin said. 'As he won't be on the offenders' DNA database.'

'How are you going to do that?' Cath asked.

'Any number of things will do, probably start with his toothbrush,' Martin replied, before turning back to Colin.

'True, but we do have a short window. The lab says they have not got enough yet to do a comparison, but should have in a day or two,' Colin said.

'Why does a delay matter now that you have Bashir?' Cath asked.

'It just means that we will have to tell Abdul's wife about Bashir – her brother-in-law's – involvement at the same time, and that could have a major effect on Bashir,' Colin said.

'The longer we can keep Bashir sweet, the more we will get out of him before it all goes tits-up,' Martin added. 'Anyway, how have you got on?'

'Thankfully, I can't find any more deaths with the red eye thingy, and I've spoken to Eleanor and the rerun will go out during the teatime regional news.'

'Excellent,' Martin said.

'I think we should all get an early night and be here as soon as the surveillance goes live in the morning. I'll join you at the hotel if you don't mind, save me some travelling to and from Manchester,' Colin said.

Cath and Martin said that would be fine, they could enjoy a meal together; tomorrow could be a long day. Martin would be having an early night. As soon as he collected his firearm, he would have to remain teetotal until he handed it back in. 'One last thing before we head off,' Martin said to Colin.

'What's that?'

'Did you level with the Indians about Sky White, so they know what their targets are really up to?'

'I did, and Aadi said he'll check on recent drug deaths, but it won't be as easy as it is over here. Most don't end up in hospital, and therefore are unknown to the authorities, but he'll try.'

CHAPTER FIFTY-FOUR

Manning had just finished his delivered pizza and was taking a slug from his third bottle of lager when the regional news started on his brand new Ultra 4K HD flat screen TV. He was expecting Suzy home at any time, but he knew she was going to turn it around and head off to her mate's flat pretty quickly as it was poker night here, which was why he'd eaten early. Gazza, Joey and a couple of the boys were due to start arriving soon. He had a couple of handguns on the coffee table of which he'd spent the last hour cleaning and oiling. Apart from the obvious reason, he found the task therapeutic, and when completed there was an added fascination in feeling the weapons' action all slick and smooth. He also checked the springs in the magazines which all felt good. He knew loads of dickheads who left their guns with ammunition still in and over time the constant pressure on magazine springs weakened them and left them ineffective. Manning had never had a self-loading weapon fail to load a round properly and didn't plan to start now. In fact, he often polished the ammunition too to remove any dirt and impurities which could interrupt the trajectory of the bullet as it left the muzzle. He wasn't sure whether that actually helped the discharge of the round, but it couldn't hinder it. Gazza said he was a bit anal about it, and perhaps he was, but Gazza would thank him one day when someone else's gun jammed and his did not. Manning liked to keep all the guns in one place, and knew he was taking added risks in keeping them all at the barn, but there were some tasks too serious to delegate.

The doorbell rang and on checking the CCTV he could see it was Gazza and let him in. 'There are a few cold ones in the cool box,' he said, as Gazza entered the lounge. He turned the TV volume up as Gazza joined him on the settee.

'And now over to our crime correspondent, Bob Daly, with news about the drug deaths threat,' the anchor said.

'Oh, fucking hell,' Manning said, and then watched the news intensely. The piece started off with a rerun of what the tits with a gob had said the previous night.

'It's only a rerun of last night's bulletin,' Gazza said.

As if that in any way limited the potential damage this bitch might cause his virgin drug market. It only lasted a couple of minutes, and Manning was about to turn the set off when Bob Daly added a comment. 'I have been liaising with Lancashire Police and their analyst, Cath Moore, who has done all the research, and she will be helping us pull together a documentary coming soon to give a more detailed insight into this new and deadly drug called Sky White.'

Manning reached for one of the guns on the table as Gazza put his arm on his wrist.

'Don't Dan; it'll only cost you another grand.'

Manning knew it wasn't loaded anyway, so put the weapon back on the table. 'That Moore bitch is fucking killing us here, Gazza. We've got to stop her before they can do a fucking documentary.'

'I've done a quick recce today at Preston but saw fuck-all. I then buzzed her gaff again before returning, and again on the way up here, but there was no sign of life inside. Reckon she's staying away after what happened. I'll go to Preston early tomorrow,' Gazza said.

'Poker night is cancelled. Ring the boys, get Joey to cover her place overnight in case she returns. If she does, get your arse up here first, and take what you want,' Manning said, as he pointed at the weaponry on the table. 'If she's a no show like you reckon, you can tool-up early doors, before you head to Preston.'

Gazza argued that he should arm himself now, but the least time Gazza was actually carrying for, the less the risk. 'No, if Joey clocks her going home for the night, you'll have plenty of time. If not, I'll see you first thing,' Manning said.

Gazza pulled his phone out and started to make the calls when Manning's own mobile rang, it was his man in India. Christ, his timing was lousy. Manning walked into his kitchen to take the call. 'Everything okay?' he started with, a little too abruptly.

'You sound happy,' the caller said.

'Sorry, just lost a bag of sand at poker,' Manning lied, his voice calmer.

'Shouldn't be so shit at it then.'

Manning wasn't in the mood for pleasantries, so again asked his caller what he wanted, albeit as calmly as he could.

'Just to let you know that I'm on my way home soon, and without any further delays this time.'

Manning wasn't sure what delays he meant but just asked, 'And you still have the golden recipe, and it's the right one?'

'Yes, got it, and as to its authenticity, you never can be a hundred percent sure with these bastards, but they reckon it's cool now, and they did do a quick local field test as you know, why the sudden doubts?'

Manning was feeling a bit paranoid after seeing the TV thing again; he was just thinking: what else could go wrong?

The caller continued, 'It's good I'm sure, and even if it wasn't, your man Beaker in Yorkshire and his nerdy mates should be able to sort it. Or so you told me when you were more chipper. What's up mate?'

'Just don't like losing.'

'You managed to remove that little problem, yet?' he asked.

'All sorted, so no worries,' he lied, and then they said their goodbyes and Manning ended the call.

He walked back in the lounge as Gazza was finishing a call on his phone.

'All done. Do you want me to use some of the boys on this tomorrow?' Gazza asked.

'Just Joey, I want to keep it tight. If there's no sign of her at her house overnight, then tell him to get his arse to pig HQ at Hutton in case she turns up there. But tell him to be careful where he parks.'

'Will do, the approach is off a dual-carriageway so he can sit in a layby.'

'Okay. You'd better head off and get some kip in case she returns home. We need to get this done; our man in India is on his way back.'

CHAPTER FIFTY-FIVE

Martin, Cath and Colin were up too early for breakfast in the hotel, so on the way into Preston Central nick Martin picked up bread and butter from a twenty-four-hour petrol station. They arrived just as Gary Falstaff and his team were leaving. Martin waved to wish them luck. Once in their office, Colin set about sorting a brew out and Martin borrowed a toaster he knew the divisional commander kept hidden in his secretary's office. He'd have it back before the boss arrived, albeit with a few more crumbs in it.

Martin went through his emails which included one from the Telephony Unit confirming that the number Bashir had given him was indeed linked to Gary 'Gazza' Cradshaw, but it had been inoperative for some time. Then Colin received a call from Aadi in Delhi where it was early afternoon, and Colin came off the phone looking excited.

'The user of the UK mobile in India is on the move. Aadi has used a triangulation team to home in on the signal. It wasn't on for long, but they were able to isolate it. It's currently in a cab with its user and Aadi's men are following,' Colin said.

'Brilliant, where's it headed?' Martin asked.

'Towards the airport. Aadi said he will keep us informed.'

'Will he let the user run?'

'He says so, says he doesn't have enough to arrest at his end, and I assured him that we do.'

Aadi was a top man; Martin knew international enquiries could be problematic, with different countries' police often working to different agendas.

'But on the promise that we share everything with them, he's keen to arrest their home-grown targets as soon as he can,' Colin added.

A fair exchange, Martin thought. Then they received more good news via a call-in to Colin from Gary Falstaff. As soon as his team plotted up on Cradshaw's address, he was out and off in a small blue Berlingo van. An early start was a good sign that he was up to no good, he just hoped that his 'no good' related to Manning.

The three of them then continued a conversation they had had the previous evening, how to flush Manning out, if Gazza Cradshaw didn't do it for them. Cath had made a good point that having been seen, albeit glancing by Martin, in Cradshaw's failed attempt to run them down, Manning might use someone else, an unknown. Neither Colin nor Martin had an answer for that. They were only sure of one thing, and that was Manning wouldn't risk showing his own face, unless they could force him into it.

Thirty-five minutes later, Colin received a further update from DI Gary Falstaff. Gazza, as he had started calling him, had driven up into the foothills of the Pennines east of Manchester and gone straight to a large barn conversion, and then disappeared through high gates into an inner courtyard and was still there. Intelligence checks revealed that the barn complex was leased to a Suzy Crabtree who was not known to the police, and whose name drew a blank on the intelligence databases. Colin said that he'd speak to Kerry Danson and have her details put through the CHAMPS database just in case an informant had mentioned her, but it didn't bode too well. 'How is Gazza dressed?' Martin heard Colin ask, and Colin repeated his reply so they could all hear. 'Blue overalls.'

Once the call was over, Martin asked, 'You don't suppose the bastard's doing an honest day's work for once in his life?'

'Be just our bloody, luck,' Colin replied.

'I think Plan B's still a goer,' Cath said, but before Martin could respond, she outlined her suggestion that they should get the eight o'clock news headlines interrupted, if they were quick, to report an update by her on behalf of the authorities for 10 a.m. or whenever, on Sky White and why all drug users should avoid any cocaine offered which is different. Martin knew the plan had merit, but it was just so dangerous. He could see that Colin was considering it.

'How do we reduce the risks?' Colin asked.

'We could ask the TV people if we could do it at the press studio at headquarters, totally safe there, and keep a lookout on the approaches. Manning and his men may try something coming to or from it,' Martin suggested.

'Too safe,' Cath said, 'and too much risk for him to come anywhere near the police headquarters,' she added.

'Where then?' Colin said.

'Preston railway station. It's perfect as it was the scene of one of the drug deaths,' she said.

'Far too risky,' Martin said.

'I'll have you and your gun with me,' she said.

Colin's phone rang and Martin watched as he took the call, he didn't look happy. Having ended it he turned to face Martin and Cath and said, 'Gazza has left the barn and headed towards the motorway, but they've lost him.'

'You're fucking joking,' Martin said, and immediately felt a little unkind, he of all people knew just how difficult surveillance was, and how easy a loss of eyeball could occur.

'They've initiated a search pattern. One car has gone back to the barn, one to his HA, and two have joined the motorway south, and two and the bike have gone north.'

'Sounds like they are all over it, we just need a bit a luck, now,' Martin said.

Martin then turned to face Cath who was talking quietly into her mobile. He hadn't realised that she was on the phone, and on seeing him look at her, she quickly ended the call.

'We've had bad news from the surveillance team,' Colin said.

'I gathered that,' she answered.

'Who was that?' Martin asked.

'Just keeping my supervisor, Eleanor, up to speed,' she said.

'Sounded very clandestine.'

'I've no idea what you mean.'

'Hushed speech.'

'I just didn't want to interrupt Colin,' she said. But she was grinning. Martin didn't like how this was sounding.

'I hope you won't be too cross,' Cath said, dropping the grin and using that puppy dog expression she saved for special occasions.

'What have you done?' he asked.

'As discussed, Eleanor is ringing the press office now to get them to speak to their contact at the TV studios in Manchester to ask them to play along. She reckons they'll jump at it on the promise of exclusivity at the railway station,' she started. Martin instinctively looked at his watch, and inwardly groaned. It was 7.50 a.m.

Then Cath's phone pinged a WhatsApp chat noise, and Martin could only look on as she began a three-way conversation with a woman from their press office and a woman from the TV station. In thirty seconds, it had all been agreed. The woman from the TV station was to add the comments to the 8 a.m. news and an outside broadcast unit would set off immediately for Preston. They would meet at 9.30 a.m. and a reporter would do a two-minute interview with Cath to go out live for the 10 a.m. news with the railway station in the background.

'Cath, what the hell have you just done?' Martin asked.

'It'll be fine, I have you and your gun to look after me,' she said with a smile back on her face.

He turned to see what Colin's reaction was; he was already giving his chin a serious rub.

CHAPTER FIFTY-SIX

One of the problems with using Preston railway station was that the site was policed by the British Transport Police who wouldn't take kindly to them running an armed operation there without them. Colin had spent thirty minutes on the phone speaking to their duty detective superintendent who was miles away in Birmingham. Once the super realised that the press would be doing the news bulletin anyway, she agreed to help. She said she would divert a couple of their armed officers from Manchester Piccadilly who would treat it as a spontaneous firearms incident should anything untoward happen requiring an armed response. But the super wasn't happy as they had no intelligence that Manning or one of his team would attack, and if they did, they had no firm intelligence that he or anyone would be armed.

'When you put it all like that, she has a valid point,' Martin had said.

'I've had similar problems with our lot in Lancashire, but they have given us two ARVs – Armed Response Vehicles – who will be parked up close by and will also treat this as a spontaneous firearms op if events unfold justifying an armed intervention,' Colin added.

'I've had a bit more luck, arrest team-wise,' Martin said. 'I have ten hairy-arsed detectives who will be in a van parked at the side of the railway station.'

'I hope you are not including the lady detectives in that description, Martin Draker?' Cath chided.

All three laughed and it lifted the tension a little.

'What does Rogers think?' Martin asked Colin.

'Haven't told him, he's a busy man.'

It looked like Colin had recovered; now that they had half a plan in place.

By 9.20 a.m. they were all in situ. Colin was sat in a car, acting as commander on the ground and coordinating everything. The van full of detectives was in place in the short-stay car park at the side of the railway station. Cath was stood outside the railway station's main entrance, and Martin was next to her. Once the thing started rolling, Martin would sit on a bench next to the station's entrance, he would be near enough to come to Cath's assistance but be out of shot of the camera. Two armed BTP officers were on platform four, seconds away, and the two liveried Lancashire ARVs were hidden on a retail complex's vast car park opposite the side of the railway station.

The main entrance to the railway station was at the end of a short cul-de-sac about 100 metres from a main road called Fishergate, which was one of Preston's main shopping streets. There was only one way into this entrance road which was lined by waiting black cabs on one side and pick up and drop off spaces on the other. If Manning or his thugs did respond to their invitation, there was only one vehicle access, and Martin would have plenty of time to call in their armed back-up should they show.

They had managed to place a railway employee at the entrance to stop the civilian drop-off vehicles, claiming maintenance work was to be carried out. There was just the line of black cabs allowed in, BTP wouldn't let Colin stop them, said it would cause too much disruption on a 'wing and a prayer' job, which had no hard intelligence that anything at all was actually going to happen. Martin could see their point. But if any civilian vehicle breached the entrance and headed towards them then it was a threat, and could be treated as such, until they knew different.

The outside broadcast unit arrived, which consisted of one man with a camera, one woman with a sound boom and the station's crime correspondent, Bob Daly. Introductions done, they had a speedy conflab, so they knew what they were doing. Colin had insisted that the press be told the full story and given the choice to quit if they wanted. It was reasonable Martin knew, but God knows what they'd do if the press did. Fortunately, they were up for it as long as they could keep the camera rolling. This could go tits-up in so many ways.

Colin had parked on the one-way system so he could give advance warning of any approaching motors that didn't look right or seemed to be approaching the station. The latest update from the surveillance team was not good news. No sign of Gazza or his blue Berlingo van. Martin had a last word with Cath at one minute to ten as she was preparing herself. He could tell that she was a little nervous; the bravado mask of hers had slipped. But she was not alone. He sighed and took his position on the bench. Every inch of his body tense, his senses on full alert. He heard Colin via his radio earpiece calling all teams to order.

Martin glanced around at all the people coming in and out of the railway station, going about their business blissfully unaware of anything amiss. In fact, this was the worst possible place to do this, far too many members of the public who were far too close. He knew that if this was a pre-planned firearms operation working from reliable intelligence, they would never have got the authority to do it here.

Then Martin noticed a bright lamp illuminate Cath's face, and the lady with the boom mic held it up on a big stick just above her head. The cameraman was behind his viewing lens and Martin heard Bob Daly start his script, 'Good morning viewers, I'm coming to you live from Preston railway station . . .'

Martin ignored Cath as she started to reply to Bob's questions, as he scanned the faces of every person passing on foot while keeping one eye 100 metres ahead on the junction with Fishergate.

Then Martin saw a blue van, a small one, start to enter the entrance to the station, before being waved down by the attendant. It pulled up. Martin was on his feet and put his hand inside his jacket and took hold of his holstered Glock handgun. He held it in position as he watched. Then he heard Colin over the radio, warning the others of the approaching vehicle. But with the comment that it had two females in it, both in their early twenties. Martin relaxed his grip slightly, and then watched as the van reversed and carried on down Fishergate. False alarm.

Martin breathed out and called Colin over his radio to confirm that it wasn't their targets. He could hear Colin repeat his words to the rest of the team on comms. He looked up on noticing the lamp go out. The interview was done. He walked over to the group and thanked Bob and his team who all looked disappointed; they then started to pack their gear up. Cath thanked them too and then joined Martin on the bench. They had prearranged to wait a further fifteen minutes in the event of a no-show, but not to let the outside broadcast unit realise this. Safer for them.

'Well, that's a bugger,' Cath said. 'Looks like Plan B has crashed and burned.'

'We've no way of knowing whether Manning saw the

news headlines earlier or not. It was always a punt,' Martin said, as his heartrate returned to normal.

'I know, and Bob said the station put it out at nine, and half nine. I hope that didn't spook them,' Cath said.

'They probably didn't see it. In some ways I'm glad, it could have been a premier league fuck-up had it worked,' Martin said.

At 10.15 a.m. exactly, Martin heard Colin stand everyone down and thank them all for their assistance at such short notice. He turned to face Cath. 'Come on; let's get back to the office.'

CHAPTER FIFTY-SEVEN

Martin glanced at the dashboard clock as they neared the police station, it was just after ten thirty, and the adrenalin of the failed operation had easily burned off the toast from earlier. That reminded him, he'd forgotten to put the toaster back, a bit late now. He'd have to try and sneak it in and hope the boss's secretary didn't grass him up. But as his stomach growled, he asked Cath if she fancied a bacon butty. He'd found a place with Colin some time ago near the police station which excelled in all things fried. They even did a huge circular soft bun the size of a small dinner plate which they stuffed with all sorts and were affectionately known by the local cops as 'chest-clutchers', such were their calorie count. He wasn't sure Cath would try one of those, but he knew Colin would be up for it.

'Sounds like a plan,' she said, so Martin continued past the nick.

Martin drove onto the A6 heading towards the north-end of Preston. Just through some major traffic lights he activated his left indicator to pull into a quiet side street which had the rears of several commercial buildings backing onto it. 'Bugger,' he said.

'What?' Cath asked.

'It's gone; we've missed it.'

'Pardon?'

'Didn't I say that it was a mobile food van?'

'No, you didn't, I wouldn't have agreed if you had.'

'Ah, but you'd have changed your mind once you'd tasted their ware,' Martin said, as he pulled the car over. The road was a short cul-de-sac adjoined on both sides by solid windowless walls, and the back of a car park at the end which was fenced off. He pulled up to allow him to do a three-point turn as his stomach growled in greater protest now it wasn't to be fed as expected.

'Surely, the police canteen will be open now?' Cath said, just as Martin's phone rang via the car's Bluetooth, it was Colin. 'Sorry, Colin, I had planned a treat for you—'

'Where are you?'

'Don't know the name of the street; it's where the chest-clutcher van usually is—'

'Get the fuck out of there now,' Colin shouted.

But before Martin could reply he saw a blue Berlingo van pass them and pull in front. Then the back doors burst open and out jumped Daniel Manning pointing a shotgun straight at them.

Martin quickly spoke what he could see and was starting to reach for his holstered weapon, when his driver's window shattered. Stood there was Gazza who had used the butt of a handgun to break the glass. Martin had one gun pointed at his head, and the approaching shotgun pointing from the front. He knew it was fruitless to try and draw his weapon at this point while facing a threat from two sides. He slowly slid his hand back out of his jacket. The fact that he was covertly armed was his only trump card. He didn't want to waste it.

He glanced at Cath, but she was transfixed on Manning who had now approached her side of the car. She screamed as the glass in her window shattered and Manning's sawn-off shot gun approached the side of her head.

'Both you fuckers keep your heads looking forward and your hands on your laps,' Manning barked.

They both complied and Martin glanced at the car's computer console, the call to Colin had ended. He just prayed he had heard enough. But would any response to it be in time?

'The tits with a gob,' Manning started. 'You have no idea how much trouble you and your boyfriend have caused me.'

Martin instinctively looked at Manning on hearing him refer to Martin as Cath's boyfriend. Immediately, he felt the butt of Gazza's weapon strike the back of his head along with the instruction to face the front. Martin complied as he tried to ignore the throbbing pain now emanating down his neck.

'Look, guys, you do know that if you off us, you'll be running for the rest of your lives. Whoever you are?' Martin said. He had added the last bit in a vain hope that if they didn't think he knew who they were, then they may be tempted to just do one, unidentified.

'Nice try,' Manning said, 'but you know who we are as you haven't asked what this is all about. Have you detective?'

Martin swallowed hard. He prayed that Colin had heard enough, all he could do was to try and keep them talking.

'Sorry we missed you at the railway station, but we reckoned you may have had a little reception waiting for us,' Manning said.

Shit, Cath's plan had worked, but with unintended consequences. Then a dreadful thought hit him, he had been nearly turning into the police station yard when they had changed their mind. They must have been waiting for them there. If only he hadn't carried straight on. If only he had ignored his stomach.

Then Gazza spoke, 'Come on, Boss, we need to do one.'

'I know,' Manning answered. 'Time for you two to make like my TVs.'

Martin had no idea what that meant, then his Bluetooth kicked in. It was Colin. Martin reached the short distance from his lap to hit the touchscreen's 'Accept Call' icon.

'No fucker knows where the street—' Colin started to say, but that was a far as he got as Manning discharged his weapon into the screen. The sound of the shotgun going off was deafening inside the car, even with both front widows gone. In the instant that followed, glass and bits of the car's dashboard exploded out towards Martin and Cath. And Martin knew that they had run out of time.

If they were going to die here and now, then he was going to go down fighting. In the moment of confusion caused by the blast, Martin went for his weapon. If he could just get one of them . . . Even though Gazza was far nearer to him, he was at an awkward angle to Martin, so he decided in that instance to attempt to get a round off at Manning who was a far squarer target. It also crossed his mind that as he started to move, his actions would draw both Manning and Gazza's attention, and this might buy Cath a small amount of time. Gazza might even flee on seeing his boss shot. It was an outside chance, but he would die happy if he could save Cath. All this flew through his mind in a millisecond.

As the resound from the shotgun was still bouncing around the inside of the car, Martin went for his gun. It was the only element of surprise he had. He felt his hand reach the grip, and a surge of adrenalin shoot through him, as he eased the weapon backwards.

Then he heard more gunshots, he wasn't sure how many, but Gazza suddenly dropped from view. Martin looked up at Manning as he freed his weapon from his jacket and saw that the man's attention was no longer on them. He was looking over the roof of their car. Martin straightened his arm, his finger on the trigger.

He started to squeeze his index finger down when he heard shouts of 'Armed Police drop your weapon. Do it now'. For a further millisecond it crossed Martin's mind to shoot the bastard. Who would blame him? It would be classed as justifiable homicide, even if he knew different. A second previous it would have been lawful, now it was not. Then his conscience kicked in. He would be no better than Manning. He released his finger and lowered his weapon as everywhere went noisy. Two plain-clothed men were at their driver's side and were dealing with Gazza, and two had already floored Manning seconds after he had thrown his shotgun away.

As time caught up, he asked Cath if she was okay. She nodded, still mute. The plain-clothed men were wearing police baseball caps but weren't the uniformed ARV officers from the railway station. Martin had no idea who they were, other than their saviours. They were told to stay in the car a while longer as Manning was restrained and removed, and then Gazza was pulled clear. Martin could see that he had a bad gunshot wound to his right leg and one of the officers had used his belt as a makeshift tourniquet. The sound of approaching sirens grew louder as Martin once again checked on Cath. She recovered her speech and said he was not to worry, she'd be alright, and that they were both alive. It was all that mattered. She was right. Then Martin heard a familiar voice. 'You can get out now.' It was Gary Falstaff, the surveillance team leader.

Martin got out and hugged the guy. Then asked how he'd come to be there.

'We lost the van as you know, so two teams headed to Preston and sat outside the nick, just in case. Then we saw you drive past, and then the fucking blue van appeared from behind one of the uni students' residential blocks. Fucker must have been there ages. We followed it and then lost the bastard again at the major traffic lights just down the road. Fortunately, for you, I'm also big fan of the "Chest-Clutchers",' Gary said.

CHAPTER FIFTY-EIGHT

'Are you sure you're okay?' Martin asked Cath for the zillionth time.

'I've told you, yes, now stop fussing,' she replied, as she took a seat in their office. 'Mind you, my feelings are a bit hurt.'

Martin exchanged a look with Colin, who they had just finished briefing about the attack, and asked her why.

'Didn't you hear what that animal called me, "tits with a gob", cheeky bastard.'

All three of them laughed. Then he started with the shakes. It was a common response to a severe adrenalin-high once you started to come down. An involuntary physiological reaction, as opposed to fear, which it was often mistaken for. He put his hands in his pockets.

'You have no idea how frightening it was for me too, no one seemed to know where the hell the food van usually parked,' Colin said.

'You probably asked the wrong people,' Martin said. 'No good asking the comms operators, it's the operational cops that use it.'

'Well, I'm just glad that Gary Falstaff has a similar diet to us,' Colin said.

'Leave me out of the "us" will you, he never told me it

was a mobile fast-food van,' Cath said.

Then Colin's desk phone rang, as did his mobile. He passed his mobile to Martin as he picked the desk handset up.

Martin noted the display just said 'call' with no details and guessed it was from overseas. Aadi, he hoped, and it was. He ended the call just as Colin was replacing his desk phone handset.

'You first,' Martin said, as he handed the mobile back to Colin.

'That was the lab, they have enough DNA to search now, so have put it on the offenders' database as a matter of course, recording it as crime scene data. They need Abdul's DNA ASAP to crossmatch it to. I've explained that we have been a bit busy but promised it later today. We need to speak to his wife regarding his death anyway now, whether we like it or not,' Colin said.

Martin nodded, irrespective of how it would impact on Bashir, and his willingness to help. He took a second to consider how unpleasant the task would be. Death Warning Messages were one of the worst parts of police work; one of which you never became used to. Martin could remember the first one he'd done as vividly as the last. And each one in between, each indelibly stained on his memory. He shook the thought off; his call had contained good news, time to share it. 'The call on your mobile was from Aadi, they had lost the target within the airport,' he started to say, and then raised his hand to reassure Colin and Cath as he continued. 'But they located him later via CCTV boarding a plane. He is listed on the flight manifest as one Mohammed Khan, a UK national.'

'That's absolutely marvellous,' Colin said.

'He's totally unknown to them, and according to their UK liaison, unknown to us, but we can double-check.'

'I'll get on to that. Where is he flying to?' Cath asked.

'That's the really good news; he lands at Manchester Ringway, Terminal One, in two hours' time.'

Colin then quickly filled them in with what had happened to Manning and Gazza. Manning was in the cells screaming for his lawyer. But as Martin knew that they had him home and dry for the first murder, and now for the armed attack having been caught red-handed; he could "no comment" all he liked, he was never going to see the light of day again, especially when they'd finished building the extra cases against him for Abdul's murder and the robbery. And that was before they started on the Sky White stuff, drug deaths, and the offences involving Bashir's inappropriate use of private data.

'What about Gazza?' Cath asked.

'Again, he is stuffed, but we'll need you two to ID him as the man from the gin bar, and you, Martin, to place him at the scene outside Cath's house, if you can.'

'I recognised him from both as soon as I saw him,' Martin said.

'Definitely the gin bar man,' Cath added.

'But his leg is a mess, so he'll be under armed guard at the hospital for a while until he's deemed fit for custody,' Colin added. 'But enough of that for now, we've got to get to Manchester airport.'

Martin nodded.

'If you drive, Martin, I can work the phone en route and set up some assistance.'

Martin nodded again and then turned to Cath.

'Don't worry about me lads, I'll make a start on database checks on this fellow Khan and then I'm off to have a nice long shower and change my clothes. I'll ring you if I turn anything up.'

'Thanks,' Colin said.

'I'll catch you both later.'

Martin picked up a spare set of car keys, together with a pair of handcuffs and followed Colin out of the office.

CHAPTER FIFTY-NINE

'So, who the hell is Mohammed Khan?' Martin asked, as he accelerated down the M6.

'I've no idea, Cath has run him through all our databases and Kerry Danson has done a CHAMPS search too. A total unknown, as is the woman from the barn. Though, Gary has just texted me to say they have a search team there now and have found loads of stuff with Manning's name on it, together with a cache of firearms,' Colin said.

'Happy days, the screw on Manning's neck just gets tighter.'

'The woman's been locked up, so expect her to give up Manning as quickly as she can,' Colin added.

'She'll have to if she wants to dodge the grief heading her way.'

Then Colin took a further call, and Martin noted that he referred to the caller as "Sir", and once Colin ended the call, asked, 'Rogers?'

'Yep, I gave him a brief rundown earlier of what had happened, as in specifically the armed attack on you and Cath but haven't bothered him with all the investigative stuff. Thought I would leave that until we had firmer news,' Colin said.

'As in once people are charged?' Martin said.

'That's it, but he does want a scrum down as and when we can. He's itching to see Yates and Grantham in the cells, I think.'

Martin nodded.

'But he rang now to obviously ask how you two were, first?'

'I heard you say that we were both fine.'

'But also, to let me know that due to the drug deaths now linked by toxicology to the red-eye deaths caused by Sky White, the Home Office have expedited the use of the Statutory Instrument within the Misuse of Drugs Act to outlaw any substance which is chemically a cocaine substitute.'

'Wow, that's fast,' Martin said.

'Just shows what they can do when they put their minds to it.'

Martin knew that any use of the drug before it had been outlawed would not in itself be unlawful. Only going forward. That said, any existing conspiracy to import or deal it, would become unlawful from this point on, and voiced as much.

'Hadn't thought of that,' Colin said.

'So any conspiracies we can prove against Manning that are ongoing, will now come under the Act.'

'That screw on his neck is becoming tighter still,' Colin said.

Things are getting better and better.

Martin pulled off the M56 and started to follow the signs for Terminal One. Now, all they had to do was work out who the hell Mohammed Khan is, and how he fits into Manning's conspiracy, other than just being Manning's man over there. 'Must admit, I was wondering what offence we were going to detain Khan on.'

'Me too, if I'm honest, though I'm sure we'd have thought of something,' Colin said.

'We would, but the call from the chief makes it easier now.'

'Good timing or what?'

Twenty minutes later, and Martin and Colin were both airside in a small room near to Passport Control at the entrance of Terminal One. They had been led there by a Border Force officer and were awaiting his boss. Martin looked at his watch as it clicked over to 3 p.m. *The plane should be at the gate by now.*

The door opened and in walked a uniformed Border Force officer with two stars on his epaulettes. Martin didn't know whether the two stars equated to a police rank of inspector, but he was obviously a senior officer. He was a portly man in his 50s and had the look of an ex-cop about him. He said his name was Steve Millson. Introductions over he asked them what their intentions were.

'We want to arrest him on suspicion of being involved in a conspiracy to import a Class A controlled drug,' Martin said, and saw Steve's eyes light up.

'Which one?' he asked.

'Sky White,' Martin answered.

'Never heard of it, you sure it's controlled?' Steve asked.

'It wasn't an hour ago,' Colin said, and then went on to explain.

'Will he be carrying any on him?' Steve asked.

'Not that we are aware of, Steve, but if you want to get the old rubber gloves out before you hand him to us, be our guest,' Martin said.

'Right you are,' Steve said, then the radio clipped to his shoulder burst into life, 'Mohammed Khan detained, sir, and is being taken to Examination Room C.'

'Roger that, en route,' Steve replied, and then left the room.

A further twenty minutes passed during which time a

junior officer entered the room and placed a small holdall on the table, and announced that it was Khan's only baggage, and it had been searched with a negative result. Martin smiled and the officer left.

Martin was becoming a little impatient and was wondering how long it took to look up someone's backside, or whatever they did on these intimate searches. He guessed it was the resulting paperwork that took the time. Then the door opened again, and Steve walked in.

'We have searched Mr Khan, with a negative result. He has refused to answer any questions with regard to the purpose of his trip; he's all yours now, gents.' Steve handed over a UK passport to Martin, who shoved it in his pocket.

Steve looked back through the open door and said, 'In here.' A second later a further Border Force officer led Mohammed Khan into the room, and Steve nodded and then both officers left, closing the door behind them.

'Mohammed Khan?' Martin said. But he wasn't really asking a question, just speaking in disbelief and staring at the Asian heritage man in his thirties stood there, who looked equally stunned.

Martin looked at Colin, who was just staring at the man. The dead man stood before them.

'Abdul, what the fuck are you doing here?' Martin eventually managed to say.

Abdul didn't respond, but neither did he try to style it out as Mohammed Khan.

Martin pulled the passport he'd just been given from his pocket and looked at it, it was a good likeness, but it was not Abdul. Probably borrowed it from a friend. 'Well, Abdul, you are being arrested, obviously, for conspiracy to import Class A drugs,' Martin said, as he reached for his handcuffs. But before he could give him the full caution, Colin recovered his voice.

'Well, if you're Abdul the ex-informant, which you are, then who the fuck was the poor bastard in the boot of the burned-out car?'

CHAPTER SIXTY

Abdul refused to reply to Colin's question, and Martin knew it had been an instinctive one, which they could not follow up on until they reached an interview room at Preston nick. Any further questioning of Abdul while they were en route would be classed as an illegal interview and ruled inadmissible. The journey therefore was a silent one. Martin was dying to chat with Colin about what may or may not be going on, but not with Abdul sat in the back.

That was until Colin's phone rang. He took the call, listened and then thanked the caller before turning to face Martin with further surprise etched on his face.

'That was the lab,' Colin said.

Martin was about to suggest he wait until they were alone before elucidating further; they were only five minutes from the custody suite, but Colin spoke as if he was unable to hold back.

'They have a hit on the DNA from the body.'

'Colin?' Martin said, warningly.

'It's some low-level criminal called Michael Staining. Whoever the hell he is.'

The name rang a bell with Martin, but it was a faint memory.

Then Abdul in the back piped up, 'I'll tell you who he is; he's a grassing bastard who deserved all he got. Not that I had anything to do with it. I was in India, as you know.'

Now it was Martin's turn to break the speech embargo, '"Grassing bastard", that's a bit rich coming from you.'

'Yes, but he was a real one,' Abdul replied.

It was all Martin could do to stop himself from launching further into Abdul; it would have to wait for the interview room. He noticed that Colin had gained his composure too, and Martin was glad to see the police station gates up ahead as he indicated to turn in.

It took thirty minutes to book Abdul into the custody suite, Colin had left Martin the job, it didn't take two of them. As soon as he was processed and locked up, Martin headed back to their office and passed Ian Laverty in the corridor. Laverty, the uniformed inspector in charge of policing the Avenham district of Preston. They nodded at each other, and then it hit Martin where he had heard the name Michael Staining before. He rushed to his office and burst in to find Colin at his desk. 'I know who the body in the boot was,' he said.

'Yeah, some thug called Michael Staining,' Colin said.

'Or "The Flag Abuser" as we've been calling him,' Martin said. And immediately saw the recognition on Colin's face.

'Abdul's Muslim-hating neighbour, with the flag of St. George plastered all over his house,' Colin said.

'The one who has never been in lately every time the local cops go round to see him,' Martin added.

'But why kill him?' Colin said.

'No idea, come on, let's ask Abdul.'

***

It took twenty-four hours before Abdul eventually opened up. It was the sticking of his brother Bashir's witness statement in front of him that finally did it. He exploded. Apparently, he hated his brother, always had. Hated his arrogance and narcissism, though according to Abdul, Bashir was too 'up himself' to fully realise. He couldn't wait to drop his brother in it. Providing information on all the drug runs that Bashir had done for Manning and him. Also, how they had recruited Bashir due to his inflated claims of access to all things IT in the police force. And how it had been Abdul's idea to risk Bashir on his last visit to India, to test the Sky White importation method.

The interview team assigned to Manning, had regular conflabs with them between the numerous interviews so they could play each off against the other. A time-honoured tactic which still worked. 'You'll never guess what so and so is saying about you now', et cetera, et cetera.

Abdul also admitted that he had 'allowed himself' to be recruited as an informant in order to try and discover if anyone was talking about Manning, his gang or even Abdul. Though he knew no reason why he should have been on anyone's radar. But did soon realise that the whole informant handling and management system was far more secure than he would have guessed, so he failed to identify any grasses. But he had always suspected his offensive neighbour, Staining, who took far too much interest in him, which was why he fingered him to Manning. He had to give Manning something to chew on and hated Staining regardless of whether he was snooping on him or not.

Abdul claimed that he had no idea that Manning would kill Staining, notwithstanding his pathological hatred of grasses. They were always going to blow out Bashir, Grantham and Yates once they no longer needed them. This was anytime now. Martin realised just how good an actor Abdul was when he thought back to when he and Colin had first met and interviewed him in the underground bunker. He also realised he was as ruthless as Manning.

Martin was unsure who was the most conceited, Bashir or Abdul? At least Bashir was showing genuine remorse and was horrified at the thought of Abdul being dead. The same could not be said the other way round.

Yates and Grantham were arrested, as were Minty and the pretend Minty, and again, they were all played off against each, and were all duly charged with a variety of offences.

The local superintendent granted a twelve-hour extension to Abdul and Manning's custody time limits, such was the amount of evidence to put before them. Gary 'Gazza' Cradshaw made no comment during any of his interviews and was charged with his part in the criminal conspiracies, and with the two attacks on Cath and Martin.

Manning, in total, was charged with two murders and two attempted murders, and the drug related conspiracy on top of joint charges relating to his use of Bashir, and the robbery.

It was forty-eight hours before anyone came up for breath, whereby all the prisoners had been charged and refused bail. It was now time to arrange a scrum down with the chief. But before they could do it Rogers came marching into their office, just as Colin and Martin were preparing to call it a day and meet Cath for a celebratory drink or three.

'Bloody fantastic job, gents,' Rogers said as he swept in.

Martin let Colin give the chief all the details and when he had finished, he asked about the Indian side. 'Aadi and his team have mopped up all their targets, and destroyed the lab, they also found plenty of heroin and real cocaine, so they are happy bunnies,' Colin said.

'Any idea who the rest of Manning's robbery team are?' Rogers asked.

'His girlfriend, Suzy, has given a lengthy witness statement, naming them all. She was often in the background being ignored when they had their many planning meetings at the barn,' Colin said.

'In the cells?' Rogers asked.

'Not yet,' Martin said, 'but I've just come off the phone to GMP, who are arranging to give them all the good news at first light tomorrow.'

'And what about the recipe for this demonic drug?' Rogers asked.

Colin nodded at Martin as he had dealt with that. 'The documentation we found on Abdul was indeed the recipe for Sky White; but they had been sold a dummy by the Indians, either that, or it is impossible to create flawless synthetic cocaine,' Martin said.

'How do you mean?' Rogers asked.

'According to the lab, this recipe would have created a worse batch than the prototype. Forget bulging red eyes and eventual death. This new recipe, which had been tweaked from the original, would, in the expert opinion of the lab's senior scientist, have induced a fatal heart attack caused by severe internal haemorrhaging within a couple of hours of taking it.

'Christ, can you imagine what effect a widespread distribution of that would have had?' Rogers said to no one in particular.

Martin didn't really want to contemplate that, and then his mobile rang. He excused himself and took the call.

'Is this DS Draker?' a male voice asked.

Martin said that it was.

'My name is Gerard Kirby, the solicitor representing

Gary Cradshaw.'

'Yes.'

'My client wishes you to know how sorry he is for the attacks which happened against you and Miss Moore, but will at trial, be providing evidence of his coercion by Daniel Manning,' Kirby said.

Martin wasn't interested in Kirby or his client's feeble apologies, especially when it was just a preamble to a crooked defence. He was about to tell him to fuck off, when Kirby spoke again, and what he said surprised him. He acknowledged it and then ended the call.

He quickly told Colin and Rogers what had been said leading up to the last comment. And then added, 'He says if we send someone to do a covert intelligence interview with Cradshaw once he's been committed for trial, he'll give us Manning's lab, which is in Yorkshire, and all the names of those running it, in return for a brown envelope to the sentencing judge in order to mitigate the length of his sentence.'

'Do we have to comply?' Rogers asked.

'We don't, but if we can't identify the lab before then, we may have to. Not that we think they have seen the recipe, but they need nicking anyway,' Martin said.

'And if we have to deal with this weasel, what will be the outcome?' Rogers asked.

'He'll get a proportionate reduction of sentence by the judge. But to be honest, he's looking at twenty to twenty-five years as it is, so five less is no great loss, and it's in the public's interest to find the lab,' Martin said.

'Christ, these informant types are hardly worth the trouble,' Rogers said.

Martin could only agree with him, but knew that as problematic as they were, they often gave the best intelligence which otherwise would pass by the ears of the police. They were a necessary evil. Even though most only became an informant once they were nicked and in deep shit.

'Well, let's hope you can identify the lab by normal investigative means, so you can tell that scumbag where to go,' Rogers said. And then added, 'I don't suppose detectives still go for a celebratory drink in these modern times, after cracking a huge case?'

'I'm afraid they do,' Colin said.

'Excellent, the first five rounds are on me,' Rogers added.

Martin then texted Cath to bring an overnight bag with her, they wouldn't be getting back to Manchester tonight.

ACKNOWLEDGEMENTS

I'd like to say a huge thank you to Louise Mullins and Michael at Dark Edge Press for taking *Inside Threat* and commissioning the new DS Martin Draker series. I'm hugely excited about the project, of which this is the first of four planned novels.

The support I have received throughout the process has been incredible. I thank Heather Dubay for casting her erudite eye over the manuscript and a special thanks to Caz Bower for her in-depth and insightful copy editing followed by a proofread which has transformed this story into the book you see today.

My thanks also to Jamie Curtis for his outstanding cover design and for the collaborative approach he offered me. My ongoing thanks to Robert Jones for his work as Social Media Marketing Manager, and to Liz Hearne who is Head of Publicity.

Also, my thanks go to all others at Dark Edge Press involved in the production, promotion and sale of this book.

And not forgetting to say thank you for the support from so many other authors, too. It has been amazing.

And last but always first; thank you to all my readers.

Thank you all.

Roger, who lives in Lancashire, served with the Lancashire Constabulary, the Regional Crime Squad and the National Crime Squad, before leaving in the rank of detective inspector. His covert unit received local and national acclaim for its successes against heroin and crack cocaine dealers.

He'd led the C.I.D. in Preston and had been in charge of a dedicated informant unit. Previous experiences included work on many murders and other serious crimes. He served nationally and overseas in Europe and the Far East. He was commended on four occasions.

After leaving the police force, he got a proper job, as a writer of crime fiction.

His first two novels – *By Their Rules* (2013) and *A New Menace* (2014) were published by Pegasus, and his next three by Lume Books, which are: *Nemesis* (2016), *Vengeance* (2017) and *Hidden* (2019).

His novels have over 1200 ratings/reviews on Amazon and Goodreads averaging 4.5 stars and his work has attracted the Amazon Number 1 Bestseller status in their main listings on three occasions.

He is also developing a TV crime drama titled *The Fixers* and when he is not writing, he enjoys riding his motorcycle, playing the guitar, and starting to work out what greenhouses are for.

Love crime fiction as much as we do?

Sign up to our associates' program to be first in line to receive Advance Review Copies of our books, and to win stationary and signed, dedicated editions of our titles during our monthly competitions. Further details on our website: www.darkedgepress.co.uk

Follow @darkedgepress on Facebook, Twitter, and Instagram to stay updated on our latest releases.

Printed in Great Britain
by Amazon